W9-AOQ-120

GHETTO GASTRO

BLACK POWER KITCHEN

Ghetto Gastro
Black Power Kitchen

Jon Gray, Pierre Serrao, and Lester Walker

With Osayi Endolyn

Foreword by Dr. Jessica B. Harris

Photography by Nayquan Shuler and Joshua Woods

Artisan Books
New York

Library of Congress Cataloging-in-Publication Data is on file.
ISBN 978-1-64829-016-9

Design by New Studio

Published by Artisan
A division of Workman Publishing Co., Inc.
225 Varick Street
New York, NY 10014-4381
artisanbooks.com

Printed in China on responsibly sourced paper
First printing, September 2022

10 9 8 7 6 5 4 3 2 1

To our families, especially our mothers: Denise, Roxanne, and Elizabeth

To the communities that nurture and inspire us, and to our ancestors who blazed the trail

Peace to the Gods and the Earths

FOOD FIGHTS

DR. JESSICA B. HARRIS

Food is often taken to be a neutral topic of conversation, something to talk about with colleagues or strangers while avoiding the contentions that may come with deeper topics like politics or religion. But in the African American world, food has always been a difficult subject: one that brings with it a history of struggle and strife, one that can evoke generations of want and decades of pain.

The story of food in the African American world has always brought with it a subtext of fight: the fight for land rights, for parity and equity, fo dignity within a profession that was traditionally relegated to those o African descent until it became lucrative and then was snatched back with the door slammed in the faces of those who had labored long a the stoves and had a foundational hand in the creation of food that is now acknowledged worldwide as American. This tale of food and Black Americans is now being told by a group of young men who are fight- ers: warriors in the struggle to reclaim a culinary heritage and affirm its proper dignity and its proper place in history.

I do not remember when I first heard about Ghetto Gastro. It was several years ago. My initial thought was *Interesting name; I wonde how they put that together?* As time went by, I heard more mentions o Ghetto Gastro, but they were usually in the realm of art or some type of performative occasion: They had presented at an event or launched something at another. It was only recently that they came fully into my ken as bona fide members of the culinary community. After finally meeting Pierre Serrao, Jon Gray, and Lester Walker, I leaned in and began to listen. And what I heard made me feel as though I had some spiritual children on a planet I didn't know with whom I had miraculously reconnected.

Black Power Kitchen is a book that explains those connections. In its pages, the members of Ghetto Gastro and writer Osayi Endolyn set out what is a culinary manifesto about the nature of Black food. The introduction, "Food Is a Weapon," is a call to arms and an explanation of the fight that is inherent in their push-the-envelope name. The book goes on to remind readers of the battle that food has been for Africans in the United States and indeed in the American hemisphere and the world. The authors begin by centering us in their place; and their place is and will always be the Bronx—New York City's most urban borough. (And I say that as someone who was born in Queens, lived in Manhattan for two decades, and can currently claim more than thirty years in Brooklyn!) They walk us through the streets and into the mom-and-pop restaurants, pizza parlors, delis, and bodegas and present an array of the borough's food in detailed recipes with evocative headnotes that let us experience the tastes of their part of town.

From there, they take us on a stroll through the magnificently named "Durag Diplomacy," continuing the culinary journey throughout the African diaspora, and then double back to give us a look at Black American culinary history. On the way, they present us with notables who, in insightful interviews, add to the total picture. We hear from, among others, Nigerian chef Michael Elégbèdé of ÌTÀN in Lagos, writer and filmmaker dream hampton, Black Panther activist Emory Douglas, and Thelma Golden of the Studio Museum in Harlem. Each conversation expands the notion of Black food by mapping out the interlaced threads of culinary history in the African diaspora in the American hemisphere. The dialogues combine with the recipes to help redefine the terms "African" and "American" in a global context and then place the cultures and their foods on the table.

Many will have difficulty defining the book, although why books need to be categorized is beyond my comprehension. *Black Power Kitchen* begins as a cookbook—a compilation of wonderfully detailed recipes that are mainly plant based and allow the reader to sample the foods discussed. But from the first pages, it is apparent that it is so much more than a cookbook. *Black Power Kitchen* is perhaps first and foremost a love song to the Bronx, but it is also a treatise and a travelogue, a history of Black people and food, and a challenge that is both culinary and cultural. It adds serious schooling by presenting difficult truths about the current state of food. There's hard talk about the lack of food availability and access in our communities and reminders about the abysmal food of the prison industrial complex, along with thoughts on diet and health and a plea for making healthy foods more affordable and available. However, the book doesn't end with this serious and necessary information. *Black Power Kitchen* also reminds us that while the road may have been stony and the journey arduous, while there have been many food fights along the way, it has not been without joy. The joy of family and friends and the stops along the way for relaxation and celebration are all acknowledged, as is the need for self-care.

In *Black Power Kitchen*, the Ghetto Gastro collective has created a work that contains a world, one in which the past, the present, and the hope for a better future are expressed through food and folks, recipes and reminiscences. This is what the culinary warriors are fighting for. It's a work to read, to cook from, to contemplate, and to savor.

FOOD IS A WEAPON

We are Ghetto Gastro. Welcome to our Black Power Kitchen.

Let's first deal with what usually needs to be dealt with. Our name makes a lot of people uncomfortable. It's not our intent to polarize for the sake of ceremony. In fact, we were all young boys when we learned that our existence itself could be polarizing to folks who didn't know us. "Ghetto" is used as a derogatory term to dismiss and separate cultures from their mainstream counterparts. Ghetto is used as a way to cue discomfort, to cue the Other. When that unknowable thing is over there, you don't have to deal with it, you don't have to be with it. That's what ghetto is supposed to do—dehumanize.

You recognize this unsettling feeling because you might not be sure if it's polite to say the words Ghetto Gastro. (You can and we hope you do. Watch out, though, say it three times fast and we just might run down on you. Ya dig.)

You feel this discomfort because you might have worked tirelessly to get out of the ghetto, surviving difficult circumstances to create a more sustainable life. Or you might wonder why someone would be proud to claim an identifier that could sound off-putting to outsiders. You might already have a sense of what we're up to but might question our credibility. We get it. It's wise to be suspicious. Ghetto has been whitewashed and commodified, used for gimmicks and a particularly Americanized performance of Blackness. (You can look to projects like *Thug Kitchen*, authored by a white duo with zero appreciation for the criticism they received at the time, for a pulse on what we do not cosign or respect. After brother George Floyd was murdered by police in the streets of Minneapolis, the brand changed their name.)

It's simple. For us, ghetto means home. It's a way to locate our people, not just in the Bronx of New York City, where we as a group formed (more on that in a moment). It's a way for us to connect with our folks in the Global South, whether their ghettos are called the hood, the slums, the projects, or the inner city. When we say "ghetto," we are saying to our people "we see you" while simultaneously indicting the systems of neglect and apathy that created the conditions we've been forced to reckon with.

In the ghetto, food is a denominator of class and a reminder of what you can and can't have. Food is weaponized against people in the ghetto when they have easier access to soda and chips than fresh produce. When subsidized commodities like sugar, wheat, and soy make buying oranges and greens unaffordable, something is deeply wrong. Food weaponized against people is watching generation after generation fall to diabetes and cardiovascular disease. These are our people. And for decades they've been given an unfair shake.

Ghetto isn't just about struggle and disenfranchisement, though. Ghetto is the flower blooming in the sidewalk cracks. Ghetto is our love language, a patois so specific and rooted in place that if you know, you can hear when someone is from the Bronx or Brooklyn or Harlem. Ghetto is our aura, our style, our stease. It's our music, our beats, built on the backbones of jazz, rhythm and blues, and dancehall. There's a reason why Donny Hathaway, Stevie Wonder, and Rick James all sang songs about the ghetto.

Ghetto isn't about excluding people. It's about telling the rest of the world, we are here, we've been here. We're going to serve what we feel like dishing out especially when many fail to acknowledge our existence.

Ghetto is so you don't forget who you're talking to. Ghetto is so we center where we're from and why we do what we do.

Ghetto Gastro is often described as a culinary collective, which is a little vague, we know. But we are a difficult crew to contain within boundaries. We take a multidisciplinary approach to our work that draws from the visual arts, music, fashion, and social activism to curate experiences as diverse and inspirational as the people and cultures who created them. We use food as our medium to connect cultures and conceptually open borders.

We started in 2012, throwing parties in NYC. Jon has his roots in fashion and art. Pierre and Lester are formally trained chefs. Jon and Lester are originally from the Bronx and grew up as neighbors. Pierre has Bajan roots by way of Connecticut. We've all dabbled in the streets, you know. Fortunately, we found other interests and opportunities that were more fulfilling.

We discovered that we had friends across creative industries who loved to dine, loved beautiful, interesting, thoughtful food but couldn't find experiences that spoke to them. We launched with a late-night series called Waffles and Models, and it was exactly what it sounds like. Loud, delicious, and beautiful. As our popularity grew, so did our mission. We didn't just want to be cooking up good eats and sending folks home. Some of us are parents now. We wanted to make a lasting impact on families and our people. We wanted to surprise and delight but also challenge and innovate.

We found that we can be thoughtful about where we cook, what ingredients we select, how we describe a dish. We've learned about the elements that enhance the dining experience, from live music or DJs to art installations. We've worked with some of the biggest brands in fashion and design. We've brought big Bronx energy to the Place Vendôme in Paris to the TED stage in Vancouver to the harbor of Hong Kong, China. We route funds back to our community in the form of mutual aid. We've partnered to sell limited runs of specialty items and big pushes of cookware appliances. We're building a retail food brand, Gastronomical, using plant-based ingredients that originate from Africa, Asia, and the Americas, the ancestral roots of the cultures that enrich us. We're not just trying to sell people stuff. We are intentional with what we do, when we do it, and who we do it with.

We don't have a brick-and-mortar restaurant (and we don't plan on one), so we can be nimble. We can think about big concepts autonomously instead of pointing folks to a location where the rent is too damn high. Not having a restaurant has aggravated gatekeepers in food media who seem mystified that a food-centered mission can exist beyond a permanent dining space. Chefs cook outside of restaurants, ya dig? Ideas about food can translate to other genres. We're of the mind-set that you don't necessarily have to offer a tasting menu to be provocative. And like many of the homegrown organizations and institutions who partner with us, we've learned that if we don't look out for our folks, no one else will. We're doing our best and learning along the way.

While we know that not everyone can access our products, we want the people from our community and from communities like ours to know that they deserve fun things just like anyone else. And we also understand that luxury, while nice, does not transform systemic injustice or resolve the internalized suffering that comes from navigating poverty and police abuse. It's a balancing act and one we constantly navigate. Money itself is not our aspiration. But until we can count on a social fabric that empathizes with and cares for all human beings equitably, we know that money is a tool that can effect real change. We know this because we've written some of the checks. We see the difference it makes. In our worldview, everybody eats.

If it's beginning to feel as if this is not the makings of a typical cookbook, that effort, too, is intentional. Our approach, based on how we've learned to create and innovate in our own lives, is to take a nontraditional path. We've often been forced to the

VANS
GHETTO
GASTRO

margins, like many of our Bronx siblings, and we have worked our way to the center by changing the conversation. It would be out of character to enter this space of food storytelling by attempting to connect with you in a way that doesn't look, feel, or sound like us. We make our own lane. We've had to.

Black Power Kitchen is reflective of our style and sensibility, offering recipes that emerge from long-standing traditions but with the Ghetto Gastro nod. Some of the recipes are approachable to those new to cooking, and others will excite and challenge advanced cooks. As Black people, so few of whom have had the opportunity to present their food story to you in this genre, we feel it's our responsibility and privilege to show you our range.

We are dynamic, like the cultures that influence us. One of the ways that food (culture) is weaponized is when gatekeepers reduce stories to one thing. But there have always been a multiplicity of narratives around a dish and its preparation, around a historical event and the retelling of it.

We don't speak for everyone in the Bronx. We don't represent all Black people. We don't define what ghetto might mean to others. But this right here is Ghetto Gastro. You're in our realm now. Have a seat.

BLACKNESS AS ABSENCE

You don't have to look far to find metaphors that align darkness with something that's negative, lacking, scary, odd, or devoid of good. In novels and poetry, lullabies and the news; listen to an artist talk or attend an art school peer critique—it's everywhere. As people who have dark skin, we reject the idea that being dark is the same as being something to fear. There is a reason James Brown wrote the song "I'm Black and I'm Proud" and catchphrases like "Black Is Beautiful" emerged in the United States as the Black Power movement took off. We all have been asked to subscribe to the belief that darkness is bad and whiteness is good (even as we consistently observe white people pursue elements of Blackness, from emulating our skin tone, changing their hair, surgically enhancing themselves, and so on). If we stand any chance at transforming our society from one born of racism to one that becomes antiracist, every arena demands review. We must interrogate and challenge these so-called inherent beliefs, these "inevitabilities" of language. Such beliefs emerged from societies that created social, political, and economic advantages for white people who supported penalizing Blackness at all costs. We refuse to further penalize ourselves and our community by using design elements, illustrations, symbols, or language that perpetuate the BS.

THE ENSLAVED, NOT SLAVES

Our food culture in the United States and beyond was permanently transformed by the transatlantic trade of African people. Our personal and collective histories are shaped by this period in ways that we're still unpacking. To talk about these influences, we must reference this period of Black enslavement, and in doing so, we want to call out a purposeful language choice.

We all grew up hearing and using the word "slave" as a catchall term for Black people forcibly brought to the Americas. But in recent years, as our understanding of this complex era has evolved (no thanks to school history books), we've changed how we refer to our ancestors. While in specific settings it may be appropriate to use the term "slave" to identify how a person was historically labeled, we adamantly avoid this language as a way of describing human beings who were deprived of choice. It is an insufficient term to broadly describe Black people in the Americas who were denied freedom by white people.

We focus instead on the act being done *to* someone, versus the circumstances someone may have found themselves in. What we're saying is, a person *is enslaved by* an oppressor. A person is not born identifying as a slave and does not choose the life of enslavement. We tip our hats to folks like Michael Twitty and Ta-Nehisi Coates, who in their work have informed many about this crucial cultural pivot.

This issue is about more than semantics, especially for Black folks. But no matter your heritage, we urge you to examine the weight of your words. In saying "enslaved Africans" or "enslaved Black people," we bring awareness to the constant presence of white oppressors who remain unaccountable for their acts of terror and violence in any meaningful systemic way. That realization alone is worth the extra letters, and we encourage you to use them.

IN CONVERSATION

In each chapter, we feature one or two conversations with figures who are important to the life and evolution of Ghetto Gastro. These artists, writers, chefs, and creators speak to the themes in each chapter, tying in their personal lives and craft. From Bronx beats to land ownership, from jet setting to feeding people, these conversations drill deep. The gems our folks drop expand on and affirm our own practice. We trust their wisdom will move you.

FEATURED ART

In addition to the stunning photography that captures our food and community, we are proud to feature artists who not only inspire us but are pushing visual language forward. Image making is a radical act, even more so when you don't see yourself or your experiences reflected in the fine arts canon.

WE ONLY LAYER FLAVOR (W.O.L.F.)

We have a saying around here, coined by Lester, the lingo wizard. As you spin through these pages, it might seem like we're doing the most. We lean on pantry items like homemade Chili Oil (page 292) and Aunt Millie's Green Sofrito (page 290). Some of these items can be made in advance, portioned out, and kept on hand (the freezer is your friend). Some dishes require planning ahead and coordinating refrigerator space. Read through the recipe first, don't just go grabbing stuff off the shelves. You'll get the vibe. We will sometimes ask a lot of you to essentially end up with grilled chicken, but if you commit, you'll respect it because it's lit like a Bic. It's going to be *fire* grilled chicken (see Twerk n Jerk, page 103). You cannot compete with the waves of spice, sweet, crunch, or heat that come with time, attention, and intention. Depth cannot be substituted! We're never flexing to show off. Our methods, while at times a bit chef-ish or unorthodox to the typical home cook, are actual Ghetto Gastro methods. In our testing, we made accommodations to account for your home kitchen, but trust that we're not giving you any limitations or imitations.

A NOTE ON PLANTS

We use plant-based protein and some dairy-free ingredients in our recipes (we still use dairy; it can depend on our aim). This can strike people we encounter in and outside of our communities as odd (and some vegetarians fundamentally don't mess with the human-made alternative ingredients; we overstand that). But we're pushing on a few things. For one, Black people throughout the African diaspora have long maintained plant-based diets. There's a rich and storied modern history of plant-based eating among Black musicians from the jazz era to the hip hop era alone. (Look it up!) But because of knowledge and access gaps in our food system, many don't know this. It pains us to know that folks who are systemically deprived of this intel, these options at the grocery store or on the menu, look like us.

We're aware that in the United States, plant-based meat and dairy alternatives don't often land in bodegas and corner stores until the community becomes a lot less Black. Even high-quality real meat can be hard to find. Using these products illustrates that our culture is a viable market for healthy options, too, and we implore makers in the space to consider to whom they're selling and what impact they aim to have on the planet.

COMMON INGREDIENTS

We recommend using the following ingredients for best results in our recipes:

Coconut milk: All coconut milk is full fat, which adds body and richness to a number of dishes.

Flaky sea salt: When we call for flaky sea salt, we're talking about Maldon. It's high quality and so flavorful, you'll wonder what that table salt ever did for you or your taste buds.

Plant-based butter: Use whatever you prefer or can get your hands on—any plant-based butter will do fine. Note that sometimes we use dairy. We make these decisions based on the intent of the recipe. At the end of the day, do you.

Plant-based proteins: We're not talking about tofu, seitan, or tempeh, but rather plant-based proteins that can easily swap in texture for ground meat or sausage, as examples. We'll grill up mushrooms any day (see Maroon Shrooms, page 96), but if you aren't a meat eater, sometimes it's nice to have the texture of meat, minus the negative environmental and human labor impact. You won't find any pork or beef recipes here, which generally reflects our personal diets and what we cook as a crew. (But if we're in Japan, at least one of us will bust down that Wagyu!)

Sugar: Perhaps no food has been weaponized more than cane sugar—its painful history as a product that the African enslaved grew and processed is haunting. Their labor made sugar a global commodity, and it continues to be a ubiquitous ingredient and a foundational element of the chemistry behind many basic cooking methods.

With that in mind, nearly all the sugar listed in this book is raw cane sugar. Commonly sold as piloncillo, demerara, muscovado, or turbinado sugar, it's minimally processed and closest in flavor to the raw sugarcane that our ancestors might have stewarded.

Raw sugar has hints of tangy molasses and notes of caramel, a less acute sweetness, and a lower glycemic index than the white granulated sugar most commonly found in processed foods and baked goods. In instances where some finesse is needed for baking, we suggest the more finely milled product sold as organic cane sugar, which is made with pure evaporated cane juice that hasn't been bleached or stripped of its raw qualities. Bottom line: When it comes to sugar, shit ain't so sweet. Know the 'ledge and choose your source wisely.

TOOLS YOU CAN USE

Opinions on what a ready-to-go kitchen comprises can vary widely based on your background and cooking skills. For example, the mortar and pestle is ubiquitous in cultures from Europe to Asia, Africa to South America. It's one of the oldest cooking technologies in human history, and chic enough for fancy brands to make pricey stoneware versions. But if you didn't come up with people manually pounding herbs or spices or, in larger versions, starchy tubers like yams, you may not know what one is. (Now you do. Know the 'ledge.)

Don't feel overwhelmed. Building a home kitchen that reflects your evolving interests and abilities is a journey, not a destination. This book is for you because you picked it up. There is something here for you at your comfort level right now, and something you might aspire to try later. Enjoy the ride and cook what makes sense for you. This list is more for setting expectations than telling you to throw down cash just to eat.

Conical strainer
Dehydrator (some air fryers also have this function)
Fine-mesh strainer
Food processor
High-powered blender
Ice cream maker
Immersion blender
Juicer
Kitchen scale
Mortar and pestle
Nut-milk bag or cheesecloth
Outdoor grill
Pimento wood chips
Pizza peel
Takoyaki pan and pin sticks
Tawa and dabla

GHETTO
GASTRO

LOBSTER TAILS STEAMED 28.00
SHRIMP COCKTAIL
WATERMELON
SALAD
MIXED VEGETABLES
ITALIAN BREAD
RICE
FRY SECTION...
FILLET
RED SNAPPER
WHITING
SMELTS
PRICES OF ALL ITEMS
3
PORGY 12
LOBSTER
SHRIMP

The Makings of a Ghetto Gastro Dish

IBRAHEM HASAN
BRONX BARREL, 2019

Our cooking ethos is guided by a few important principles: It's gotta be right and to the bite. Done with finesse, but make it look effortless. Our food is delicious and beautiful. Intentional and subversive. And always with that swag, as in the Triple Cs.

TRIPLE Cs

Triple Cs is quintessential Ghetto Gastro, so it deserves to stand on its own. It features seared cornbread, crab salad, and caviar.

CORNBREAD

Native Americans, Africans, and ancient Mesoamericans made cornmeal and its many iterations a core food. We can look to johnnycakes, corn pone, spoon bread, and cornbread as the expression of Indigenous and enslaved peoples. Somehow, the cultures that put in the work and sacrifice, ultimately building global economies, are the ones that get exploited. Native American, Black, and brown communities are among the most food insecure in the United States. Even still, our innumerable contributions are the foundation of global wealth.

CRAB SALAD

When our political representatives take actions that divest resources from our communities, we're told it's like crabs in a barrel. The metaphor suggests that if we're all going down, no one can get out. But that analogy is insufficient because crabs belong in and around water. And maybe the crab isn't trying to block the other one's freedom. Maybe they're all trying to link up and help each other get out.

CAVIAR

Caviar—black gold—is thought of as the pinnacle of European luxury. But caviar originates in the Middle East and Asia, an example of how incomplete histories can alter our view about who gets to enjoy what.

CONTINUED

Serves 12

INGREDIENTS

For the cornbread

14 ounces (3½ sticks/400 g) unsalted butter, plus more for greasing

2 cups (240 g) tipo "00" flour or all-purpose flour, plus more for dusting

5½ cups (900 g) frozen corn kernels

1 cup (250 g) unsweetened oat milk

3 large (150 g) eggs

1 cup (160 g) cornmeal

1 cup (200 g) organic cane sugar

1 tablespoon kosher salt

1⅛ teaspoons (5 g) baking powder

½ teaspoon (3 g) baking soda

For the crab salad

1 pound (455 g) peekytoe crabmeat, cleaned

2 tablespoons chopped fresh chives

3 tablespoons crème fraîche

1 teaspoon lemon zest

9 ounces (255 g) beluga caviar or osetra caviar (the amount is your preference)

PREPARATION

Make the cornbread

Heat the oven to 375°F (190°C). Grease two 9 x 5 inch (23 x 13 cm) loaf pans with butter and dust them with flour, tapping out any excess.

In a heavy-bottomed pot, melt the butter over high heat. Add the frozen corn and cook until golden brown, about 15 minutes. Transfer the mixture to a blender, add the oat milk, and blend on high until smooth. Add the eggs and blend again until smooth. Set aside.

In a large bowl, stir together the flour, cornmeal, sugar, salt, baking powder, and baking soda.

Add the wet ingredients to the dry ingredients. Mix well. Pour the batter into the prepared pans.

Bake for 40 minutes, until the cornbread turns golden and the top begins to crack. Remove from the oven. Set the pans on trivets or a wire rack and let cool completely.

When the cornbread has cooled, heat a large skillet over medium-high heat.

Turn the loaves out of the pans and set them right-side up on a cutting board or flat surface. Using a serrated knife, cut the loaves into equal slices about ½ inch (1 cm) thick.

Working in batches, place the cornbread slices into the heated dry skillet, leaving space between the slices. Sear each slice until golden brown on both sides, 1 to 2 minutes per side. As they finish, set aside on a rack.

Make the crab salad

In a large bowl, combine the crabmeat, chives, crème fraîche, and lemon zest. Stir gently to combine. Use immediately, or cover and chill for up to 2 days.

To plate your Triple Cs, divide the crab salad evenly among the cornbread slices and spread it evenly over the surface. Top each slice with a dollop of caviar and enjoy immediately.

CORN
BREAD
MORTON
IODIZE SALT

from scratch
sweet as honey
in the rock
revolutions are stewed and sautéed
on stove tops every movement starts
in sweaty kitchens
while passing plates and peppering pallets
bless the dressing and the well-dressed
it starts in you
with you
and for you.
a community-led recipe
the truth is best served at room temperature.
food is a vibe
a tone
a tune
a mood
the marching orders
an appetite for belonging
a dance with pots and pans
the thick smell of care
lingering in a room.
never mind the measuring
a pinch
of heart
a sprinkle
of courage
let us gather
one by one
eyes glistening
seasoning a perfect silence
meals that moan
make you wanna shout
the way
closed mouths don't get fed.

—aja monet

CHASE HALL
RON AND THE CRAB, 2022
ACRYLIC AND COFFEE ON COTTON CANVAS
18 x 12 in.

wel come to the BX

When we think of the Bronx, we think of home. When we say BX, we think of the birthplace of hip hop, which is to say, the undisputed cultural influence of our lifetime, brought to you by working-class Black and brown kids. (This ain't hyperbole. They're spittin rhymes in multiple languages and emulating our style all over the world.)

We've got delis and bodegas within walking distance. We've got massive apartment buildings and single-family homes on tidy, tiny lawns. Diverse food cultures abound on White Plains Road and Arthur Avenue, from the roti shop to the cannoli spot. Immigrant culture is ubiquitous here. We've got Albanians, Vietnamese, Cubans, Jamaicans, Ghanaians, Pakistanis, and countless more. The expressway is jammed; the elevated trains are probably running behind. When we think of the Bronx, we think of music on loud sound systems because if you've got the beats, you gotta shake the streets. From the North Bronx, in Baychester, high-rise windows show off stunning sights of the Hutchinson River feeding into Eastchester Bay, which frame the dense treetops of Pelham Bay Park. We are the greenest borough in the city of New York. But that doesn't mean everyone gets to experience the idyllic trails or beautiful wildlife preserves in the same way.

When we think about the Bronx, we know it's full of many different kinds of people, many different experiences. But if you haven't been to the BX, or you've only experienced certain sides of it, you're probably more familiar with places that get a one-sided shake. Like certain wards down south in New Orleans, favelas in São Paulo, the shantytown in Joburg, or the ghetto in Port-au-Prince, there are far too many parts of the Bronx that struggle against divestment and systemic oppression. We're not talking about "underprivileged" communities, which is an indirect way to say what they really are: intentionally deprived.

In the financial capital of the world, many people in the Bronx go to bed hungry every night, while police are tasked with ticketing "unlicensed" street vendors for selling produce at affordable prices. The Bronx is not a food "desert," because deserts are natural occurrences. But our borough is affected by food apartheid, a social system of inequality that limits access to affordable, healthy food and makes state-produced poverty a personal burden.

In a city where thousands come from around the globe to pursue their academic and artistic education, the school-to-prison pipeline in the Bronx couldn't be more clear. We have been in schools where a painted line down the center of a hallway separates children who are forced to walk silently, single file, between classes. We've seen a cafeteria labeled as a "mess hall," as it might be in prison. An outdoor play area, if it's even used for such activity, is labeled "the yard." Around the corner from the South Bronx High School complex, which currently houses two distinct schools, is the Horizon Juvenile Center in Mott Haven. It's classified as the most restrictive facility of its kind for youth. Imagine walking by a place where your friends or family might be locked up and alone, while you're on your way to school. Only then can you have a sense of what it's like to come of age in the South Bronx.

Our community deserves so many more resources than it gets. But we come from hardworking, determined folks. We find beauty and make magic in the struggle, because the alternative is to succumb to great odds. We're less concerned with convincing others that the Bronx is worthy. We already know what it is, YERRRRR! We are invested in impacting tangible change that shifts the reality, the narrative, for folks in our community. And we are proud of where we come from, imperfections and all.

The food in this chapter takes you on a tour of the place Ghetto Gastro was born. We set it off with Chopped Stease (page 29), our take on the classic bodega sandwich. We hit you with a little Chinese takeout with Jade's Palace (page 45), our take on General Tso's. The Nutcrackers (page 64) will get you feelin nice, and if you don't know, trust you will soon. Mobb out with the GG goons. We chop it up with A$AP Ferg and Thelma Golden, whose respective links between our crew, Uptown, and Black culture help frame our work and the legacies we are proud to reflect. Ferg has brought that interdisciplinary energy since day one, banking certified-platinum hip hop tracks alongside innovations in fashion and making moves on the screen. Thelma Golden has been a pivotal curator in the arts world for more than three decades and leads the Studio Museum in Harlem, the premier global institution for visual art by artists of African descent, as director and chief curator.

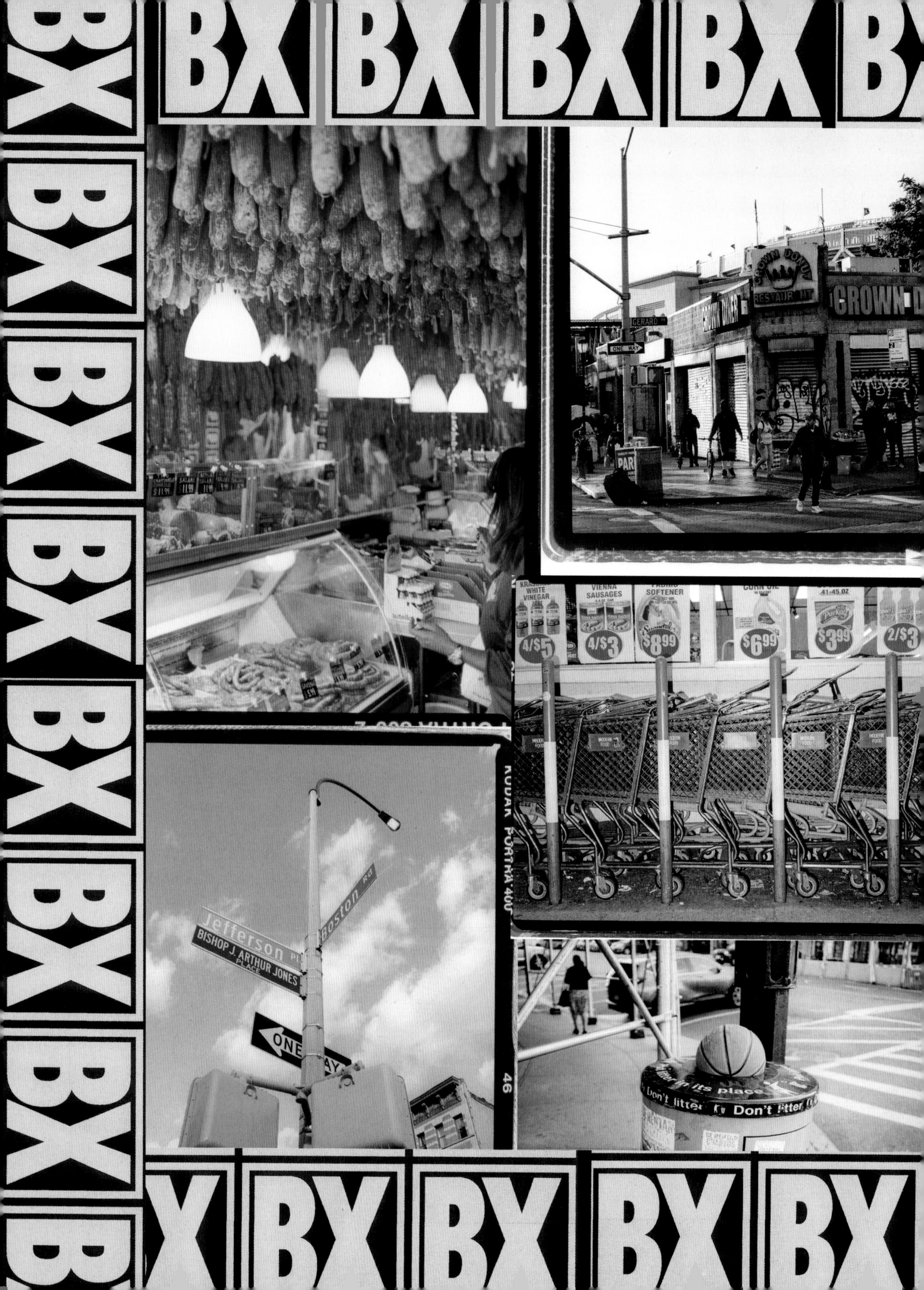
BX BX BX BX BX
VIENNA SAUSAGES
FABRIC SOFTENER
WHITE VINEGAR
4/$5
4/$3
$8.99
$6.99
$3.99
2/$3
41-45 OZ
CROWN DONUT
CROWN DINER
GERARD
ONE WAY
Jefferson Pl
BISHOP J. ARTHUR JONES PLACE
Boston Rd
KODAK PORTRA 400
46
Don't litter
BX BX BX BX BX

BX BX BX BX BX
Prospect Av
GAUCHOS
Fordham CENTER

CHOPPED STEASE

Seems like we've been eating chopped cheese our whole lives. Our favorites were from delis like Hajji's on 110th (also known as Blue Sky Deli). It's a hood staple, one that until recent years, you'd find only Uptown.

For $4 or $5, any short-order bodega cook can style it how you like it, but the classic build is ground beef cooked down with onions and American cheese, then topped with tomatoes and shredded lettuce on a hero or roll. It's a sandwich that's been extensively rapped and written about, argued over, and widely consumed. Some make comparisons to other sandwiches, but we're not doin that (this is not the time for Philly cheesesteak debates). Like a lot of foods that emerge from neighborhoods and cultures where many are systemically deprived of wealth, the chopped cheese is a blue-collar dish. It's gonna fill you up, get you right. And like many iconic foods, especially those from Black and brown cultures, the chopped cheese is not without its social complexities.

As the class makeup of the BX and Uptown has shifted to attract richer, whiter populations in recent years, the chopped cheese found its way into the hands of folks who didn't grow up on it like we did but rather often "discovered" the sandwich and, naturally, loved it. It wasn't long before chopped cheeses appeared downtown and across the bridge in Brooklyn, at restaurants, not delis, and sometimes at more than triple the deli price (and on the wrong bread!).

In the United States, inexpensive food can often mean it's actually unhealthy. A widespread lack of care for our environment, agricultural policies that subsidize certain commodities over fruits and vegetables, commercial rents that make running a restaurant in practice a real estate business—these all factor into a $4 beef sandwich that's no long-term investment in your body. The cost to source antibiotic-free, sustainably farmed meat, organic produce for the fixins, and bread made from high-quality non-GMO wheat would make it unrealistic for most businesses to maintain the low retail tag. But study this: Here's a class issue exacerbated by racism. Poor people get a sandwich they can afford that's not nourishing, and wealthy people get offered a healthier, more expensive version that might not even resemble the real thing. Some of us Black folks looked up to see a product of our environment appear in news stories as if it just got invented, a relentless American refrain.

Our take on the sandwich that's come to symbolize so much in our community is the Chopped Stease. At Ghetto Gastro, we aim to keep pushing the conversation, remixing, repurposing, subverting where we can. Stease is about that layered flavor, that BX energy. We have to big up where we're from, and that means claiming the parts that helped shape us. No disrespect to the OG chopped cheese, but it's only right we add our own stease. Respectfully.

CONTINUED

Makes 4 sandwiches

INGREDIENTS

1 tablespoon vegetable oil

4 hero rolls or French dinner rolls, sliced in half lengthwise

3 tablespoons plant-based butter

1 cup (125 g) cipollini onions, diced

1 pound (455 g) plant-based ground meat

1 tablespoon flaky sea salt, plus more to taste

1 teaspoon freshly ground black pepper

9 ounces (255 g) plant-based American cheese

½ cup (110 g) Aquafaba Aioli (page 290)

1 cup (75 g) finely shredded iceberg lettuce

1 heirloom tomato, sliced

PREPARATION

In a large nonstick pan, heat the vegetable oil over medium heat. When it begins to smoke, add the rolls, cut-side down, and toast, gently pressing them against the pan, until the insides develop a golden brown hue and crisp up, about 1 minute. You might need to work in a few batches; don't crowd the pan. As the rolls are toasted, remove them from the heat and set aside.

Add the plant-based butter to the same pan and increase the heat to medium-high. Add the onions and sweat them until they begin to soften, about 2 minutes. Add the plant-based ground meat and season with the salt and pepper. Cook, using a spatula to break up the meat as it cooks, until browned, 5 to 6 minutes, then layer the cheese onto the meat. Use the spatula to "chop" the cheese into the meat. Chop it! Stir to combine, then remove from the heat.

Take the bottom half of each sandwich roll and spread a layer of the aioli onto it, then add some lettuce. Load on the meat-and-cheese mix, then top with sliced tomato, plus a sprinkle of salt. Finish with the top half of each roll.

To serve it up deli-style (and for a less messy eating experience), wrap the sandwich in a sheet of parchment paper, then in a sheet of foil. Order up! Serve immediately.

JORDAN CASTEEL
ICE, 2018
OIL ON CANVAS, 78 x 60 in.

GREEN "FOR THE MONEY" JUICE

Around our way, we say "Green for the money, gold for the honey." For us, greens represent resilience and abundance. Plus, you can't beat the essential health benefits.

Green Garden Juice Bar and Health Food Store is on White Plains Road. It opened as Brother Roy's Green Garden in 1983 at a different location (it's always going to be Brother Roy's to us), but the juice bar is a beloved Black-owned gathering place that promotes health and wellness. For youth used to seeing smoke shops and liquor stores on countless corners, this West Indian spot is where you find like-minded people knowledgeable about nutrition.

Brother Roy's is across from an elevated train, facing the New York Housing Authority's Gun Hill Houses. The energy is chaotic on the streets. In the shop, it's like an oasis. You smell the fresh fruit. You hear patois that reflects Caribbean roots. A mural dedicated to Brother Roy stretches across one wall.

Green "For the Money" Juice is inspired by this juice spot. The black seed oil, extracted from black cumin seed, is slightly bitter, a little spicy, and balances well with the blend. You can find black seed oil at natural food stores, or online (see Resources, page 295). Drink it cold, so start with fruit that's been refrigerated. Health is wealth.

Serves 4

INGREDIENTS

2 cucumbers, halved
6 celery stalks
8 curly kale leaves, stemmed (your preference of kale)
2 cups loosely packed (60 g) baby spinach leaves
2 (1- to 2-inch/3 to 5 cm) pieces fresh ginger
2 large (or 4 small) Granny Smith apples, cored
2 tablespoons fresh lime juice
Black seed oil, for finishing

EQUIPMENT

Juicer

PREPARATION

Working in batches as needed, use a high-powered juicer to juice the cucumbers, celery, kale, spinach, ginger, and apples, one ingredient at a time. Pass the juice through a fine-mesh strainer into a carafe or pitcher, discarding the pulp.

Add the lime juice and stir to incorporate.

Pour the beverage into glasses. Garnish each with 3 small dots of black seed oil. Serve and drink immediately.

LYNETTE YIADOM-BOAKYE
THE ALMONDS, 2020
OIL ON CANVAS, $29\frac{1}{2}$ x $27\frac{3}{4}$ in.

YOU GOT THE JUICE NOW

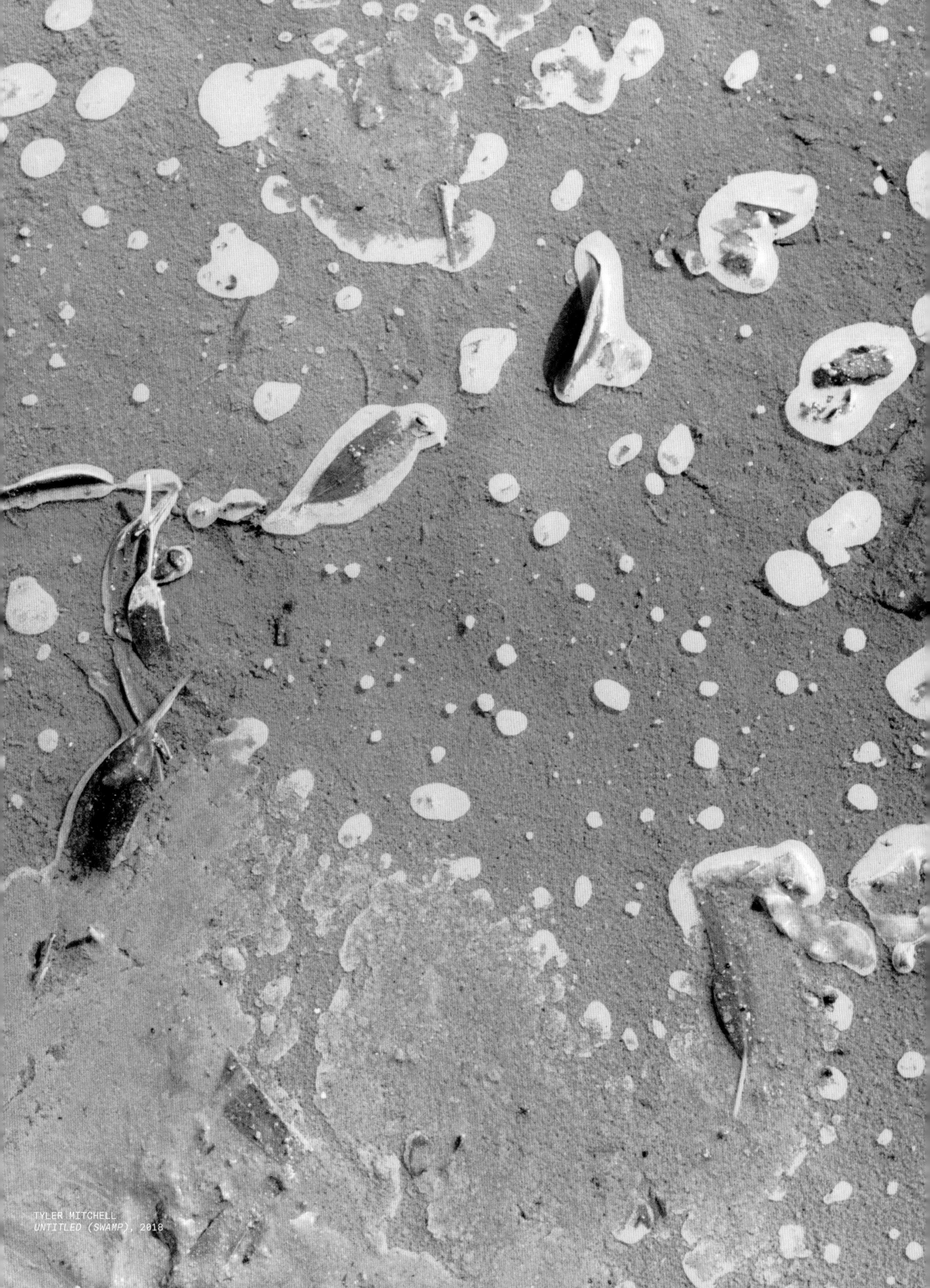

TYLER MITCHELL
UNTITLED (SWAMP), 2018

COCO LOCO

Summertime Uptown, you've got several tasty options to beat the heat: Piragua, a fruity shaved ice classic from our Boricua fam; Mister Softee ice cream trucks; or coco helado, coconut ice offered in a range of flavors.

Mister Softee shows up in late spring. But when the coco ice is outside? That's when it's dumb hot. When we spot the Delicioso Coco Helado carts, it's often an abuelo slinging the treats for $1 to $2 (as the Bronx emcee Fat Joe says, "Yesterday's price is not today's price!"—those joints were 50 cents when we were coming up). Get your coco, cherry, mango, or if you're feelin a little spicy, you can taste the rainbow. Coco helado is essential when the humidity is high, when open fire hydrants flood the streets and multiple generations sit on stoops.

This coconut ice cream is inspired by our childhood memories Uptown. It calls for coconut puree, which is a frozen product (see Resources, page 295). Defrost the puree in the refrigerator a day or two before you want to make the ice cream. Once it's defrosted, do not refreeze what's left. You can use the remaining coconut puree as a substitute for coconut milk in Limonada de Coco (page 160) or add it to curries or other sorbet recipes.

Makes about 1 quart (1 L)

INGREDIENTS

4 cups (375 g) unsweetened shredded coconut

4 cups (500 ml) coconut milk

1¾ cups plus 2 tablespoons (185 g) organic cane sugar

1½ cups (375 ml) frozen coconut puree (such as Boiron brand), thawed

EQUIPMENT

Ice cream maker

PREPARATION

Heat the oven to 350°F (175°C).

On a sheet pan, spread the shredded coconut into an even layer. Toast the coconut in the oven for 3 to 5 minutes, until it develops a toasty aroma and is lightly browned.

In a large pot, bring the coconut milk and sugar to a simmer over medium heat. Turn off the heat. Add the toasted coconut to the warmed coconut milk and steep until the liquid has cooled to room temperature, about 2 hours. Using a fine-mesh strainer, strain the liquid into a large bowl.

CONTINUED

Add the coconut puree to the infused coconut milk and whisk thoroughly to completely dissolve the puree. Pour the mixture into a large bowl or container. Cover and refrigerate the ice cream base overnight, or for about 8 hours. You want to allow the coconut flavor to develop.

Transfer the chilled ice cream base to your ice cream maker and follow the manufacturer's instructions for preparation. The texture of the ice cream should be smooth and creamy. Transfer the ice cream to a freezer-safe airtight container and freeze until the ice cream sets, usually 2 to 4 hours, then serve.

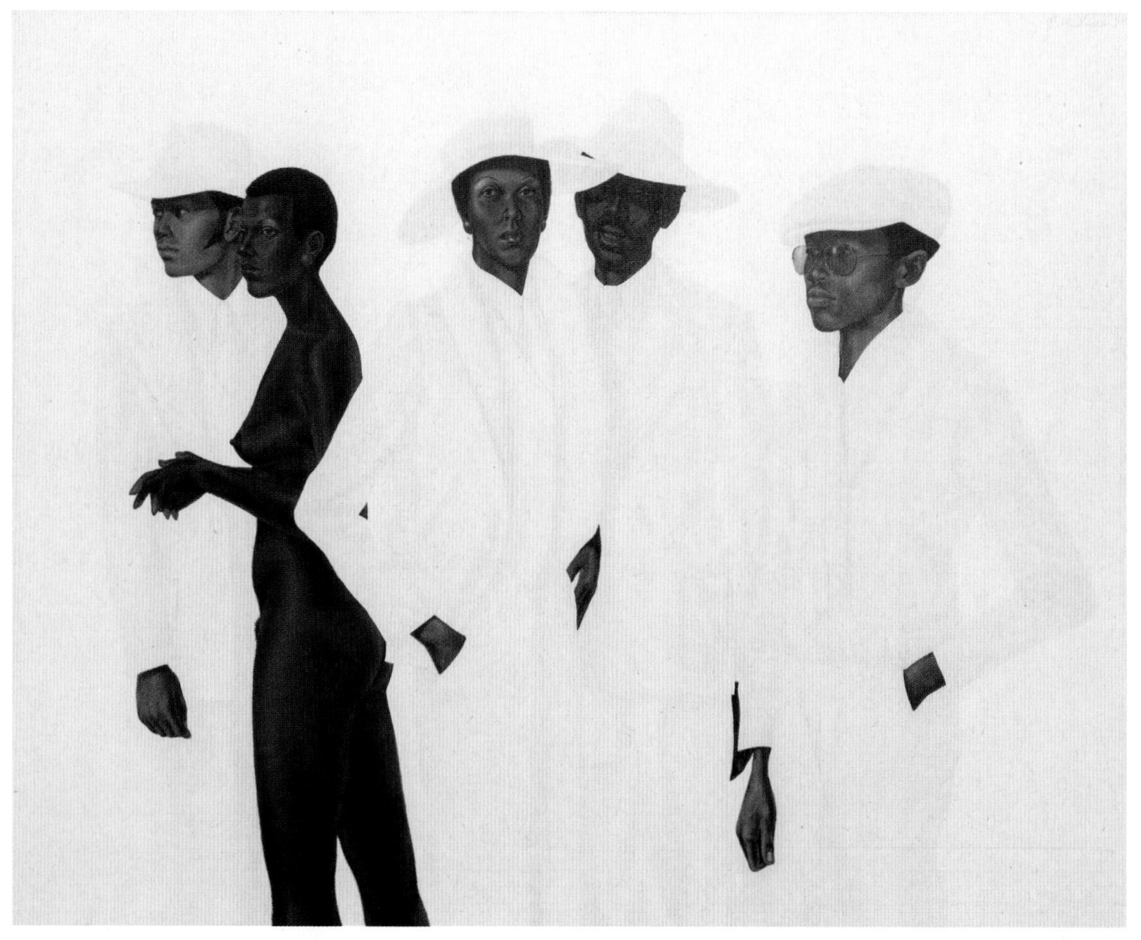

BARKLEY L. HENDRICKS
WHAT'S GOING ON, 1974
OIL, ACRYLIC, AND MAGNA ON COTTON CANVAS, $65\frac{3}{4}$ x $83\frac{3}{4}$ in.

BRYAN FERNANDEZ
EL HELADERO, 2020
ACRYLIC PAINT, ALUMINUM FOIL, MISCELLANEOUS PAPER, OIL PASTEL, PLASTIC BAGS, GLOVES, MEDICAL MAKE, FABRIC, CARDBOARD, COTTON BALLS, LEATHER, 48 x 48 in.

SEAFOOD CITY

New York City is far more geographically diverse than most people realize. City Island, or what we call the "Hood Hamptons," is right past Pelham Bay and south of Orchard Beach (aka Chocha Beach). It's one of those "if you know you know" spots.

One and a half miles long and only half a mile wide, it's a small strip that, for a number of reasons, never saw the big development that some speculators planned. The original stewards of this region, the Lenape people, fished and hunted on what was then called Lenapehoking long before Dutch colonizers arrived. It's been a sought-after destination by outsiders ever since. Today, City Island is renowned for its plethora of seafood.

Particularly in the spring and summer, it feels like everyone goes to City Island. We refer to our time there as being at The Office because we used to go as a team to catch up, game-plan, and chill. Thanks to a single point of entry, traffic is wild; the queue of cars can reach all the way back to Orchard Beach. Folks angle to get their fixes, from lobster tails to little neck and cherrystone clams, and heaping plates of fritto misto—fried shrimp, scallops, or calamari. On the libation side, cognac coladas and planter's punch are fan favorites. Two popular restaurants across the street from each other have serious cult followings: Johnny's Reef (we love their clam strips) and Tony's Pier (might have the better fried shrimp plate), and mention of either can engage folks in lengthy, if sometimes hilarious, philosophical debates over which is best. We ain't here to pick sides, but we here to provide the vibes. Now heat that oil and let's ride. Prego.

CONTINUED

Serves 4

INGREDIENTS

For the romesco

¾ cup (85 g) grated Parmigiano-Reggiano cheese

1 cup (120 g) hazelnuts, roasted and skinned

1 roasted red bell pepper (canned, or roasted over the flame on a gas stove, seeded, and peeled)

¼ cup plus 2½ tablespoons (95 ml) extra-virgin olive oil

1½ tablespoons sherry vinegar

4 or 5 garlic cloves

½ cup (8 g) fresh flat-leaf parsley

1½ teaspoons flaky sea salt

1½ teaspoons smoked paprika

For the fritto misto

8½ cups (2 L) vegetable oil

4 whiting fillets

9 ounces (255 g) squid, tentacles removed, bodies sliced into rings

9 ounces (255 g) prawns, head on

4 cups (1 L) buttermilk

1 cup (150 g) semolina flour

Leaves from 1 bunch basil

Lemon wedges, for serving

PREPARATION

Make the romesco

In a blender, combine the Parmigiano-Reggiano, hazelnuts, roasted pepper, olive oil, vinegar, garlic, parsley, salt, and paprika and blend until smooth. Set aside.

Fry the seafood

In a deep fryer or a deep pot, heat the vegetable oil over medium-high heat until it registers 350°F (175°C) on an instant-read thermometer (adjust heat as needed to maintain). Line a plate or two with paper towels and set nearby.

Clean all the seafood and pat dry. Pour the buttermilk into a large bowl. Submerge all the seafood in the buttermilk and leave to soak for 5 minutes.

Put the semolina in a separate bowl. Remove the seafood from the buttermilk and gently shake off any excess liquid. Working in small batches, toss the seafood in the semolina to coat, making sure you get an even coating and that the semolina gets inside the cavities and crevices of the seafood. Place the dusted seafood in a strainer and tap lightly to shake off any excess semolina.

When the oil is hot, fry the basil first, letting the leaves get just crisp, about 1 minute. Remove with a slotted spoon or spider, then let them drain on the paper towel–lined plate.

Working in batches, fry the seafood until it's golden brown. Transfer to a paper towel–lined plate to drain. After each batch, make sure to leave time for the oil temperature to return to 350°F (175°C) before frying the next round of seafood.

Garnish the fried seafood with the crispy basil and serve with the romesco and fresh lemon on the side.

KODAK PORTRA 400
ORCHARD BEACH
...PLEASE
CASH ONLY
...served with french fries...
CLAMS
OYSTERS
SQUID (CALAMARI)
FROG LEGS 10
WE FRY ONLY WITH VEGETABLE OIL
...cole slaw ...lemon
CHICKEN FINGERS
CHICKEN
CHICKEN LIVERS
CHICKEN WINGS
...PLEASE PAY WHEN SERVED
SNOW CRAB LEGS $32.00
MOZZARELLA STICKS $7.00
FISH STICKS $14.00
ONION RINGS
THANK YOU!
75 YEARS.....
OF SERVING YOU
PRICES HAVE CHANGED
QUALITY NEVER!
CLAM BAR...
LITTLE NECKS
CHERRY STONES
PLEASE PAY
1 DOZEN
½ DOZEN
4

Thank You
Enjoy

JADE'S PALACE

What we affectionately refer to as hood Chinese spots are small hole-in-the-wall takeout restaurants, unique expressions of American Chinese food. Redlining, a shameful decadeslong practice ruthlessly coordinated by predominantly white lawmakers, white-owned banks (many still doing dirt in Black communities today), and real estate agents, resulted in covenants and restrictions limiting where people of color could rent, own homes, or open businesses.

Folks talk about the segregated South, but this practice is common throughout the country. Generations of this systemic oppression created communities where many Black Americans and non-white immigrants ended up in the same places, struggling among one another for resources that were plentiful for white residents in other neighborhoods. Often these communities are afflicted by divestment (it's not a coincidence that they lack beautiful parks, well-lit and tree-lined streets, or consistent sanitation).

In the early twentieth century, the failure of Reconstruction and its broken promises to Black Americans emerging from slavery, mixed with racial terror and the dawn of Jim Crow laws in the Deep South, produced the Great Migration. Spanning more than fifty years, this exodus of resistance created larger groups of Black people in the Northeast, Midwest, and western areas. But up north, Black people were still often limited to where they could dine. Chinese-owned restaurants were proliferating throughout the United States, a result of an imported labor pool that built the American railroad system. These spots didn't necessarily serve Chinese-based cuisine but were among few dining spaces outside of the Black community that served Black patrons. The flavor profiles of these menus, evident in the selections available at the hood spot today, reference African American soul food and Spanish food canons. (Here when we say "Spanish," we're speaking as New Yorkers taking cues from our local community, referencing part of the Afro Latin diaspora with deep roots in the city, including the Dominican Republic, Puerto Rico, Cuba, and so on, who refer to themselves this way. We're not referring to white Spanish people of European background.)

The hood Chinese restaurant is ubiquitous in Black hip hop culture. For decades, references to dishes have appeared in song lyrics; there's even a brown and green Timberland boot that's been dubbed "beef and broccoli." The tan joints are called "sesame chickens." These are not the spots where you look for traditional Cantonese dumplings or classic Sichuan noodles. You're gonna find chicken wings next to egg foo yung. Chinese sweet tea served in plastic quart containers. Nobody's complaining about MSG (real talk, everyone should stop complaining about MSG). Everything comes in a to-go box because even if the spot is large enough for tables and chairs, you're probably not staying long.

Take a closer look, and the politics are often complicated. These restaurants serve neighborhoods that are underfunded and over-policed; the takeout joints are cash only, the aesthetics are typically grim. You're gonna see bulletproof glass.

DOUBLE DRAGON 龍
INESE FOOD FREE DELIVERY TEL:718-367-3366/530
FRIEDRICH
PARTY TRAYS
BANDEJA DEL PARTIDO
You Can Choose Any Dishes From The Menu

Tensions exist. Animosity can be subtle or overt, but we know that it stems from the same source: capitalist-driven white supremacy, concealed in the myth of the American Dream. Black folks and Asian folks are often forced to compete with each other, when we benefit so much more from solidarity. That can be hard to remember day-to-day where resources are finite and scarcity dominates.

From a distance, some dishes or flavor combinations can strike self-proclaimed purists as "odd," or "weird"—a word that has no place in food descriptors. But we gotta remember that every menu serves somebody's tastes, which are a reflection of where people come from, where people end up, and what people can access. One iconic dish from the hood Chinese joint is General Tso's Chicken. Our take uses cauliflower because that's how we do, and we've named it after our local spot, Jade's Palace.

Serves 2 to 4

INGREDIENTS

For the General Tso's sauce

½ cup (120 ml) Mushroom Dashi (page 292) or vegetable stock

¼ cup (50 g) organic cane sugar

3 tablespoons dark soy sauce

2 tablespoons Shaoxing wine or dry sherry

2 tablespoons Chinese rice vinegar

1 tablespoon cornstarch

1 teaspoon toasted sesame oil

2 teaspoons peanut oil (or vegetable or canola oil)

2 garlic cloves, minced

1 piece fresh ginger, about 1 inch (3 cm) long, peeled and minced

2 teaspoons minced scallion whites

8 small dried red Chinese chiles

For the fried cauliflower

About 6 cups (1.5 L) vegetable oil (enough to submerge the cauliflower so it deep-fries), for frying

⅓ cup plus 2½ tablespoons (60 g) all-purpose flour

1 cup (150 g) cornstarch

½ teaspoon (2 g) baking powder

½ cup (120 ml) water

½ cup (120 ml) vodka

1 head cauliflower, chopped into 1- to 2-inch (3 to 5 cm) chunks

Flaky sea salt

Sesame seeds, for garnish

6 to 8 scallion greens, sliced into 1-inch (3 cm) pieces, for garnish

Cooked rice, for serving

Lime wedges, for serving

PREPARATION

Make the sauce

In a large bowl, combine the mushroom dashi, sugar, soy sauce, wine, vinegar, cornstarch, and sesame oil. Stir with a fork until the cornstarch has dissolved and no lumps remain. Set aside.

In a large skillet, combine the peanut oil, garlic, ginger, scallion whites, and red chiles and heat over medium heat, stirring, for about 3 minutes, until the vegetables are aromatic and soft but not brown.

Stir the sauce mixture once more, then add it to the skillet. Make sure to scrape out any sugar or starch that has sunk to the bottom of your bowl. You want all this good stuff to balance the flavor. Maintain your medium heat. Cook, stirring, until the sauce boils and thickens, about 30 seconds. Remove the sauce from the heat and transfer back to your large bowl.

Fry the cauliflower

In a large heavy-bottomed pot, heat the vegetable oil over medium-high heat until it registers 350°F (175°C) on an instant-read thermometer (adjust heat as needed to maintain). You need enough oil in the pot to fully submerge the cauliflower pieces, which you're going to fry in small batches.

In a bowl, whisk together the flour, ½ cup (75 g) of the cornstarch, the baking powder, water, and vodka. Pour the remaining ½ cup (75 g) cornstarch into a wide shallow bowl. Working in batches, coat a few cauliflower pieces with the cornstarch and dip them into the batter. Gently shake off any excess batter.

Add the battered cauliflower pieces to the hot oil and fry until the batter is crispy, about 3 minutes. (This batter is light and crispy, so it will not turn a golden brown color.)

Use a spider or slotted spoon to remove the cauliflower from the pot, and set the cauliflower aside to drain on a wire rack set over a sheet pan. (You can keep the fried cauliflower warm in the oven at 350°F/175°C while you're frying the remaining batches.) When all the cauliflower is finished, add it to the bowl with the General's Tso sauce and toss to coat. Season with salt to taste.

Sprinkle with sesame seeds and the scallion greens. Serve with rice and a lime wedge.

INTERVIEW WITH

A$AP FERG

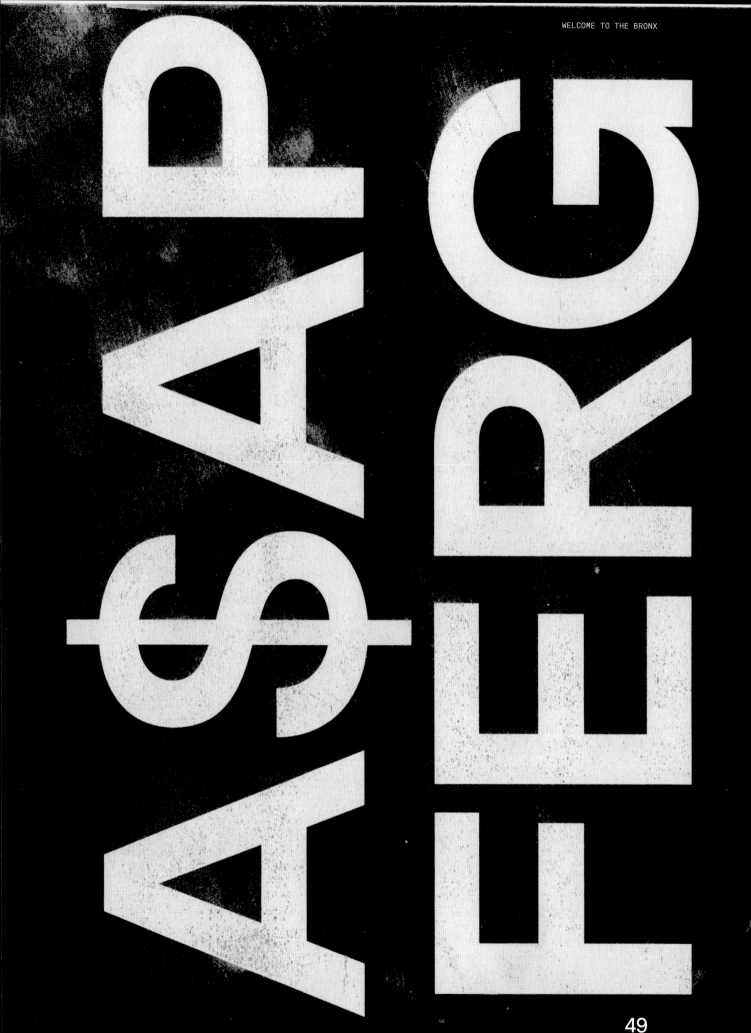

Harlem native A$AP Ferg is best known as one member of the New York hip hop collective A$AP Mob. His father was a graphic designer who, through his own company, designed the logos for music labels like Bad Boy Records and Uptown Records (both Harlem-founded). Ferg expanded on these early lessons in merging design, art, and music by blending the arts with fashion and hip hop. He collaborates on projects from sneaker and streetwear releases to working with brands in fine jewelry and luxury beverage. He's always got his eye on bringing Harlem to the rest of the world, much like we're about biggin up the BX.

Ghetto Gastro: You're a Harlem cat. But what comes to mind when you hear "the Bronx"?

A$AP Ferg: I think about the place where hip hop was birthed through gang culture, as something positive that came out of that environment. Instead of the kids warring with each other, they figured out break dancing and "battling" each other. I think about the pioneers bringin the speakers out for the block parties.

I think about "Planet Rock" [by Afrika Bambaataa and the Soul Sonic Force], one of my favorite songs.

Harlem and the Bronx are distinct, but there's a long history of cultural exchange.

They're both rich in culture, it's rich in the soil. You go to the Bronx and it's a lot of Puerto Ricans, a lot of Black people. It's similar in Harlem—I'm from 143rd and Amsterdam, where it's predominantly African American, but you go to Broadway and it looks like you went to the Dominican Republic.

The music changes, you get the Spanish music happening. You got the little stores where women could buy their jeggings, the hair salons, all of that. We grew up with a lot of those Spanish guys. We was shopping at the same spots, going to the same schools. You know, when my moms wasn't cooking, I was eating Spanish food.

What are some of your favorite food memories between the BX and Uptown? You probably got some City Island stories.

Oh, City Island is crazy. City Island is one of those places that we all go to. Everybody.

We call it the "Hood Hamptons."

That's a good comparison. It's a getaway with affordable seafood. That was the first place I ate frog legs with my dad. He was like, "Yo, we going to get some frog legs." He made it this big event. I've got fond memories. The snow crab legs with the seasoning and the butter and all of that.

How has your experience of food changed as you've traveled more and eaten in other countries?

Well, my dad was Southern, from North Carolina. He moved to New York at an early age. My mom's family is Trinidadian. I grew up eating "American" food: soul food, Chinese food, Italian—pizza. I think my palate changed, from the quality of food.

In the United States, we eat, like, these big chickens. You go to the chicken spot and it's this ginormous, gigantic chicken wing. And you go to London and the chicken wing is smaller [because it was raised differently]. The quality of the food changed.

And then I learned about farm-to-table. I learned that you could go to the farm and check out the livestock and you can see how they raised the animals before you eat. That was an eye-opening experience.

In Australia, there's a huge plant-based and vegan culture. When I went plant-based for a while, it was actually perfect when I was touring over there. They were super creative in how they prepared their food.

Uptown, we have a unique point of view with plant-based eating because of West Indian culture, especially Rastafarian culture and Ital cuisine, the juice bars.

For sure. I definitely grew up going to the juice bar. Uptown we have juice bar culture. That's the only reason I'm able to make a song called "Green Juice" and do activation with Styles P with Juices for Life [a Bronx-based juice company], and sell merchandise like signed T-shirts. We would hang out at the juice bar. We'd hang out at the corner stores, but it's probably even cooler at the juice bar because we're actually replenishing our bodies, drinking good juices, eating healthy food.

My father was going through kidney failure and he started eating at a lot of juice bars. They diagnosed him with mild diabetes, so he couldn't eat too much salt or sugar. He started getting food from the juice bars, but that shit was smelling so good, I wanted to taste his food. He was getting curry chickpeas with the rice.

This is the one on 125th, the Uptown juice bar by Madison?

One Twenty-Fifth between where?

Between Fifth and Madison. That was the only juice spot that had hot food Uptown.

Okay, yeah. I'm going to say it's that spot. Now, every day I eat at the juice bar. Like if I'm not going to a major dinner on some fancy stuff, I'm going to eat at the juice bar. It's good prices and you're going to feel full and you're gonna feel good about what you ate.

We first linked in the fashion realm. You were coming to the first Freestyle Friday parties. You've been part of this thing from the beginning.

It's funny, because when I was coming to y'all's house, I felt like even though I was early on it, I felt like I was super late to the party. That's how much energy y'all generated in the town, like that's how excited I was for it.

I was like, *damn*. I'm here in the spot, but I'm wanting to know all the history. What made y'all come up with the ideas, the inspiration for the food, the inspiration for the name. One of those early dishes had the hood Crown boxes—

Oh yeah! The chicken spot joints played off the Crown to-go boxes.

Yeah. It's avant-garde food inside these hood boxes. And I'm like, yo, the aesthetic is totally me. When I came to the game, I was like, I'm going to be the dude that'll show up at a fashion show with gold grills, a black hoodie, and a durag. And that was translated through your food. The titles of y'all's foods—it's like if food could rap, that's what it was. And that's what it *is* to me. It's poetic, it's true to who you are, and it speaks to people just like us. That's why it resonated with me.

You guys are always introducing history. When I made "Shabba," a lot of kids thought I was Shabba. But like, if they google "Shabba," then one of the heroes pop up beside me, you know what I'm saying? Shabba Ranks, the Jamaican artist, the legend, the icon, one of the dudes that pioneered the game with dancehall music, he pops up when they're searching my name. If you make history with history, you're going to be history. That was Onyx on my first album. You guys align y'all selves with great brands from the Rick Owens to Audemars Piguet, down to A$AP Ferg. I love the whole avant-garde route meets us.

The first time Jon heard "Shabba," Rocky hadn't even recorded his verse yet. Jon knew,* my boy is next. *Let's talk about the Denim Library.

This is how young I was and not knowledgeable. There was a young man named So, probably in his late thirties. I'm still learning, I'm still learning my roots. But Denim Library was a hub. So was one of the first entrepreneurs, besides my dad, I seen with his own establishment. He had a store called Denim Library. So was a young man, probably late thirties at the time. And he had accounts like True Religion, Antique Denim, Robin's, William and Brad, Red Monkey. Any type of jean, all the fly stuff, it was in the Library.

And then So had a designer that was in this crazy glass casing. It was these custom shirts called "Jon Gray." I would come in the store and see all this stuff. I'm just looking, 'cause I can't afford none of this stuff. I'm looking and this case, it just popped out to me. All this time, I'm thinking this person, it's a white dude. It's a white, old dude with gray hair. 'Cause that's all I'd ever seen as a fashion designer, old and white, like on that level. When I met Jon, So introduced me to homie. I'm like, *Ooh shit!* This dude is young. He looks like me. How did he wind up getting an account with So, being in this store among all these pillars of fashion design?

It gave me hope for my endeavors. I could see myself in this space more now because I seen somebody else do it. When Ghetto Gastro started, it was out of nowhere, Jon didn't tell nobody. I was like, *Ooh, I get him. He's like a curator-type dude*. It's not just the music, it's not just the food, it's not just the clothing. It's lifestyle.

You were printing shirts downstairs at Denim Library and showing paintings at Black Ink. We gotta let the folks know you went to New York's High School of Art and Design. You're the same, though, you got a lot of different interests.

We are the same. I would love to have time to focus on culinary arts, travel to Patagonia, cook with different people and all of that. You know what I'm saying? I'm like watching *Chef's Table*, I'm looking at Tinker Hatfield–designed sneakers, then I'm gettin into a Rothko documentary, then I'll watch some Tupac, Death Row Records shit. This is all my world. I'm pretty sure you wrote a rap before. You probably laid some shit down!

Back in the day, after* 8 Mile *came out, Jon started writing raps. He was inspired, yo!

We come from a place where you gotta be creative. We gotta make it out. It was times I had to make duck sauce sandwiches, or mayonnaise sandwiches just to eat. You know! That tuna fish. That shit was bussin! You gotta get creative and we gonna try everything.

I had a lot of great people to look up to, like my dad. He was just the biggest influence. He took me to the China man to get the embroidery done to the shirts. Then he took me to the African dudes at the market to do the heat transfer. He took me to the Indian guys to pick up the shirts, and he took me to the Jewish guys to get the silkscreen and paint and the screens made. I learned how to make a product.

When they sellin drugs outside, I didn't have to go that route 'cause I had information. I think that kids, they lack information and then they put their energies elsewhere. I was printing Bad Boy Records' shirts for *Making the Band*. D-Block, Black Rob, and LL Cool J—this was when I was in high school, after school. When my father got sick with kidney failure, I took on the business. I was doing four hundred shirts front and back, manually. This is before automatic machines.

Yeah that's some real skills.

Come on now! I threw that Justin Timberlake album, the one that Timbaland produced. I threw the Pharrell, the N.E.R.D. *In Search of . . .* I be trapping T-shirts. You know what I'm saying? In school, I was printing shirts and I was taking the shirts to school and selling them to the dudes. But I was like making the boy joint and I was making a girl joint to match. I would go up to the girls, match they sneakers, and then the dudes would be forced to buy a shirt and buy the girlfriend a T-shirt. Early on, I equated art to money. I want to look fly. I want to be exclusive. I want to be able to monetize off my exclusiveness. That's how I always looked at it.

That's my dad in me, and my mother is a hard worker as well. She was very locked in and focused, she graduated college. And with those two, I just, I'm a beast. How to move, you know, if shit going down on the block. You heard the gunshot; it was fights happening. I knew not to go that way. A lot of kids was running to see what happened. That shit never made sense to me.

What does "Ghetto Gastro" symbolize for you?

"Ghetto Gastro" is like *Trap Lord*. It's like "Hood Pope." It's like "Cocaine Castle." Like with my music, it's a juxtaposition of the kids that come from hardship with the avant-garde, the upper echelon, the finer things.

What do you feel when you hear "Black Power Kitchen"?

I'm thinking about the Black Panthers running a program to feed kids back in the day. I'm thinking about empowering our people on what to eat, how to eat, where to eat, because we've been conditioned for so long to eat a way that's not healthy for us. It represents strength. It's a strength for you to eat the way you eat with Ghetto Gastro. You say "food is a weapon," right? Not a weapon for destruction, but for us to build. That's what that Black Power Kitchen is.

HIGHBRIDGE PLANTAIN PATTY

Highbridge is a neighborhood in the Bronx that's connected to Washington Heights in Upper Manhattan by way of the pedestrian High Bridge. The blending of cultures across this physical landscape is rich, and like the bridge, we're linking collards and platanos in this recipe, flavors of the West African and Caribbean diasporas.

These patties have a nice sweetness and a spicy punch. They also take some time, because you'll need to ferment the plantains for the filling for up to one week, which adds a tangy depth to the flavor. If you're cooking in a warmer climate, it may take less time for the plantains to ferment. Keep checking on them. They should smell sour but not rancid, so don't let it go too far. You can also refrigerate the plantains to stop the fermentation; they'll keep for up to five days.

The recipe also calls for Greenbacks, our braised collards dish that's packed with flavor and benefits from a long cook time. Don't rush these steps. Trust, you won't be disappointed. We suggest using store-bought empanada shells for ease of use. Follow the instructions on the package, if available. Otherwise, a general guide is to bake the patties at 375°F (190°C) for 20 to 22 minutes.

CONTINUED

Makes 45 to 50 patties, depending on shell size

INGREDIENTS

8 very ripe plantains (5½ pounds/2.5 kg)

For the habanada pickles

5 habanada peppers

5 tablespoons (75 ml) rice vinegar

½ teaspoon raw cane sugar

½ teaspoon flaky sea salt

For the patty filling

1⅓ pounds (600 g) Greenbacks (braised collard greens, page 226), minced

1 cup (240 ml) Aunt Millie's Green Sofrito (page 290)

3 scallions, thinly sliced

2½ tablespoons thinly sliced fresh cilantro leaves

1 heaping tablespoon finely grated fresh ginger

2 tablespoons lemon zest

2 tablespoons white miso paste

40 to 45 store-bought empanada shells (preferably 5-inch/13 cm)

PREPARATION

The key is to ripen the plantains until they begin to ferment, so start with plantains that are as ripe as you can find. Place 6 of the plantains (you'll keep 2 fresh) in a paper bag and leave them in a dark place in your kitchen for 5 to 7 days, until they soften and begin to exude liquid. (Alternatively, you can ferment the plantains in a mason jar or resealable bag; the jar might work better if you're in a warmer climate. Just remember to open the jar or bag daily to "burp it"—meaning release the gas inside.) Once the fermentation is done, make the dish right away or refrigerate the fermented plantains until ready to use, up to a week.

Pickle the habanadas

The same day you start fermenting the plantains, place the whole habanadas in a mason jar.

In a small saucepan, bring the vinegar to a boil, then add the sugar and salt. Reduce the heat to low and simmer for 10 minutes. Remove from the heat and allow to cool for 10 minutes. Pour the liquid into the jar to cover the habanadas. Screw on the lid and refrigerate for 7 to 10 days before first use.

Make the patty filling

When the fermented plantains are ready to go, you can start the mixing process. Peel the fermented plantains and the 2 fresh, ripe plantains and finely chop them. Transfer to a large bowl and add the braised collard greens. Add the habanada pickles, sofrito, scallions, cilantro, ginger, lemon zest, and miso and mix well.

Now your filling is ready for the empanada shells. (Alternatively, the filling can be stored in an airtight container in the refrigerator for up to 2 days or in the freezer for up to 3 months.) Add 2 heaping tablespoons (55 g) of filling to the center of each empanada shell. Gently fold the shell in half to enclose the filling and use a fork to press down along the edge, crimping and sealing the shell.

Cook the patties according to the instructions on the empanada shell package, or follow our suggestions mentioned in the headnote. Once the patties are cooked, allow them to rest for 5 to 10 minutes so the filling has time to cool, then serve and enjoy immediately.

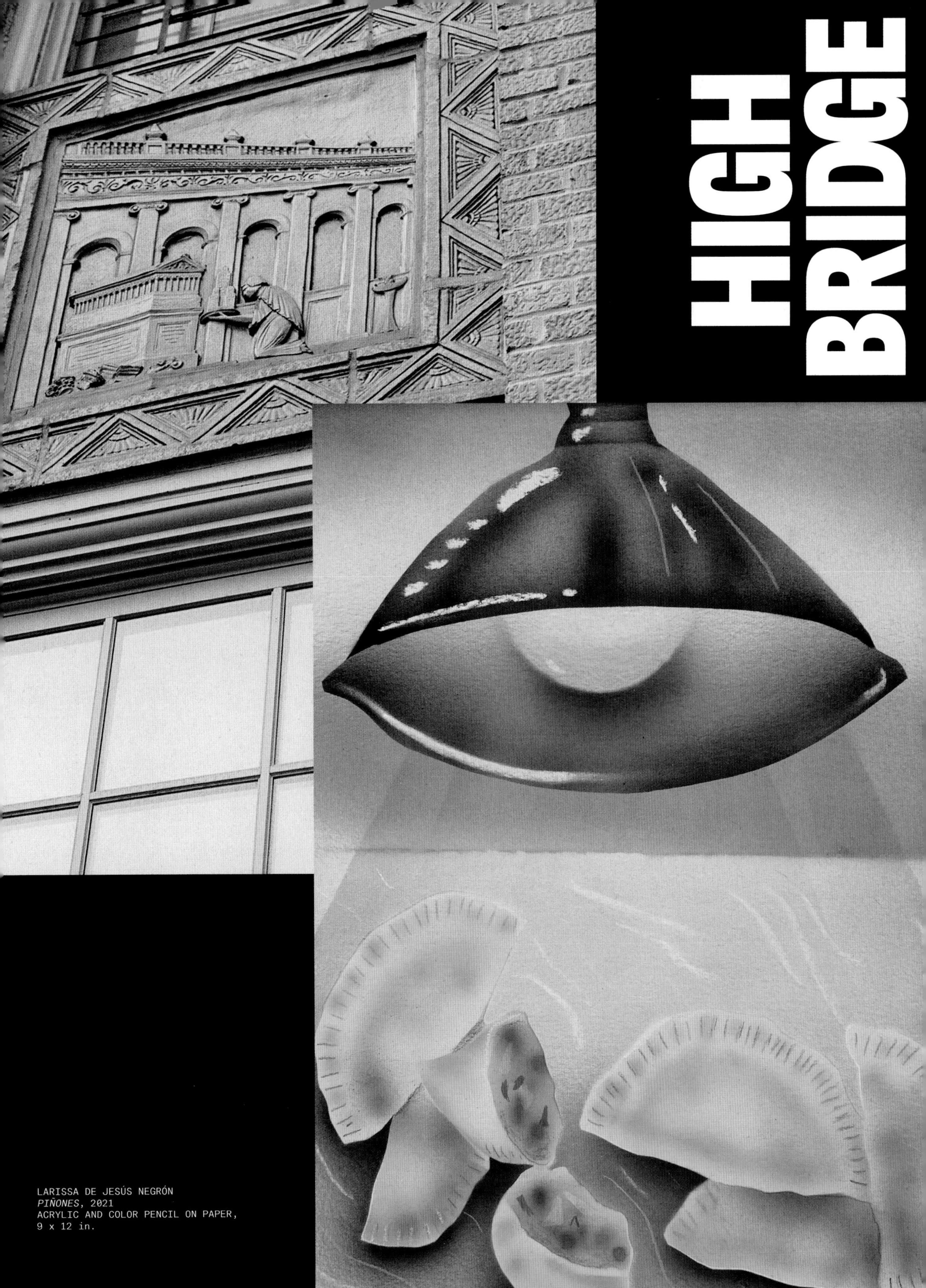

LARISSA DE JESÚS NEGRÓN
PIÑONES, 2021
ACRYLIC AND COLOR PENCIL ON PAPER,
9 x 12 in.

LEMMEGETASLICE

Pizza has long been a go-to meal for folks all over the United States. But for those who grew up in New York City, it's hard to exaggerate its cultural resonance. Here your preferred slice and purveyor can reveal where you're from and who you rock with.

Nick's Pizza on Gun Hill Road is known for their thick cheese. Full Moon on Arthur Ave has the semolina crust. There was a mega-slice joint by Westchester Square. You could feed a family of three off a single slice, no doubt. Pizza spots were the after-school hangs. Back in the day for a buck fiddy, you'd get your slice then head to the arcade in the back to play video games with the homies. This was before you could tap into a multiuser game from your iPhone. For folks watching the wallet, when you really didn't have the cash for fancier meals, a pizza slice could hold you down without making you feel left out.

You're gonna start your dough the day before you want to serve the pizza, giving it time to proof (the fermentation period that allows the dough to rise) and develop a chewy bite in the finished product that we love so much.

CONTINUED

Makes two 16-inch (40 cm) pizzas, to serve 8

INGREDIENTS

For the dough

3¾ cups (500 g) bread flour, plus more for dusting

2½ teaspoons flaky sea salt

1⅓ cups (330 ml) lukewarm water (65° to 70°F/18° to 20°C)

1 teaspoon agave syrup

1½ teaspoons (6 g) active dry yeast

Extra-virgin olive oil

Semolina flour, for dusting

For the toppings

½ cup (120 ml) tomato sauce

1 cup (90 g) low-moisture shredded mozzarella cheese

10 fresh basil leaves

PREPARATION

Make the dough

In the bowl of a stand mixer, combine the bread flour and salt.

In a small bowl, mix the water, agave, and yeast. Make a well in the flour and pour in the yeast mixture. Mix with a wooden spoon until the dough starts to look shaggy; this may take 3 to 5 minutes.

Attach the bowl to the stand mixer and, using the dough hook, mix on medium speed for 3 to 4 minutes, until the dough is a uniform mass and cleanly pulls away from the sides of the bowl.

Dust your work surface with flour, turn the dough out of the bowl, and shape it into a ball. Transfer the dough to a container with a lid, cover, and allow it to sit at room temperature (60° to 70°F/15° to 20°C) for 2 to 5 hours, until it doubles in size.

Turn the dough out onto your work surface. Using a scale, divide it into 2 roughly 10-ounce (285 g) portions and shape each portion into a ball. Using a pastry brush, lightly brush each dough ball with olive oil. Place the dough balls in a container with a lid, cover, and let rest in the refrigerator for 24 hours.

Assemble the pizzas

Heat the oven to 500°F (260°C). If your oven has an option to reach a higher setting, use that. Position an oven rack in the second-highest position and place a baking steel or stone on the rack to heat. We want the stone to get ripping hot. Allow the oven to heat for 45 to 60 minutes before baking. Take the dough out of the fridge and let it sit in a warm spot while the oven heats; when it's ready to be shaped, it should look relaxed.

Cook one pizza at a time. On a countertop, stretch one ball of the dough into a roughly 16-inch (40 cm) round. Lightly dust a pizza peel with semolina, then transfer the stretched dough to the peel. (If you don't have a pizza peel, you can use the back of a sheet pan or a cutting board.)

Dollop about ¼ cup (60 ml) of the tomato sauce over the dough, and spread it evenly in a circular motion, going from the center of the dough toward the outside. Sprinkle half the mozzarella on top.

Using the peel, slide the pizza onto the baking steel in the oven. Bake for 2 minutes, then rotate the pizza and bake for 3 minutes more. Turn on your broiler for about 90 seconds, until the pizza develops a golden, slightly charred crust. While the first pizza is in the oven, get the second one ready to go, using the remaining tomato sauce and mozzarella.

Using the peel, remove the pizza from the oven. Repeat the previous step to bake the second pizza. Top each baked pizza with half the basil leaves and allow the pies to rest for at least 1 minute before serving. Slice and enjoy immediately.

Sam's Famous PIZZA
ESTABLISHED 1962
150
SAM'S FAMOUS PIZZERIA
212-348-9437
Family

TRIBORO TRES LECHES

In the early 1970s, the Bronx became the first borough in New York City's history to reach a majority Black and Puerto Rican demographic (we recognize that a lot of our Borinquen siblings identify as Black). Today, the Bronx has the largest concentration of Puerto Ricans of any city in the world, particularly in neighborhoods like East Tremont, Mott Haven, Hunts Point, and Castle Hill.

We've never had to go far to experience delicious Puerto Rican cuisine, but we had an unforgettable tres leches dessert in San Juan. La Casita Blanca has been around for decades (big up to José Parla, our Cuban brother who grew up in PR, for the recommendation). They offer all the fixins of a traditional criollo restaurant—bacalao guisado, whole grilled pescado, plantains, rice, and beans. Their version of tres leches is light but creamy and rich, with the perfect touch of sweetness. We'd argue that tres leches is to Puerto Ricans what red velvet cake is to many Black Americans. It's a pillar of the culture that you'll find at the panaderías alongside flan and other classics, even as its origins are believed to be in Nicaragua or Mexico. A spongy cake generously drenched in three milks (condensed, evaporated, and fresh), our version replaces the dairy with oat milk, almond milk, and a coconut yogurt–based crème.

In the coconut crème, we use superfine sugar, which should not be confused with powdered sugar. Superfine sugar (also known as caster sugar) has a fine quality that dissolves easily and won't make the crème gritty like regular granulated sugar can. We also use xanthan gum in the coconut crème to act as a thickener and emulsifier. It's widely available, usually in the baking section of grocery stores.

HUGO McCLOUD
PINEAPPLE EXPRESS, 2020
SINGLE-USE PLASTIC MOUNTED ON PANEL, 70 x 60 in.

CONTINUED

Serves 16

INGREDIENTS

For the cake

Nonstick spray
1⅔ cups (400 ml) almond milk
1⅔ cups (400 ml) oat milk
1 (14-ounce/400 ml) can coconut cream
½ cup (150 g) agave syrup
3 tablespoons amaretto syrup
2 cinnamon sticks
2 whole cloves
1 cup (100 g) cake flour
½ cup (50 g) corn flour
Pinch of flaky sea salt
6 large (300 g) eggs
¾ cup (150 g) cane sugar
2 teaspoons vanilla extract

For the coconut crème

⅓ cup (80 ml) aquafaba (from one 15-ounce/425 g can of chickpeas)
3 tablespoons plus 1 teaspoon superfine sugar
½ teaspoon xanthan gum
⅔ cup (150 g) unsweetened coconut yogurt

For serving

1⅔ cups (200 g) diced pineapple
Zest of 1 lime

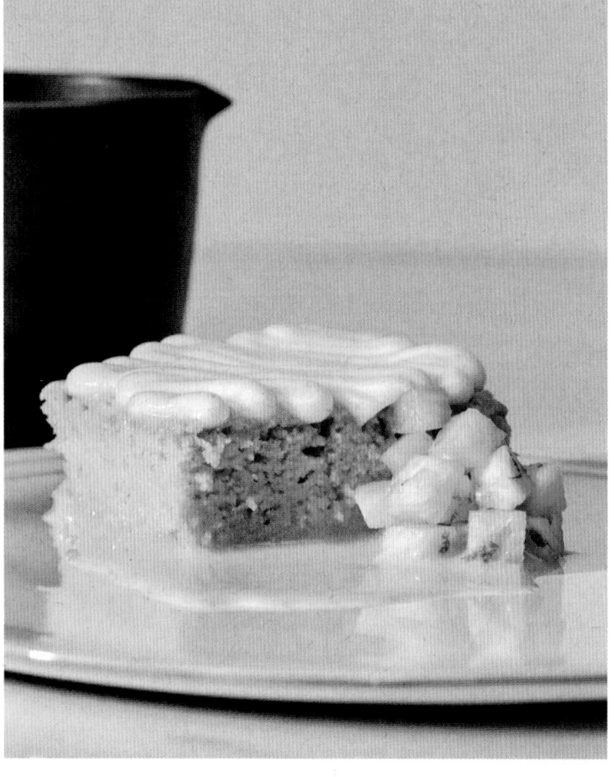

PREPARATION

Make the cake

Heat the oven to 400°F (200°C). Lightly coat a 9 x 13 inch (23 x 33 cm) baking pan with nonstick spray.

In a medium saucepan, whisk together the almond milk, oat milk, coconut cream, agave, and amaretto syrup. Add the cinnamon sticks and cloves and bring to a boil over high heat. Reduce the heat to medium and simmer for 3 minutes. Remove from the heat and let steep for 10 minutes, then allow to cool to room temperature. Strain the infused milk mixture through a mesh sieve into a bowl and discard the solids. Set aside.

In a medium bowl, mix the cake flour, corn flour, and salt. Set aside.

In the bowl of a stand mixer fitted with the whisk attachment, beat the eggs on medium-high speed until they're light and frothy, about 3 minutes.

With the mixer running, gradually stream in the cane sugar and beat until the mixture becomes voluminous and airy, about 4 minutes. When it's ready, the mixture should leave a ribbon that slowly dissolves when it falls off the end of the whisk and back into the bowl. Rub a small dab of the mixture between your fingers—it should be grit-free, which tells you the sugar has been fully incorporated. Add the vanilla and beat until it's incorporated.

With the mixer on low speed, gently add the flour mixture and mix thoroughly to incorporate.

Pour the batter into the prepared pan and bake on the center rack for 30 minutes, or until the middle of the cake springs back to the touch. Transfer the pan to a wire rack and let the cake cool for 15 minutes.

Using a fork, poke holes all over the cooled cake. Gradually pour the strained milk mixture over the entire cake. Cover with plastic wrap and refrigerate for 6 hours or up to overnight.

Make the coconut crème

In the bowl of a stand mixer fitted with the whisk attachment, whisk the aquafaba until it becomes stiff, about 1 minute (you're basically making a meringue). Add the superfine sugar and whisk until the mixture becomes glossy. Add the xanthan gum, whisk until stiff, then turn off the mixer.

In a separate large bowl, whisk the coconut yogurt. Remove the bowl from the stand mixer and fold the aquafaba "meringue" into the yogurt. Refrigerate until ready to use.

Use a spatula to evenly spread the coconut crème over the top of the cake. Slice the cake into rectangles and serve topped with the pineapple and lime zest.

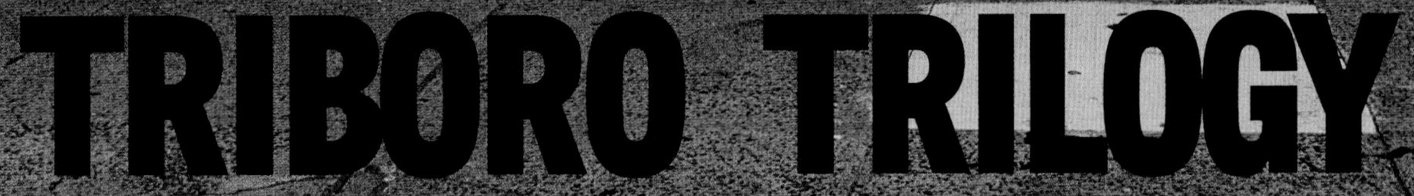

TRIBORO TRILOGY

NUTCRACKERS

Summertime in New York City means the underground nutcracker market is in full force. From the bodega to the beach, you'll find entrepreneurs moving units of pre-batched cocktails, sold by flavor or color, depending on the dealer. If this sounds illegal, it most definitely is, but we can't knock the hustle (especially in an outdated and biased alcohol-licensing system).

Nutcrackers are an undeniable part of the culture, from Washington Heights and Harlem to Flatbush in Brooklyn. You'll hear the vendor call, "Nutcracker!" or "Nutty!" Or you'll spot the goods by their short, capped plastic bottles, sold at barbershops, concerts, or summer parades. Some are even branded after favorite cartoon characters. The creativity that goes into standing out from the crowd deserves props.

Each recipe makes 1 cocktail

BLUE

INGREDIENTS

2½ ounces (75ml) coconut water

1½ ounces (45 ml) cognac

¾ ounce (20 ml) blue curaçao

¾ ounce (20 ml) lemon juice

PREPARATION

In an ice-filled shaker, combine the coconut water, cognac, curaçao, and lemon juice. Shake until the drink is chilled. Strain into a glass and enjoy immediately.

ORANGE

INGREDIENTS

2 ounces (60 ml) apple juice

1½ ounces (45 ml) cognac

1 ounce (30 ml) Aperol

1 ounce (30 ml) ginger beer (store-bought or see page 243)

PREPARATION

In an ice-filled shaker, combine the apple juice, cognac, Aperol, and ginger beer. Shake until the drink is chilled. Strain into a glass and enjoy immediately.

HENRI PAUL BROYARD
NFA, 2021
ACRYLIC ON LINEN,
20 x 16 in.

INTERVIEW WITH

THELMA GOLDEN

As a native New Yorker who's spent her lifetime writing new narratives into the discourse of American contemporary art, there are few who can capture the diversity and poignancy of Uptown Black culture like Thelma Golden. Long a friend to Ghetto Gastro, Thelma understands what it means to work within and beyond institutions. Since joining the Studio Museum of Harlem in 2005 as its director and chief curator, she's led the way in creating community across disciplines, and through her observance of how art impacts people. Thelma has poetic insight into how using creative disciplines (such as art and the culinary) can shape identity and ideas of social sculpture.

Ghetto Gastro: In your work at the Studio Museum, what has it meant to you to be part of a conversation that is both chronicling history and also creating it? Speaking to Black people, while mirroring Black culture within the community?

Thelma Golden: Let's just start with the biggest question ever! You know, it is a real privilege. It's an honor that comes with deep responsibility to steward an institution like the Studio Museum in Harlem as an art museum, yes, but also a cultural and community anchor.

Some of the reason it's a privilege is because it's an institution that was formed by founders who were at once deeply invested in carrying the history of Harlem, the history of Black art and artists, the history of Black people and culture, from the past into the present. But they also were deep futurists, because they were projecting into a moment that didn't yet exist. In 1968, when we were founded, I believe they were looking back at the Harlem Renaissance, claiming that. They centered their relationship to creating a space, an intellectual space, a physical space for Black art within this construction, arguably one of the most important in the twentieth century, the Harlem Renaissance. But they also, I think, imagined this moment that we're in now, and were creating an institution that had resilience and durability to form and reform itself in the ways in which the culture always has.

What has that meant in a place where so many have been divested from and restricted from seeing themselves in such institutions, even elsewhere in the city? What kind of effort and communication does that take to let people know, "This is here for you"?

It means creating a space and a spirit of welcome. It means creating opportunities to understand new visions of value. It means creating the opportunity for different ideas about what autonomy, self-determination, can and do look like. But it also means operating within a space, always, that's self-defined. At the Studio Museum, like other Black-led, Black-founded, Black-serving culturals in Harlem, something that we all believe is that we are carrying these ideas all the time. It's not episodic, right? Historically or culturally. It's about what it means to be rooted and sited in and of community, always.

Let's get into the interchange between Harlem and the Bronx. Sometimes we use "Uptown" to speak to both areas, because it feels like we're cousins.

Yeah, I know. That's what Bronx folks do! 'Cause y'all always trying get that Harlem adjacency—no, I'm joking. Here's the thing: I *do* think about it as Uptown. No, for real. I do think about it as Uptown because when we're talking about these geographies, what in many ways we are talking about are these places that have been defined differently, but in many ways, similarly, through their relationship to Black culture.

Now, yes, Harlem lives in many ways differently [than the Bronx]. And that is something I am always conscious of as I embrace Uptown as a concept. When I think artistically, for example, when I think of artists, communities, I think of the Bronx, Harlem, Washington Heights, all as one. But I do think it's important to imagine, and that's why what Ghetto Gastro has done is so important, because the Bronx has suffered from a kind of mythology. That mythology always has to be revised, right? Especially when we're talking about Black and brown communities, the ways in which the Bronx has to be claimed into its complexity, not sort of shrunken into what have been these representations and depictions of others.

Harlem exists in other ways that are complicated, because the mythology around Harlem comes from the ways in which it looms large and stands in for many people, for Black American culture writ large. That's the beauty and the treasure of what moments like the Harlem Renaissance have meant, when you can think about the ways in which the culture of Harlem, the culture of Black folks in Harlem, becomes representative.

In the current moment, in many ways, I see what's going on in the Bronx, particularly in the southern parts of the borough, and it's Harlem twenty years ago.

Right.

So if we imagine it in that way, then it also provides possibilities of thinking about the importance of institution building as these communities shift and transform the idea of rooting and having institutions that have the possibility of permanence. That's significant and important. In a personal way, when I think about the origin story of so much late-twentieth-century and early-twenty-first-century Black culture in New York City, we are talking about things that live, grow, and have happened in the Bronx and Harlem.

I include Brooklyn and Queens in that mix, when we think outside of these geographies that are defined by the boroughs themselves, when thinking about New York City in all the ways Black culture shows up.

We were in Venice, and we were with David Adjaye and Kunlé Adeyemi. We met Okwui Enwezor. We had dinner at this restaurant on San Marco Square.

Okwui asked Jon where he was from. Jon told him about Ghetto Gastro, and Okwui knew about us, saying, "When I moved to New York in 1986, the first place I lived was in the Bronx." He was attracted to the Bronx because of the work that was happening at Fashion Moda, and it's where he could afford to live at the time. [Adjaye and Adeyemi are both globally renowned for their innovations as designers and architects. Adjaye is from Ghana; among his most notable projects is the Smithsonian's National Museum of African American History and Culture, in Washington, D.C. Adeyemi is from Nigeria, where with his firm he developed the Makoko Floating System in Lagos, a modular approach to address development in climate change. Enwezor was a curator from Nigeria who pivotally remade the contemporary art field from an African perspective, recognizing African diaspora artists while challenging institutions to curate fuller, more accurate narratives; he died in 2019.]

And as you know, to talk about Black culture, we do have to talk about these cross-continent relationships. The Bronx was and is still a very strong community of West African immigrants. It's that place in the past, and even in the present, where Okwui could go and say the Bronx had the only good Nigerian food in the city. Others might argue with that! But the Bronx had a relationship that he knew of and understood because of its relationship to an immigrant community. Food is often the way we can trace where we've been, where we went, and where we've come from, where we're going. How that shows up in our communities is incredible.

In your work documenting and developing artists, how do you see Ghetto Gastro operating in and around the food space?

I see Ghetto Gastro in relation to how, in the contemporary art world, we think about relational art or relational aesthetics, and this participatory action where things exist as they are created. While rooted in the Bronx, my sense of Ghetto Gastro is that they're all over. That it is global, that wherever it lands, it is bringing where it's from with it, but it's also responding to wherever it is. So perhaps highly twenty-first-century in that way.

What's important about that is, from my perspective as a curator, thinking about visual art by artists of African descent, this idea of geographies is critical to understanding past, present, and potential futures as they relate to aesthetic innovation that marks our culture.

Are there artists or periods that come to mind when you think about that cyclical nature of telling our own stories?

There are lines that can be drawn between different periods and ideas. Rooting in community definitely speaks to political and cultural ideals of the 1960s. In the moment that Studio Museum was founded, 1968 in Harlem was a big year—the Dance Theatre of Harlem and the National Black Theatre were also founded. Then just one year later, El Museo del Barrio in East Harlem. Many of our organizations come in that sixties period. They use "museum" in our name. So that was consciously looking at the museum field as a whole but also creating something totally new. That's where Ghetto Gastro is in the culinary space: looking at the field, acknowledging it, having reverence for its traditions while reimagining them, reinventing them, remaking them.

I do see ideas of Ghetto Gastro being aligned to efforts visual artists have been making to create institutions. Projects like Theaster Gates's Rebuild Foundation or Art + Practice, which is Mark Bradford's organization in Los Angeles, or what Rick Lowe created with Project Row Houses in Houston, and many others. There are people like Vanessa German and Julie Mehretu, visual artists that have seen what it means to create space, often in places where the intersection between art and community is strong and can be an avenue, a lever, to create greater access to democracy.

I know you all have lots of relationships to artists as individuals, but I want to draw the line between the larger effort that others have made and will make. I'd love to speak to the culinary aspect and where that lives and sits within this larger space of creativity, from a perspective of the culinary as a creative pursuit and whether that creativity comes out of necessity.

When we think about Black culinary history, we understand that a lot of the creativity came out of necessity. But we can also see culinary as it relates to creativity, and that creativity being a way in which the self is expressed. Think about the home cooks. Those people who cooked for us in the domestic sphere who expressed their brilliant creativity through the culinary.

That's a great point, especially because the creativity as self-expression, as a kind of playfulness, can be a point of departure for some. But we deserve that too, right? We have this history of struggle and necessity, survival. But there's also always been a space to create levity and be celebratory, to do things just because.

Yes. What's important about a project like Ghetto Gastro is that it ties deeply to the way in which food in and of itself is a way that we create community. The ways in which we engage in community. In the idea of food culture, to eat is a way to understand culture at large, which is how I feel about art.

I often say to young people, you can travel all over the world looking at art. Like, when I'm engaging with our young folks Uptown, I say, go to the museums all around the city, and through that experience, you experience aspects of all these different cultures, past and present, through art. Food offers very much the same experience.

When we talk about where we are in our culture, and all the ways that we can talk about what comes from the disconnection between people, food culture is one of those ways that we can re-create and reinvent. I have always been aware of how much people's own personal stories one can narrate through food. When you narrate through food in that way, it becomes a way to understand someone's life—where they've been, where they lived, who they are.

Growing up, my food life was very involved with the fact that my mother did not like doing home cooking. My mother, born in 1930, she was one of those women—that home-cooking thing was work and she was not going to do that. However, my grandmother, my father's mother, lived with us. My mother was born and raised in Bed-Stuy [in Brooklyn], my father was born and raised in Harlem. So that's even more complicated than the Bronx-Harlem relationship. That was an intermarriage! Okay! When my parents got married in '63, that was a big deal. So my mother, not interested in home cooking, she was good with the Stouffer's, the TV dinners, we could have fast food. All of it. Because that was all freeing for her. My grandmother, however, who came to this country from Jamaica in the twenties, she worked as a domestic worker, primarily in the Bronx, on the Grand Concourse.

The OG New York Fifth Avenue.

Exactly. She worked a little bit on the Upper West Side, but her families were mostly in the South Bronx. So much of the food that I grew up eating was food that she learned to cook in those kitchens, to cook for the families she worked for. Some of the names of the things were wrong because they came through her Jamaican. It was only years later that I'd be like, *Oh, that's what that was.*

Maybe that's something that Ghetto Gastro is giving back to folks. It's letting them claim their stories and themselves because by engaging in this community, in the culinary, you're allowing others to claim a relationship to their individual journey, their family history.

That individual framing is partly why food is such a contested space. Because people feel so much sovereignty and identity attached to "Well, we had this, and this is what we did, and that's not how it was." It becomes an indicator of power, or an attempt to reclaim lost power. We don't always get the opportunity to reflect, as you said, to claim ourselves and to see the diversity in our foods, even among our own communities like Bed-Stuy or Harlem, in a society that's always conflating us.

Right. All these categories, we have to claim them. I mean, there was a whole moment, you know, in the '60s and '70s, where many Black artists resisted the term "Black art." Not because they were trying to deny their culture but because of the way that was a small box. It was not as big and broad and expansive. I think the same thing about Black food. Like how wide and deep it is. We are talking about many different iterations of the culture.

We should talk about Ghetto Gastro in terms of this idea of hybridity. How we can bring things together that we don't understand necessarily as being aligned or even adjacent but that then are brought together. What happens in deep creative collision is an interesting way to think about Ghetto Gastro.

Yeah, "collision" is one of our favorite words. Think of all the magic that happens. In the Bronx, the history of hip hop, alone.

The sample, the remix. But also powerful ways of thinking about reinvention. I speak from the world of the visual, but I even think of collision in terms of language: "ghetto," "gastro."

Yeah. People don't think that the two words belong together. It's a polarizing phrase.

That's right. We can talk about what I'd call the "conceptual underpinnings" of what you're doing and where that comes into conversations in the broader space of culture.

Tell me this. I remember a long time ago, we had a conversation that you all were pursuing other physical spaces.

Yes. Looking at Theaster Gates's earlier work reminded us that we can start small and that ownership is important.

I love the pop-up thing conceptually. But the problem is—we need to look at these lessons of history in 1968, when the group of people who brought about Studio Museum, people like Barbara Ann Teer at National Black Theatre and Arthur Mitchell, they bought these buildings.

The only reason the Studio Museum can be in the midst of building a new beautiful building by David Adjaye is because back then, they bought at a time when people were running away from Harlem. And they invested as cultural organizations, not as businesses. It meant that we get to stay. The typical story would have been that we all would have had to leave because we would have been priced out.

You're right to think about buying as a way to stake a claim. That means you can have a longer runway for your impact for what you're doing. I think it's important. I think that's a kind of real activism.

What resonates with you when you hear "Black Power Kitchen"?

Of course, when I hear "Black Power Kitchen," I think of the history of the Panthers and their food movements, what now we refer to as food justice, which were at the core of the Black Power movement. But I would even broaden it from that, because it also indicates the larger tradition of where we can put the idea of feeding the people, as in right relationship to community.

Whether that happened through political actions of the Panthers or with community groups, our churches, these micro or macro movements take on the idea of feeding folks. And through that, it creates for people a sense of being able to engage in their own humanity.

AFRICAN ROOTS

AFRICA ROOTS

AFRICAN ROOTS

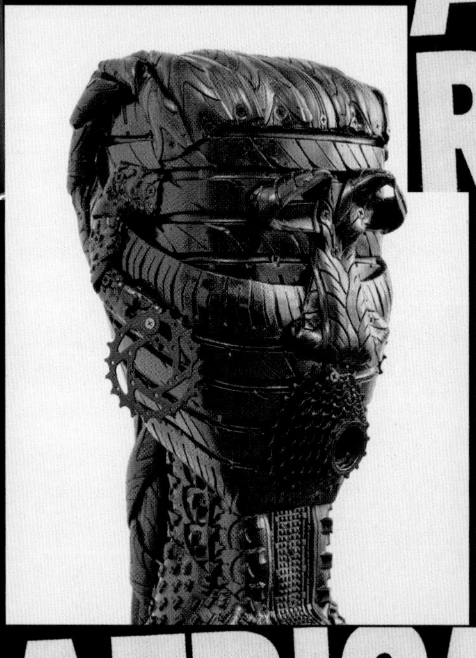

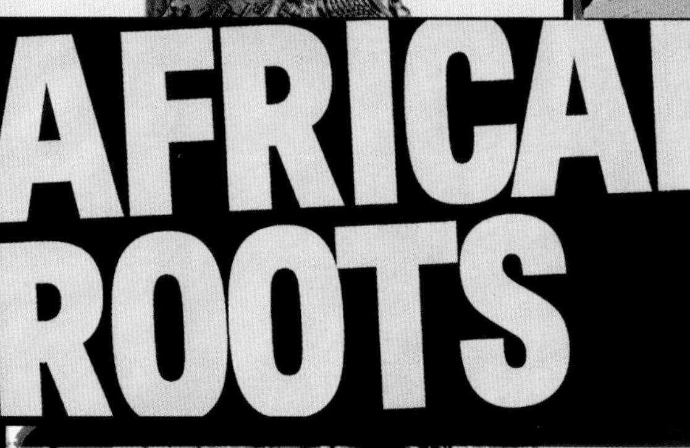

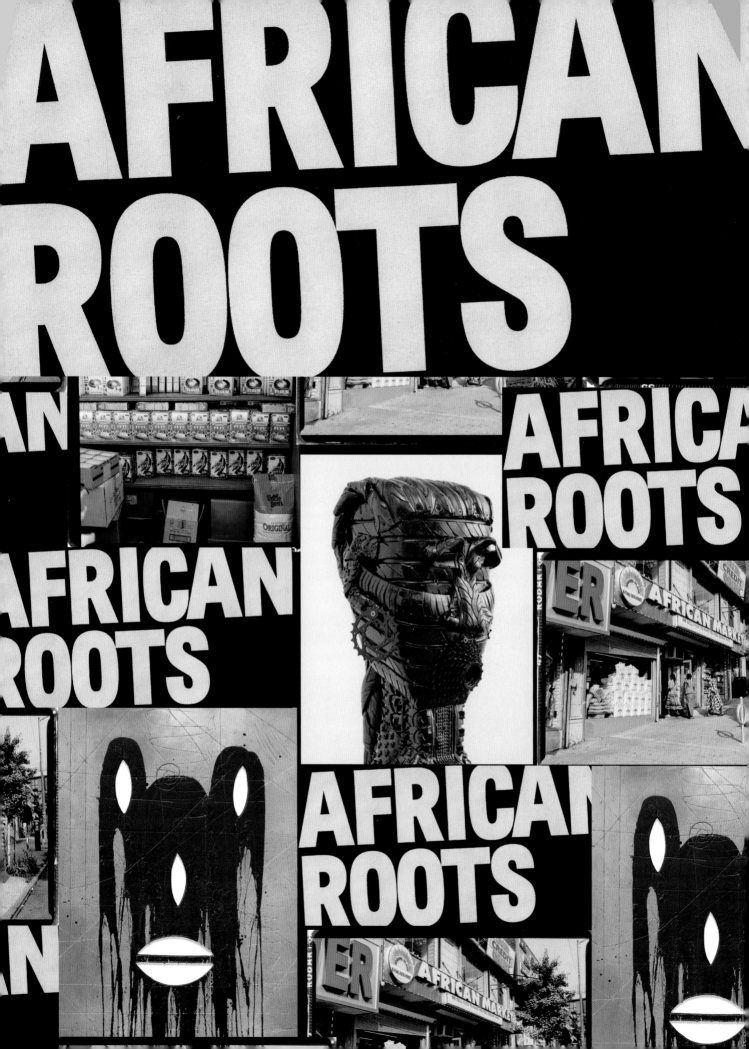

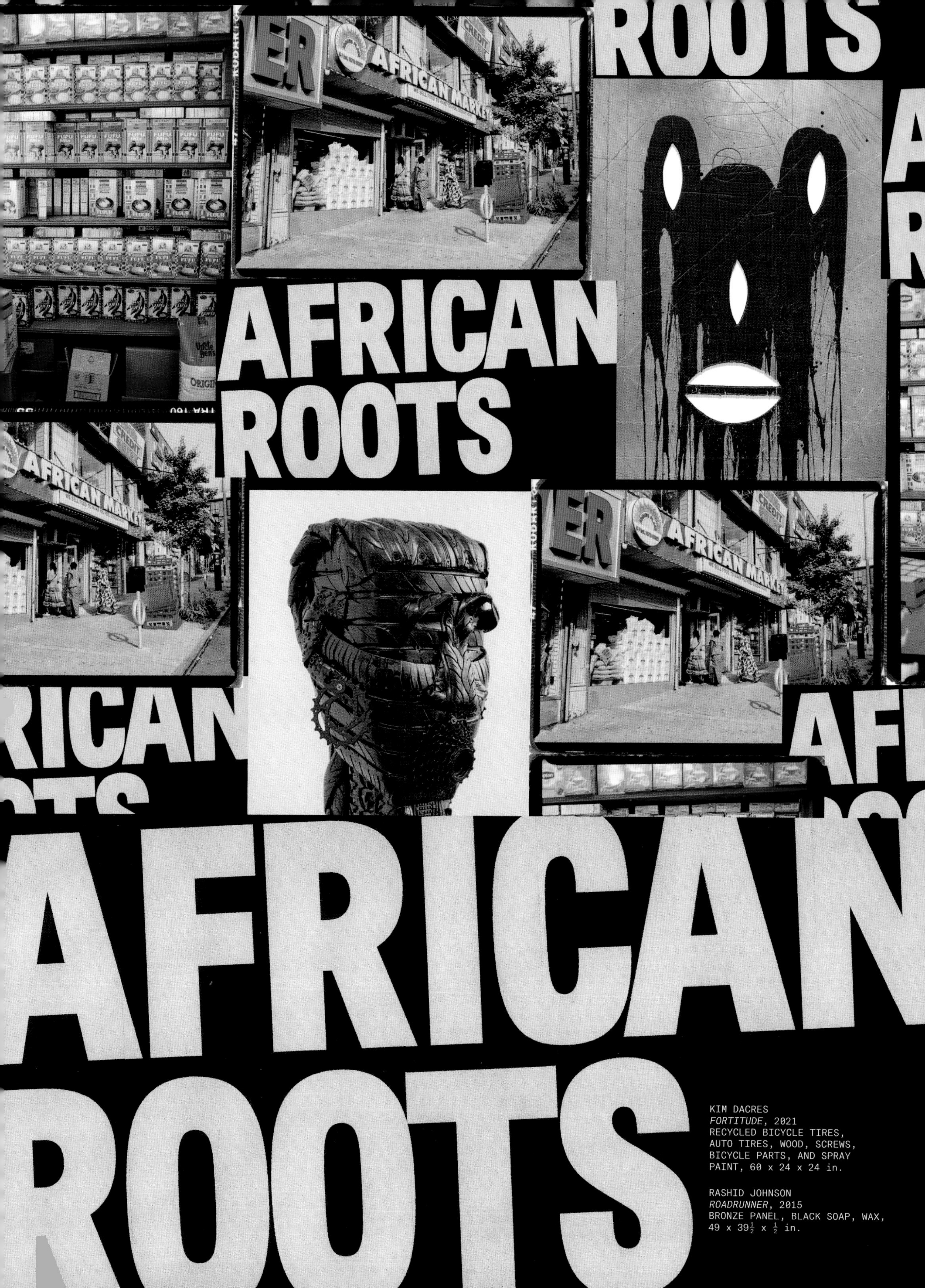

KIM DACRES
FORTITUDE, 2021
RECYCLED BICYCLE TIRES, AUTO TIRES, WOOD, SCREWS, BICYCLE PARTS, AND SPRAY PAINT, 60 x 24 x 24 in.

RASHID JOHNSON
ROADRUNNER, 2015
BRONZE PANEL, BLACK SOAP, WAX, 49 x 39½ x ½ in.

MING SMITH
PRELUDE TO MIDDLE PASSAGE (ÎLE DE GORÉE, SENEGAL), 1972
ARCHIVAL PIGMENT PRINT,
36 x 24 in.

Africa figures large in our evolving relationship to Black American history and our Blackness as an identity. The continent and its wide reach are hard to quantify. A symbol of source and origination, Africa is home to our planet's first people. It's a place with striking beauty and diversity of language and culture, food and ritual, landscape and terrain. It is modern and forward-looking, yet also honors tradition as tribal, regional, and national treasure. Even as an imperfect mix of borders and boundaries, Africa continues to be the world's most-tapped resource. For centuries, its children and natural elements have sparked and maintained the flame of inspiration and commerce around the globe. We're proud to descend from a profoundly large and complex place, one that continues to innovate and have powerful effects on its diaspora. Consider our hometown: Immigrants from Africa account for about 4 percent of New York City's population of those born abroad, but they make up 10 percent of the immigrant population in the Bronx alone.

We came up in a community that, between our households and the block, was a reflection of multigenerational experiences and cultures: from the Caribbean (Jamaica, Haiti, Trinidad and Tobago, Barbados, and Saint Vincent and the Grenadines, to name a few) to Gambia, Senegal, Ghana, Ivory Coast, Sierra Leone, Liberia, and Nigeria, right next to the migration of Black Americans from the South and Midwest, defining Black New York culture and aesthetic. No matter the reason for mass movement, one common bond remains true for most newcomers: Upon arrival, people want to find their tribe. When you combine that basic human need with systemic practices that limit where folks can go, you get communities where like recognizes like. For those open to the possibility, the Bronx can be experienced as a hot spot of the African diaspora, one that has inspired musical forms like hip hop, one that can host contemporary art exhibitions from international artists, and one where food moves as people do, getting remixed and redefined as our stories evolve.

The artist Kehinde Wiley once said in an interview, "While we want to celebrate a pure or perhaps imagined African identity, artists at their best navigate multiplicity. We're tricksters. We're able to exist at the crossroads. Africans have evolved the aesthetic of nomads. To be able to create an identity under duress is the defining feature of an African aesthetic, even an African American aesthetic." We relate to this notion of living at a crossroads, as Black Americans who work with food and other disciplines in ways that challenge expectations across industries. We relate to feeling like tricksters being born in the United States and having that function as an asset abroad but not always benefiting from what this country has to offer when we're at home. We see this multiplicity in indigenous African ingredients like yam, okra, rice, and watermelon, which arrived en masse on ships that transported our ancestors, to eventually be integrated into agricultural practices throughout the Americas. We can taste the nomadic energy in cooking practices that adapt over time to new ingredients, different climates, cross-pollination of language and style, and the undefinable thing that makes something "Black"—you know it when you see it. At least, we do.

Without our African roots, Black Power Kitchen cannot exist in any form. Not as an idea, not as a functional space in our homes, not as a traveling concept. The food in this chapter reflects our thinking about how ingredients like sorrel (hibiscus), stewed hearty greens, and tubers like dasheen, yam, and sweet potato have appeared over centuries in similar ways throughout the diaspora and how these dishes sustain us. We tap in with chef Michael Elégbèdé, a Lagos native who trained professionally in the United States before returning home to launch his own test kitchen. He reflects on the symbiotic nature of African and Black American creators and the power in claiming and affirming each other. We're interested in traditional recipes and how, as Ghetto Gastro, we can contribute to ongoing conversations on the plate. The Bronx has long been a home to Africa, and Africa in its many permutations is within us. You're going to learn that even if you don't identify as Black, Africa is in you, too.

BANANA LEAF FISH

Banana leaf fish is poppin on Ngor Beach, just outside of Dakar in Senegal. We touched down to attend Kehinde Wiley's Black Rock artist residency opening. But if you know Ghetto Gastro, you know we're always looking for the spread. On the beach, we ran down on folks serving fresh-caught fish steamed in banana leaves. We can't overstate the impact of seeing such a beautiful, majestic place with tangible references to African American and Afro Caribbean cultures.

Pierre grew up in Connecticut but spent parts of the year in Barbados with his family. The energy on Ngor Beach feels similar to the Bajan island vibes, from the food to the music. This black snapper dish is inspired by both places.

Use a whole cleaned fish, head on. Traditionally, looking at the whole fish has been a way to confirm its freshness and quality. Functionally, a whole fish (bones, skin, minus the guts) will be more flavorful and juicy than fillets, particularly in this preparation. The fish steams inside a banana leaf, or "en papillote," as the technique is called in some kitchens. If banana leaves are new to you, check Resources (page 295) for shopping tips. We also use green seasoning, a customized, homemade blend of herbs and spices found in households throughout the Caribbean. This version is a standard Bajan approach. We finish with a robust, herbaceous vegetable stew spooned over the fish. Maybe it's a fool's errand to try to recapture a serendipitous beach day, but we're gonna give you our best shot.

CONTINUED

Serves 4

INGREDIENTS

For the green seasoning

1 onion, coarsely chopped
1 large scallion, chopped
3 garlic cloves
1 cup loosely packed (14 g) fresh cilantro leaves
1 cup loosely packed (14 g) fresh flat-leaf parsley
1 tablespoon loosely packed fresh thyme
1 tablespoon fresh marjoram
½ habanero chile

For the fish

4 banana leaves, large enough to fully wrap the fish (or use parchment paper)
2 (1¾-pound/800 g) whole black snapper (or another type of snapper), cleaned, heads left on
1 tablespoon flaky sea salt

For the caper butter

8 tablespoons (1 stick/113 g) unsalted butter, at room temperature
2 tablespoons capers, rinsed, drained, and diced

For the sauce

3 tablespoons plus 1 teaspoon extra-virgin olive oil
1 large yellow onion, diced
5 garlic cloves, grated
1 medium red bell pepper, diced
2 medium zucchini, diced
¼ cup plus 2 teaspoons (100 g) chickpea miso paste
2 small tomatoes, chopped
2 scallions, thinly sliced
½ habanero chile, finely chopped
2 fresh bay leaves
3 tablespoons fresh marjoram
3 tablespoons fresh thyme leaves
1 cup (240 ml) fish stock
1 tablespoon plus 1 teaspoon tomato sauce
1½ tablespoons Worcestershire sauce
2 teaspoons coconut aminos (such as Coconut Secret)
Flaky sea salt
2 limes, cut into wedges, for serving

EQUIPMENT

Kitchen twine or toothpicks

PREPARATION

Heat the oven to 400°F (200°C).

Make the green seasoning
In a food processor, combine the onion, scallion, garlic, cilantro, parsley, thyme, marjoram, and habanero. Pulse until the ingredients create a homogeneous paste. Set aside.

Make the fish
Trim the thicker edges off the banana leaves. To make the banana leaves more pliable so it's easier to wrap the fish, wilt each leaf over an open flame for 10 to 15 seconds per leaf. (Alternatively, you can drop the leaves into a pot of boiling water for 10 seconds and then chill in a bowl of ice and water to stop the cooking.)

Lightly pat the fish dry. Liberally season them inside and out with the salt and green seasoning; you want to use up all the seasoning.

Use the banana leaves to make a parcel for each fish: Place one fish on each wilted leaf, then top each with another leaf. Tuck the sides of the top leaf under the fish, then bring up the sides of the bottom leaf to completely enclose the fish, and secure the leaves with kitchen twine. If you don't have twine, use toothpicks (soaked in water for 15 minutes so they don't burn). Try to avoid gaps in your wrapping so liquid doesn't leak out.

Place the fish parcels on a wire rack with a sheet pan underneath to catch any drips and bake until cooked through, about 25 minutes. To test for doneness, gently insert a skewer into one wrapped fish—you should meet little resistance.

Make the caper butter
In a medium bowl, mix the butter and capers until the capers are fully and evenly incorporated. Spread the butter onto a sheet of plastic wrap. Roll the butter into a log, wrap in the plastic wrap, and set aside in the refrigerator.

Make the sauce
In a medium saucepan, heat the olive oil over medium heat. Add the onion and sauté until it softens, 2 to 3 minutes.

Add the garlic and cook for 3 minutes, then add the bell pepper and zucchini. Sauté until softened, 4 to 5 minutes. Stir in the miso and cook for another 2 minutes.

Add the tomatoes, scallions, chile, bay leaves, marjoram, thyme, stock, tomato sauce, Worcestershire, and coconut aminos. Simmer until the liquid has reduced and the vegetables are tender, about 20 minutes. Taste and add salt to your liking. Remove from the heat, then stir in half the caper butter. (The remaining caper butter can be refrigerated for up to 1 month or frozen for up to 6 months.)

Unwrap the fish and slather with sauce, then serve with lime.

JOHN RIVAS & LUDOVIC NKOTH
CHICKS N FISH, 2021
ACRYLIC ON CANVAS, COLLAGED WITH CLAY, BAMBOO, ROPE THREAD, EMBROIDERY, TEXTILE, PLUSH FISH TOYS, JOINT, CIGARETTE, BEANS, AND SHELLS, $72\frac{1}{2}$ x 60 in.

CALLALOO, WHAT IT DO

What is meant by the word "callaloo" can vary, depending on where you're from and with whom you're speaking. For our purposes, callaloo refers to a staple green-leaf-based side dish cooked with spices, okra, and pumpkin and simmered down in coconut milk. Like so many delicious foods, it is African in origin, and iterations of the dish have become representative of different Caribbean cultures, from Jamaica to the twin islands of Trinidad and Tobago.

The Trinis use the leaves of dasheen, or taro plant, for their callaloo. Jamaicans and Guyanese typically use amaranth leaves for their callaloo and different aromatics than the Trinis—like Scotch bonnet peppers, tomatoes, and onion. In some cultures, it appears soupy, almost the consistency of a paste. In others, the leaves appear more defined, all the ingredients identifiable as parts of a flavor-packed whole. If these dishes sound like the beloved collard greens found in African American cuisine, then you know what time it is.

Collectively, what we know in the Americas as callaloo derives from a dish cooked with the flavorful, unrefined red palm oil ubiquitous in West African cooking. (This palm oil, or "red gold," from the fruit of the oil palm, ethically and sustainably sourced for millennia, has little to do with the highly debated use of refined palm oil found in Western shelf-stable foods and health and beauty products.) The incredible breadth and influence of our ancestors turned provisions imported for enslaved labor into nutrient-rich dishes that sustained generations and still stand the taste test of time. Trinidad and Tobago features callaloo with crab as its national dish, a living acknowledgment of this powerful legacy.

Here we have callaloo with okra, pumpkin, aromatics, and pepper. The addition of crispy shallots, while not a traditional preparation, adds a brightness and texture to the dish.

CONTINUED

Serves 4

INGREDIENTS

For the flour mix

½ cup (60 g) tipo "00" flour

½ cup (50 g) cornstarch

½ teaspoon (2 g) baking powder

For the crispy shallots

10½ ounces (300 g) shallots (about 6 large), sliced into ¼-inch-thick (6 mm) rings

1 cup (240 ml) coconut milk

4 cups (1 L) vegetable oil

Flaky sea salt

For the callaloo

¼ cup (60 ml) grapeseed oil

6 garlic cloves, finely grated

5 ounces (150 g) shallots (about 3 large), finely chopped

4 scallions, chopped

1 bunch cilantro, finely chopped

2 tablespoons fresh thyme leaves

7 ounces (200 g) okra, thinly sliced

4 to 5 cups (10 to 12½ ounces/280 to 350 g) chopped callaloo greens (amaranth, taro leaves, or mustard greens)

7 ounces (200 g) pumpkin, diced

1 Scotch bonnet pepper, halved and seeded

1 (14-ounce/400 ml) can coconut milk

Flaky sea salt

Freshly ground black pepper

PREPARATION

Make the flour mix

In a medium bowl, mix the flour, cornstarch, and baking powder; set aside. (The flour mix can be made ahead and stored in an airtight container until ready to use.)

Make the crispy shallots

Rinse the shallot rings in cold water, then soak them in the coconut milk for 1 hour.

In a deep fryer or heavy-bottomed pot, heat the vegetable oil over medium-high heat until it registers 350°F (175°C) on an instant-read thermometer (adjust heat as needed to maintain). Line a sheet pan with paper towels and set it nearby.

Drain the shallots from the shallot rings, but keep them slightly wet; this will allow the flour to stick better.

Working in even batches, dredge the shallots in the flour mixture, then add them to the hot oil and fry until golden brown, about 2 minutes. They can burn quickly, so don't walk away. Drain on the paper towel–lined pan and season with salt. Repeat with the remaining shallots.

Make the callaloo

In a large heavy-bottomed pot with a lid, heat the grapeseed oil over medium heat. Add the garlic and cook until the garlic becomes fragrant but does not develop color.

Add the chopped shallots and cook until soft and translucent, about 1 minute. Add the scallions, cilantro, and thyme and cook, stirring, for another minute.

Stir in the okra, greens, pumpkin, and Scotch bonnet, then follow with the coconut milk. Season to taste with salt and black pepper. Stir well and cover with a lid. Reduce the heat to medium-low and cook until the pumpkin is tender, 30 to 40 minutes. Transfer to a serving dish, garnish with the crispy shallots, and serve.

LUDOVIC NKOTH
FALLEN ANGEL #6, 2021
ACRYLIC ON CANVAS,
60 x 48 in.

STEWED SEA BASS AND COU-COU

You'll find preparations of cou-cou (also known as fungi—pronounced *foon-JEE*) throughout the Caribbean. Cou-cou takes cornmeal, native to the Americas and long cultivated by Indigenous people, and mixes it with okra, imported by way of the trade of enslaved Africans.

While flying fish and cou-cou is considered the national dish of Barbados, you may recognize a popular pairing found in the American South: fish and grits.

This cou-cou is savory and creamy with a mild sweetness. Though we're using sea bass, you can apply this method to any fish or crustacean.

CONTINUED

Serves 4

INGREDIENTS

For the cou-cou

1¼ cups (180 g) polenta, coarse or medium grind
2 teaspoons grapeseed oil
4 medium okra pods, diced
½ banana shallot (⅓ ounce/10 g), finely chopped
1 sprig thyme
10 tablespoons (1¼ sticks/150 g) unsalted butter
¼ teaspoon flaky sea salt, plus more to taste

For the stew

4 sea bass fillets
Juice of 1 lime
Flaky sea salt
¼ cup (60 ml) extra-virgin olive oil
½ white onion, diced
1 teaspoon diced garlic
1 red bell pepper, diced
1 tablespoon fresh thyme leaves
1 tablespoon curry powder
½ cup (120 ml) dry white wine
1 plum/Roma tomato, diced
1 tablespoon Green Seasoning (see page 78)
¼ cup (50 g) Caper Butter (see page 78)
Freshly ground black pepper

PREPARATION

Make the cou-cou

In a bowl, soak the polenta in 1¼ cups (300 ml) water for 30 minutes. Using a fine-mesh strainer, drain the polenta and set aside.

In a medium saucepan, heat the grapeseed oil over medium-low heat and immediately add the okra, shallot, and thyme sprig. Fry for 3 to 5 minutes, until the vegetables soften but aren't browned.

Add 3⅓ cups (800 ml) water and simmer for about 10 minutes, until the okra is just cooked. Drain the okra, reserving the cooking water, and discard the herbs. Set the okra aside.

Return the cooking water to the saucepan and bring to a boil over medium heat, then simmer. Add the drained polenta and cook, stirring continuously, for about 15 minutes. You want it to be smooth.

Return the okra mixture to the saucepan. Add the butter and season with salt. Keep warm.

Make the stew

Liberally season the sea bass fillets with the lime juice and salt. Cover and let marinate at room temperature for 10 to 15 minutes.

Meanwhile, in a deep saucepan, heat the olive oil over medium heat. Add the onion, garlic, bell pepper, thyme, and curry powder and cook to slightly soften, 2 to 3 minutes. Add the wine and cook out the alcohol for 1 minute before adding the tomato. Stir in the green seasoning and caper butter.

Rinse the fish fillets to remove the lime juice and salt, then pat dry. Season with black pepper. Use a knife to score the skin side of each fillet on an angle.

Place the fillets skin-side up in the saucepan with the stew. Cover and simmer gently for 8 to 12 minutes, until the fish appears white and is firm to the touch.

To serve, spoon the cou-cou into individual serving bowls and top each with a sea bass fillet. Spoon the stew over the fish and enjoy immediately.

SOPHIA-YEMISI ADEYEMO-ROSS
OKRA AT DAWN, 2021
ACRYLIC, WATERCOLOR, PAPER,
27⅞ X 23⅞ in.

RED DRANK

Red drink, popular throughout African American culture, is related to sorrel and other beverages made from roselle hibiscus. Also known as bissap in Senegal and agua de jamaica in Mexico, many of these plant-based beverages come from African traditions and have been woven into the cultural narratives throughout the diaspora. Juneteenth, for example, is often celebrated with red drinks as part of the spread, signaling the blood our ancestors shed in order to keep going, to survive.

In the Caribbean, you'll find different interpretations of sorrel that feature ginger, orange peel, cloves, pimento (allspice), cinnamon, or sometimes a little rum. It's most popular during the Christmas holiday season, but since it's a refreshing drink with natural health benefits, there's never a bad time to drink up. You can make this recipe your own and dilute as needed to lessen the intensity.

Note: *Sorrel is the Caribbean name for hibiscus (not to be confused with the tangy green herb also called sorrel). Depending on where you live, you might find dried hibiscus or sorrel leaves in the produce section of the grocery store, in the tea aisle, or even in the vitamin section.*

Makes 8½ cups (2 L)

INGREDIENTS

8½ cups (2 L) water
¾ cup (180 ml) agave syrup, plus more as needed
½ cup (14 g) dried sorrel (hibiscus) leaves
2 (2-inch/5 cm) pieces fresh ginger, sliced
4 whole cloves
1½ tablespoons orange zest
1 cinnamon stick

PREPARATION

In a large pot, combine the water, agave, sorrel, ginger, cloves, orange zest, and cinnamon stick. Cover and bring to a boil. Reduce the heat to low and simmer for 30 minutes. Remove from the heat. Allow to cool before refrigerating. Let the ingredients steep in the refrigerator for up to 24 hours.

Strain the liquid and discard the solids. Do it twice to make it nice. Taste and add more agave as needed. Store in a jug or bottle.

ALVARO BARRINGTON
BARBADOS, BLACK BACKGROUND, 2021
MIXED MEDIA ON BURLAP IN ARTIST FRAME OF TIN AND WOOD,
225 x 225 x 10 cm

KING JAFFE JOLLOF

Jollof rice is a beloved, delicious, and at times joyously, if hotly, contested dish from West Africa. The Ghanaians, Nigerians, Liberians, and Cameroonians make it, but the Wolof people of modern-day Senegal (once known as the Jolof or Jollof Empire) established the recipe's baseline with the dish thieboudienne.

The insider's joke about jollof is that its many fans debate who deserves credit for bringing us this perfect mix of rice, tomatoes, peppers, and spice. We're not about to weigh in on the so-called jollof wars, but we're inspired by all approaches. One preparation known to many Nigerians as "party rice" can include open-fire cooking that gives the rice a smoky flavor and crispy grains at the bottom of the pot.

Iterations of jollof in the United States include the staple Gullah Geechee red rice (or Charleston red rice), a direct reflection of the people from Senegambia who were brought to the Lowcountry specifically for their mastery in cultivating the grain and establishing irrigation systems. Don't believe for a moment what you see in American history books, that European traders randomly rounded up unskilled African people. The practice of enslavement was far more dubious and strategic; the cost of transporting unwilling humans was too expensive to exist without intention. And stateside, those born into slavery apprenticed not just as field laborers (themselves, to this day, an underpaid, underregarded skilled group) but also as carpenters and stonemasons, blacksmiths and bricklayers, cooks and bakers, fishers and sailors, horse trainers and tailors. South Carolina made its preindustrial wealth off of the rice Black people grew, harvested, and milled, the outcome of which contributed to a global economy. A lot went down for us to have the pleasure of red rice, or jollof rice, in any form today.

Thinking of our influences surrounding this dish and our relationship to Africa, the fictional land of Zamunda, as featured in the Eddie Murphy film *Coming to America*, was Wakanda for our generation. The movie was a groundbreaking and lighthearted comedy when it hit the streets in 1988, and we still feel pride in the Joffer family, spearheaded by King Jaffe Joffer as portrayed by the great James Earl Jones. Since our version of jollof is a mash-up, we're shouting out this pivotal representation in American cinema that brought positive shine to the continent in ways many Black Americans hadn't seen before.

We extract robust flavors every step of the way. Use a mushroom dashi, toast all your spices, and char the bell pepper, onions, ginger, and garlic. Give yourself a day ahead to prep the dashi. And if you're new to jollof, understand that the best versions have a balanced ratio of sauce to rice. We're not looking for a saucy dish but a silky rice. Make it nice.

CONTINUED

Ardent Mills
KOKUHO RICE
Ardent Mills
Flour
KOKUHO RICE

Serves 6 to 8

INGREDIENTS

½ cup (120 ml) plus 4 tablespoons grapeseed oil
1 pound (455 g) fresh tomatoes (preferably plum/Roma), chopped
7 ounces (200 g) red bell pepper, chopped
4 ounces (125 g) red onion, chopped
1 head garlic, cloves peeled and chopped
½ ounce (40 g) fresh ginger, peeled and chopped
2 Scotch bonnet peppers, seeded and chopped
3 or 4 dried chipotle peppers, diced
1 tablespoon smoked paprika
1 tablespoon chopped black garlic (4 cloves)
1 tablespoon whole black peppercorns
1½ tablespoons Madras curry powder
1½ teaspoons ground cinnamon
1½ teaspoons cumin seeds, toasted and ground
1½ teaspoons hot sauce (preferably Tabasco)
1 tablespoon tamari
2 teaspoons soy sauce
2 teaspoons Worcestershire sauce
1 teaspoon agave syrup
1 tablespoon flaky sea salt
2⅔ cups (500 g) uncooked jasmine rice
2½ cups (600 ml) Mushroom Dashi (page 292)

PREPARATION

In a medium saucepan, heat ½ cup (120 ml) of the grapeseed oil over high heat. When the oil starts to smoke, add the tomatoes. Leave the tomatoes to sizzle in the oil for several minutes without moving them around, allowing them to char on the bottom. It's okay if they get a little burnt. After about 5 minutes, flip the tomatoes and cook until they reduce and begin to break down.

Meanwhile, in a bowl, combine the bell pepper and onion and toss with about 2 tablespoons of the oil, enough to lightly coat them.

In a separate saucepan, heat the remaining 2 tablespoons oil over high heat. Add the bell pepper and onion and leave to char for 2 to 3 minutes. Add the garlic and ginger, gently stir, and leave to char for 1 to 2 minutes more. Don't let the garlic and ginger burn.

Add the charred vegetables to the pot with the tomatoes. Add all the peppers, paprika, black garlic, peppercorns, curry powder, cinnamon, cumin, hot sauce, tamari, soy sauce, Worcestershire, agave, and salt. Stir well to incorporate the ingredients, then reduce the heat to low, cover, and cook for 20 to 30 minutes, until the mixture softens and reduces. It should look like a paste when it's done.

Transfer the mixture to a food processor or blender and blitz well to achieve a smooth paste consistency. Add a little water and blitz again. Pass the sauce through a sieve into a container. Set aside.

Rinse the rice well, then drain it. In a cast-iron skillet (to get the best char), combine the rice, mushroom dashi, and ½ cup (120 ml) of the strained sauce. (The remaining sauce will keep in an airtight container in the refrigerator for up to 1 month or in the freezer for up to 6 months.)

Cover and simmer for 18 to 20 minutes, until the rice is cooked through. Remove from the heat and allow the rice to rest, covered, for 10 minutes. Serving suggestion: roasted vegetables or fried sweet plantain.

DAVID DRAKE
STORAGE JAR, 1858
ALKALINE-GLAZED STONEWARE,
22⅝ x 72 in.

HUGH HAYDEN
SOUL FOOD, 2021
COPPER-PLATED BRASS INSTRUMENTS,
COPPER PANS AND CAST IRON WITH
CUSTOM STEEL RACK

MAROON SHROOMS

We pay homage to the OG freedom fighters. The Africans who escaped Spanish and British bondage in Jamaica, fleeing to remote areas of the island where they formed their own communities and evaded recapture, were called Maroons, from the Spanish word "cimarrónes." Maroons existed all over the Americas. Wherever there has been slavery, there have always been people finding ways to claim their freedom.

The Maroons' self-emancipation in Jamaica preceded the Haitian Revolution and state-approved emancipation in the United States. They gained legendary status for their self-reliance, their ability to resist recapture, their success using guerrilla strategies to win multiple armed conflicts against colonial entities, and their ingenuity in not only surviving but also in building communities that thrived. Today, several Maroon villages—Charles Town, Accompong Town, Scott's Hall, and Moore Town—still exist.

This dish is a plant-based hat tip to Jamaican jerk, using marinated then grilled mushrooms doused with a barbecue miso glaze. The work here is in the prep, but the cooking is a breeze. Use a grill, an acknowledgment to open-flame cooking that will set off your shrooms with a deep, smoky flavor.

Pull up to the Asian market to get kombu (dried kelp), shiro shoyu (white soy sauce), and gochujang (a Korean chile paste).

CONTINUED

Serves 4

INGREDIENTS

For the marinade

2 sheets kombu (½ ounce/15 g)
¼ cup (60 ml) grapeseed oil
1 tablespoon plus 1 teaspoon coconut nectar
½ Scotch bonnet pepper, seeded
1 tablespoon smoked paprika
2 dried chipotle peppers
4 garlic cloves
1¼ ounces (35 g) black garlic
2 teaspoons whole allspice berries
1 teaspoon whole black peppercorns
1½ tablespoons grated fresh ginger
5 tablespoons (75 ml) shiro shoyu
2 Asian pears, peeled and cored
1 Gala apple, peeled and cored
⅓ cup (80 ml) filtered water, plus more as needed
1 pound (455 g) oyster mushrooms or hen of the woods (maitake) mushrooms

For the barbecue miso glaze

1 cup (240 ml) fresh orange juice
1 cup (240 ml) water
4 garlic cloves
6 black garlic cloves (about 30 g)
¼ cup (100 g) honey
2 tablespoons gochujang
2½ tablespoons red miso paste

To serve

2 heads Little Gem lettuce, gently torn
Aquafaba Aioli (page 290)
Assorted fresh herbs (like cilantro, mint, or scallion greens), for garnish

EQUIPMENT

Outdoor grill

PREPARATION

Make the marinade

Heat the oven to 350°F (175°C). Place the kombu on a sheet pan and toast in the oven for 5 to 10 minutes, until the color becomes brown and the kombu looks visibly drier.

In a food processor or blender, combine the grapeseed oil, coconut nectar, roasted kombu, Scotch bonnet, paprika, chipotles, garlic, black garlic, allspice, peppercorns, ginger, shoyu, pears, and apple. Add the filtered water and blitz the ingredients, adding more water as needed, until the mixture has a smooth consistency.

Put the mushrooms in a bowl, liberally rub the marinade over them, and set aside to marinate for at least 2 hours and up to 24 hours.

Make the barbecue miso glaze

In a blender, combine the orange juice, water, garlic, and black garlic. Blend on high speed for 2 minutes. Pour the mixture into a large pot. Using a whisk, mix in the honey, gochujang, and miso. Bring the sauce to a boil over medium-high heat, then reduce the heat to maintain a simmer. Allow the mixture to reduce by half, 20 to 30 minutes, until you have a beautiful glaze.

Heat a charcoal or gas grill to medium-high. Place the mushrooms on the grill (if using a charcoal grill, offset the mushrooms away from direct flame) and grill for up to 10 minutes, until they develop a thorough char. Liberally brush the mushrooms with the miso glaze as they're cooking. Don't be afraid of the blackened char; it adds great flavor.

Serve the shrooms with the lettuce, aioli, and fresh herbs. For an extra pop, you can fry up sweet plantain and add it to this dish.

PAUL ANTHONY SMITH
JUNCTION #4, 2019-2022, OUT OF MANY ONE PEOPLE. R.B.G
UNIQUE, PICOTAGE, SPRAY PAINT AND ACRYLIC BEAD ON
INKJET, ON MUSEUM BOARD AND DIBOND, 40 x 60 in.

TWERK N JERK

Where Jamaicans go, so goes jerk. This style of cooking emerged from the mountainous regions of Jamaica where the Maroons (see page 96) established their secret, impenetrable communities.

Traditional jerk cooking involves generously seasoning game with bird peppers, pimento (allspice) berries, and salt, then cooking the pepper elder leaf–wrapped meat in a covered, smokeless pit over pimento wood coals. The Maroon communities needed to preserve and robustly flavor the hunted game, and the cooking method was meant to avoid detection by colonizers. While their existence was known, Maroons still had to defend themselves from recapture. Today you're more likely to see jerk chicken and jerk pork, often served with a side of rice and peas (kidney beans).

On White Plains Road in the Bronx, you can smell the scent of jerk seasoning emanating from different restaurants. You can tell if the jerk's gonna be right when you catch that whiff, especially if they're using soaked pimento wood. Our Twerk n Jerk is an homage to the traditional method. We've brought this recipe from the Bronx to the world: London, Paris, and Venice.

This recipe is fully loaded. Involve your friends and fam; more hands make for less work. Don't let the long list of ingredients discourage you. Let the flavor encourage you. You can make large batches of the dry seasoning and keep it in the stash for whenever you're ready. You can also premix the wet marinade and freeze it. (For tips on sourcing pimento wood, see Resources, page 295.) We serve this with Pineapple Confit, which adds a whole new dimension to the dish. Consider it optional. The sweetness and texture of the low-and-slow-cooked pineapple offsets the spice of the jerk and gives a tropical essence.

CONTINUED

Serves 4 or 5

INGREDIENTS

For the brine

4 cups (1 L) water

4 cups (1 L) fresh orange juice

¾ cup (255 g) honey

1 orange, sliced

1 lemon, sliced

¼ cup plus 3 tablespoons (125 g) flaky sea salt

⅓ cup (80 ml) apple cider vinegar

1 (1-inch/3 cm) piece fresh ginger, coarsely chopped

4 or 5 garlic cloves, crushed

1 lemongrass stalk, bruised and chopped

5 sprigs lemon thyme, leaves only

1 (2¼- to 4½-pound/1 to 2 kg) whole chicken

For the wet jerk seasoning

½ yellow onion, coarsely chopped

⅓ cup (80 ml) molasses

17 garlic cloves

2 scallions

1 Scotch bonnet pepper

1 (2-inch/5 cm) piece fresh ginger

2 tablespoons apple cider vinegar

Zest of 2 lemons

7 sprigs lemon thyme

For the dry jerk seasoning

3 tablespoons garlic powder

3 tablespoons plus 1 teaspoon cayenne pepper

1½ tablespoons onion powder

½ cup (25 g) dried lemon thyme

¼ cup (25 g) ground parsley

2 tablespoons muscovado sugar

2 tablespoons flaky sea salt

2 tablespoons smoked paprika

2 tablespoons ground pimento (allspice)

1 tablespoon freshly ground black pepper

1 tablespoon ground Espelette pepper

1 tablespoon ground nutmeg

5 tablespoons (35 g) ground cinnamon

3 tablespoons dried oregano

5 teaspoons ground cumin

2 teaspoons ground red chile

Twerk Sauce (recipe follows), for serving

Pineapple Confit (page 294), for serving (optional)

PREPARATION

Brine the chicken

In a large bowl, combine the water, orange juice, honey, orange and lemon slices, salt, vinegar, ginger, garlic, lemongrass, and lemon thyme. Cover and refrigerate overnight. The next day, strain the brine and compost or trash the solids. Set aside the brine.

First butterfly (spatchcock) the chicken so it's easier to season and because when it's flat, it will cook evenly: Use kitchen shears to cut along either side of the backbone, then remove and discard it (or keep it to use for making chicken stock).

Place the chicken in a large bowl or baking dish and pour the brine over the top until the chicken is submerged. Cover tightly with plastic wrap. If your space is snug, you can use the shears to cut the butterflied chicken into 2 large pieces, then transfer each section to its own gallon-size (4 L) resealable plastic bag. Refrigerate the chicken in the brine for at least 10 hours but no longer than 1 day.

Make the wet jerk seasoning

In a blender, combine the onion, molasses, garlic, scallions, Scotch bonnet, ginger, vinegar, lemon zest, and lemon thyme. Puree until smooth. Set aside.

Make the dry jerk seasoning

In a large bowl, combine the garlic powder, cayenne, onion powder, dried lemon thyme, ground parsley, muscovado sugar, salt, paprika, pimento, black pepper, Espelette, nutmeg, cinnamon, oregano, cumin, and ground chile. Stir to combine until all the ingredients are well incorporated.

Pour the wet jerk seasoning into the bowl and stir until you have a paste consistency. Important: Set aside 2 tablespoons of this marinade for the Twerk Sauce.

Remove the chicken from the bowl and allow any excess brine to drip off. Transfer the chicken to a clean bowl. Pour the jerk seasoning paste over the chicken and massage it evenly all over the bird for 5 to 7 minutes. Cover the bowl and refrigerate the chicken overnight.

The next day, pull the chicken from the refrigerator and bring it to room temperature.

Fill a chimney starter with charcoal and soaked pimento wood chips (about two-thirds charcoal, the rest pimento wood). When the charcoal is lit and covered with gray ash, pile the coals against one wall of a kettle grill. (Alternatively, set the burners on one side of a gas grill to medium-high.) Clean your grill grate and lightly oil it. Set it in place, cover the grill, and allow it to heat for 5 minutes. Set the bottom and lid vents to half open.

Lay the chicken skin-side up over medium-low heat (on the cooler side of the grill), with the legs pointed toward the hotter side. Cover the grill and cook for 30 minutes.

EQUIPMENT

Pimento wood chips, soaked for 1 hour and drained

Uncover the grill and wait 5 minutes until the coals are hot again (if using a gas grill, increase the heat to medium). Carefully lift the chicken off the grate and transfer it to the hot side of the grill, skin-side up. Cook the chicken until lightly charred, about 15 minutes. Flip the chicken and cook until the skin is crisp and charred, 4 to 6 minutes longer, until the coolest part of the breast registers 150° to 155°F (65° to 68°C) on an instant-read thermometer.

Transfer the chicken to a large platter. Allow to rest for 5 minutes, then glaze with Twerk Sauce. Have some fun carving the chicken. Get in there with a cleaver, do what you feel, hack it up as you prefer. No need to be too delicate—the prize is in the eating, not so much the presentation.

If you're serving this with the pineapple confit, plate the pineapple on the bottom of the dish, then place the glazed chicken on top.

TWERK SAUCE

Makes 2 cups

INGREDIENTS

¾ cup (180 ml) fresh orange juice

¾ cup (180 ml) pineapple juice

½ cup (120 ml) shoyu

¼ cup plus 2½ tablespoons (75 g) coconut sugar

½ cup (120 ml) vegetable stock

4½ tablespoons (80 g) double-concentrated tomato paste (preferably Mutti)

2½ tablespoons red miso paste

3 tablespoons gochujang

1 tablespoon white vinegar

1 tablespoon liquid smoke

2 tablespoons jerk marinade (reserved from page 104)

¼ cup (60 ml) white truffle oil

PREPARATION

In a medium saucepan, combine the orange and pineapple juices (if you're making Pineapple Confit, substitute these juices with the strained liquid from that recipe), shoyu, coconut sugar, stock, tomato paste, miso, gochujang, vinegar, liquid smoke, and jerk marinade. Gently bring to a boil over medium-high heat. Cook until reduced by half and thick enough to coat the back of a spoon, 20 to 30 minutes. Remove from the heat. Add the white truffle oil and emulsify with an immersion blender.

The sauce will keep in an airtight container in the refrigerator for up to 2 weeks.

Note: *If you're making Pineapple Confit (page 294) to serve with the jerk chicken, you won't use the orange and pineapple juice in this recipe. Instead, use the strained liquid reserved from the braised pineapple in that recipe.*

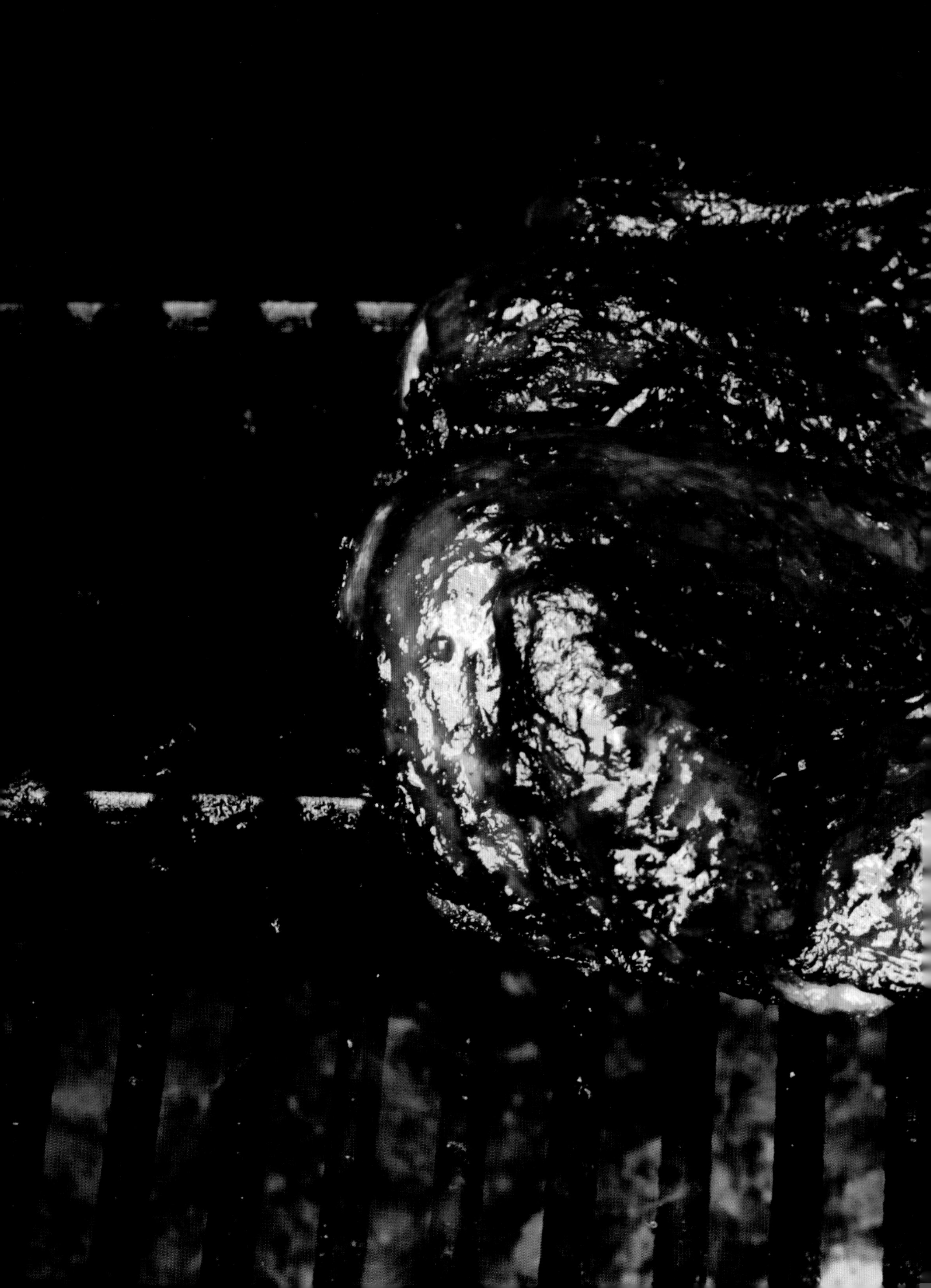

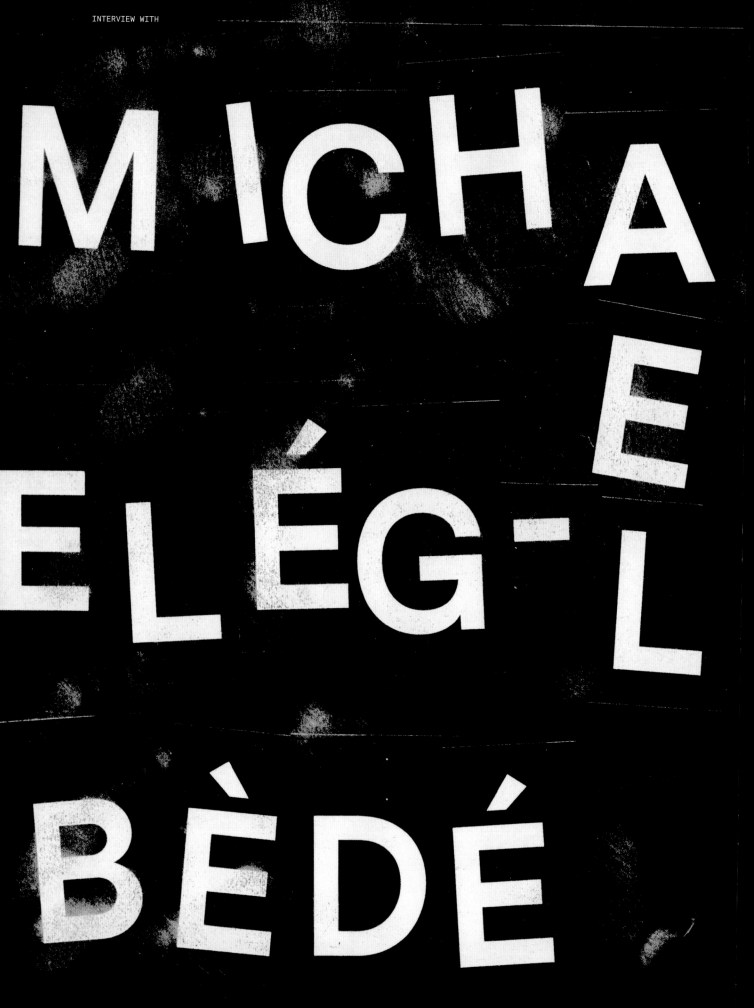

MICHAEL ÉG-L E BÈDÉ

Born in Lagos, Nigeria, Michael Elégbèdé spent his formative years in the United States. He dropped studying biology because another passion spoke to him, influenced by his chef mother and baker grandmother—his mother had gone to Cordon Bleu in Chicago, and his grandmother trained under a French chef in Nigeria. Michael went to culinary school, too, later cooking under the guidance of high-profile chefs. But it was upon returning to Lagos that he locked into his calling. He launched ÌTÀN, his culinary studio and event space in the Ikoyi neighborhood, where as owner and executive chef, he explores Nigeria's vast indigenous foodways.

Ghetto Gastro: We're finally seeing a wider, more comprehensive appreciation and knowledge base for the origins of West Africa in American foodways. How do you think about this ongoing cross-cultural, cross-generational exchange in food?

Michael Elégbèdé: In the culinary space, there's always a desire for more, a desire for new flavors, new dishes, new expressions. The oversaturation of Eurocentric cuisine has come to a point where it's just not acceptable anymore.

You have people looking to African culture and African cuisines and African American cuisines and how those intergenerational and intercontinental narratives come together. They're seeing it actually tells a better story. That has triggered the advent of increased exposure of African and African American cuisines in the global space. We've had an incredible number of people, chefs and writers specifically, paving the way for this to be able to happen.

I recently did a menu inspired by the diaspora, tracing dishes that we have in Nigeria. Bringing it back 360, seeing the correlation between suya and American barbecue, or our seafood okra in West Africa and gumbo. *Gombo* literally means "okra," and it's indigenous to West Africa.

Looking at lineages like akara, which is a bean fritter in West Africa, there is acarajé in Bahia, Brazil, which has one of the largest Yoruba communities outside of Nigeria. We have more representation, the representation of people asking questions and people trying to express themselves and express their history and ancestors—that's core to our identity, which brings more awareness to our cuisine.

You're talking about the iterations of West Africa in other parts of the world, and you've also explored Nigeria as its own base of multiplicities of food cultures. What has that exploration looked like? The shorthand in the United States is that often we tend to truncate the narratives on the other side of the Atlantic. But there's a lot that you didn't know about Nigerian food until you started looking for it.

Wow. I mean, that journey was one of the most transformative journeys in my self-identity, self-awareness, cultural awareness, and career. I found myself coming back home. I had not visited after thirteen, almost fourteen years in America. Lagos is where I grew up, but in many ways the majority of food is mass, commercial fast food. I wanted to see Nigerian food from where it's from, indigenous Nigeria, especially the north and east parts. I'd never been to those places before.

The images that we see of Nigeria are those of suffering. You see a lot of dirt. You never see the foothills that are some of the most beautiful foothills that I have seen, and I'm an avid hiker. We don't think of the waterfalls. We don't think of the plateaus. We don't think of the mountains. I was rediscovering Nigeria, getting to know Nigeria. And through the lens of food, obviously I would go to these markets. I had a driver and an assistant, and we traveled by road, which everyone was like, *Are you crazy? You're going to get kidnapped. You're going to get killed.* But I go cross-country by road everywhere else in the world. If I can't do it in my own country, then it's problematic. So we'd go to the market. I would see a range of ingredients that I'd never seen before. Obviously I'd done readings and research on the places that I was going to, and some things I might have been expecting. But these places were never described the way they actually were.

I would go to the market. I would ask about the ingredients and the ways that they use them. I thought I was just going to listen to them talk and maybe see someone cook. But everywhere I went, I was able to connect with someone in the market to cook with me. We would buy ingredients, go to their hut, their kitchen. We cooked dishes that were signatures in that remote part of Nigeria. We're a country of over two hundred different ethnic groups and that shows in the food that we eat.

A lot of techniques people affiliate with just Western or Asian cuisines, even flavor profiles, but I'd see someone sauté vegetables with irú and crayfish, just so simple. That's by the waterfront. Then you see in Calabar, you see how the food in one state changes the farther you go north. The more southern you are on the coast, the more fresh seafood they're eating, the more north you go, and it's gradual, you see how the dishes change based on what they have available to them, what they grow, what they can find. So the fresh food becomes dried, preserved seafood. They're constantly aware of seasonality.

I was mind-blown, to say the least. I learned so much about the diversity of the dishes. We have soups that are not cooked, literally, like we have our ways of making ceviche. It's called ose ani, the uncooked soup. Different parts of the country ferment differently, what they ferment, the derivatives of the fermentations, the sustainable practices of their food processing. Take palm oil, for instance, something that has been so demonized by the West, but because of the way the West uses palm oil. We don't use palm oil as an ice cream stabilizer, or in shampoo and toothpaste. We don't kill orangutans or tear down forests to extract palm oil. Here it's a small backyard thing. You're not cutting down the trees. You're just harvesting the fruit, the red part. These things that are so healthy to us, they're practiced sustainably. We use the pulp for cooking. The seed is used medicinally. The extracts of that are also used in making fire and in black soap. Every single part of the processing is used for something that is integral to the culture. That's something that's incredible. That's something that shouldn't be demonized. It gave me a different perspective on what I need to speak about and represent in spaces that I'm privileged to be in.

You said something when we met, about "children of the soil." There's this dancehall song by Sheila Rickards; in the title, she says she's "Jamaican Fruit of African Roots," which inspired the name of this chapter. Marcus Garvey established the beginnings of Pan-Africanism, and recent generations have evolved that into the Year of the Return in Ghana, homecoming trips. Folks from Europe who might have migrated are returning. What do you think of Black folks in other parts of the world experiencing Africa? What are your hopes around that? What do you feel we can do next?

It's very special to me, this topic, because I spent my formative years in the States. And as an African American—you know, when people see me, when people interacted with me, they interacted with me based on the way I look, and we know what that means, being Black in America. The power that the colonizers had over us was the power to separate. Once they separated us, they were able to control us in different ways. For me, until we realize that our narratives are not complete without each other, there's no moving forward. We as Africans: Our narratives are not complete without our brothers and sisters in the diaspora. The narratives of our brothers and sisters in the diaspora are not complete without us. And the moment we begin to think in that way, we will be able to do everything that we want to do and achieve in every single space.

I get emotional when I'm in this space of thought. I remember going to Badagry, a port for the enslaved, one of the largest in West Africa, in Nigeria. And I remember going to the Point of No Return and just sitting there on the floor. The power and the privilege that I have, to be able to come home, knowing that I can return, knowing exactly where I can return to—that strength—it was just overwhelming.

I hope to try to do that with food. I hope that in tying these blurred links, that we're able to express our rich culture, especially through what I like to think is the core of our identity, which is food. I love when I'm sitting down with friends from the American South and we start eating. If we're eating Nigerian foods, they're like, oh, this reminds me of my grandmother's this. And then if we're eating African American foods, I'm like, this is obe ata! It's like this secret code that's been passed down from generation to generation to generation. We *are* children of the soil. You cannot take away the plant from the soil. We will always be grounded to the soil that we come from. Every time we get a flavor from the fruits of that soil, you will recognize it. Because it's in the DNA, it's in the strands.

We're writing our stories in the flavors, in the techniques of where we came from. And that for me is just so beautiful. When you say, What can we do more? I want us to have more conversations on what ties us together. Let's not speak of gumbo without speaking of seafood okra in West Africa. All Black people are from Africa. I mean, we can say everyone is from Africa, but I'm speaking ancestrally, in our ethnic identity. If we have that conversation, constantly reminding the world of how much we understand our roots, then the more powerful we become.

What does "Black Power Kitchen" mean to you?

It's powerful. It's direct. Too often we are trained to subdue our power. *Oh, this might sound this way, this might be too bold.* But when I hear that, I feel powerful. I want my child to be able to pick up a book that says "Black Power Kitchen," because it's simply saying that the Black kitchen is powerful.

WHAT'S THE "YAMS"??

Yams and sweet potatoes actually have no botanical relationship, even though these terms are used interchangeably in the United States. Yams can grow to more than 40 feet long and have a rough exterior with starchy, dense flesh.

They're native to Africa and Asia and are eaten throughout Latin America and the Caribbean as well. Sweet potatoes, a root vegetable native to the Americas, are significantly smaller and have a soft interior. While yams were imported as a food supply for enslaved Africans traversing the Middle Passage, it's the sweet potato that became a stand-in for yams, due to the former's availability in North America. Africans adapted their diverse food traditions using ingredients that functioned similarly. The cultural overlap between yams and sweet potatoes remains today, for example, with holiday dishes like sweet potato casserole being called "candied yams."

In many African countries, yams are considered a highly regarded crop. For example, the Igbo people celebrate the harvest with a yam festival, extending gratitude to the ancestors and Spirit for the sustenance. We named this dish What's the "Yams"?? to acknowledge this historic lineage. Symbolically, the word "yam" comes from "nyam" (which has similar spellings in various West African languages), meaning "to eat."

The setup on this dish is inspired by Bajan souse, a traditional weekend lunch served with pickled pork and a pudding of sweet potato. Here we have a dehydrated roasted sweet potato that develops a chewy exterior texture and tender, delicate interior. And instead of a pudding, we use a cucumber-pepper juice that's bright and refreshing. If you can't find Padrón peppers, shishito peppers will work, too. This recipe takes 8 to 10 hours to fully prepare because of the time it takes to slowly dehydrate the sweet potato. Treating a root vegetable this way enhances the flavor. Don't sweat the technique. As Kendrick Lamar would say, "The yam is the power that be."

CONTINUED

Serves 4

INGREDIENTS

For the cucumber–Padrón pepper juice

1 cup (5¼ ounces/150 g) Padrón peppers, stemmed
2 cucumbers, skin on, juiced
Juice of 1 lime
1 teaspoon flaky sea salt
2 tablespoons diced fresh ginger
5 teaspoons chopped fresh cilantro
1 Thai chile

For the "yams"

4 Garnet sweet potatoes
1 cup (240 ml) coconut oil
12 sprigs lemon thyme
1 Persian cucumber, thinly sliced lengthwise
1 small white onion, thinly sliced into rounds
Ginger Oil (page 293), to finish
Espelette pepper, for garnish

EQUIPMENT

Juicer
Dehydrator

PREPARATION

Make the pepper juice

In a blender, combine the Padrón peppers, cucumber juice, lime juice, and salt and blend on high speed for 2 minutes.

Place the ginger, cilantro, and Thai chile in a bowl. Stir in the Padrón pepper mixture, cover, and refrigerate for at least 2 hours.

Make the "yams"

Heat the oven to 425°F (220°C). Place an oven rack in the middle position.

Wash the sweet potatoes and liberally poke them all around with a fork. Place the sweet potatoes on a sheet pan and roast for 45 minutes.

Remove the sweet potatoes from the oven and allow to cool for about 10 minutes. Peel them, leaving the flesh whole and intact.

Place the peeled sweet potatoes in a baking pan in the oven or in a dehydrator set to 160°F (70°C) and dry for 8 to 10 hours. When done, the outside should look a little wrinkly, but the inside should feel a little dense. Set the dehydrated sweet potatoes aside.

In a medium pot, heat the coconut oil over medium heat until it registers 185°F (85°C) on an instant-read thermometer (adjust heat as needed to maintain). Add the lemon thyme.

Fully submerge the dehydrated sweet potatoes in the oil and poach over low heat for 20 minutes, until the sweet potatoes look plump. Remove and slice them in half lengthwise. The texture inside should be slightly chewy, almost like taffy.

Place the sweet potato slices on a rimmed plate or in a shallow bowl. Cover with ½ cup (120 ml) of the cucumber-pepper juice; the sweet potato should be in a shallow bath of juice. Garnish with the sliced cucumber and onion. Finish with a drizzle of ginger oil and a sprinkling of Espelette pepper and serve.

MIGUEL LUCIANO
UNCLE KOLA, 2002
ACRYLIC ON CANVAS, OVER PANEL,
72 x 72 in.

CHUFA COQUITO

Puerto Rican coquito is a delicious holiday tradition born of coconut milk, coconut cream, and rum. Our take merges the festive beverage with tiger nut milk, which is popular in Nigeria.

Tiger nut (chufa) is a tuber, not a nut, but it still offers a nutty flavor, and tiger nut milk is a high-nutrient alternative to dairy milk. The drink horchata de chufa originated in North Africa and was brought to West Africa and Europe by the Moors. Horchata arrived in Mexico via Spanish colonization, but with rice as its main ingredient, as tiger nuts weren't imported to the Americas. Historians understand that this is how the classic rice-based Mexican drink evolved. We're inspired by these food narratives driven by the movement of people and the ingredients they had available or substituted, and by the cyclical nature of food origins that so often return to the African continent in ways we're not actively educated about. To make the drink, start soaking the tiger nuts and begin your citrus syrup the day before. To find tiger nuts, see Resources (page 295).

CONTINUED

Makes 6 cups (1.5 L)

INGREDIENTS

For the chufa milk

1 cup (150 g) tiger nuts
4 cups (1 L) hot (not boiling) water

For the citrus syrup

3¼ cups (780 ml) water
3½ cups (750 g) light brown sugar
Zest and juice of 3 oranges
Zest and juice of 3 lemons
½ cup (50 g) fresh lemon thyme sprigs

For the egg base

15 large (250 g) egg yolks
½ cup (120 ml) filtered water

For the drink

1¼ cups (300 ml) dark rum, plus more if needed
1 cup (240 ml) filtered water
1 cup (240 ml) cashew cream

EQUIPMENT

Nut-milk bag or cheesecloth

PREPARATION

Make the chufa milk
In a bowl or food storage container, submerge the tiger nuts in cool water to cover by 2 inches (5 cm). Cover the bowl with its lid or plastic wrap. Soak for 24 hours at room temperature.

The next day, line a fine-mesh strainer with a double layer of cheesecloth and set it over a deep bowl. Drain the tiger nuts. Add them to a blender with the hot water and blend on high until smooth and homogeneous, about 2 minutes.

Carefully strain the blended nuts with a nut-milk bag or cheesecloth into a container, squeezing the pulp to extract the remaining liquid. Cover and refrigerate until ready to use.

Make the citrus syrup
In a saucepan, combine the water, brown sugar, orange zest, orange juice, lemon zest, and lemon juice and bring to a boil over medium-high heat. Remove from the heat, then add the lemon thyme and allow to steep overnight. Strain the syrup, discarding the solids, and set aside.

Make the egg base
Bring 4 inches (10 cm) of water to a boil in a large pot. Set a large heat-safe bowl over the pot so that the bowl rests above the boiling water. Add the egg yolks, ¾ cup (180 ml) of the citrus syrup, and the filtered water. Cook over medium heat, whisking continuously, for about 15 minutes. Make sure to scrape the sides of the bowl to keep the eggs from overcooking. The base should thicken to a smooth consistency. Remove from the heat. Allow to cool to room temperature before chilling the egg base in the refrigerator.

Make the drink
In a bowl, whisk together 2 cups (480 ml) of the egg base, 1¼ cups (300 ml) of the chufa milk, the rum, filtered water, and cashew cream until smooth. Taste and adjust with more rum to your preference. Strain the mix through a fine-mesh strainer into a container with a lid. Keep cold and serve chilled.

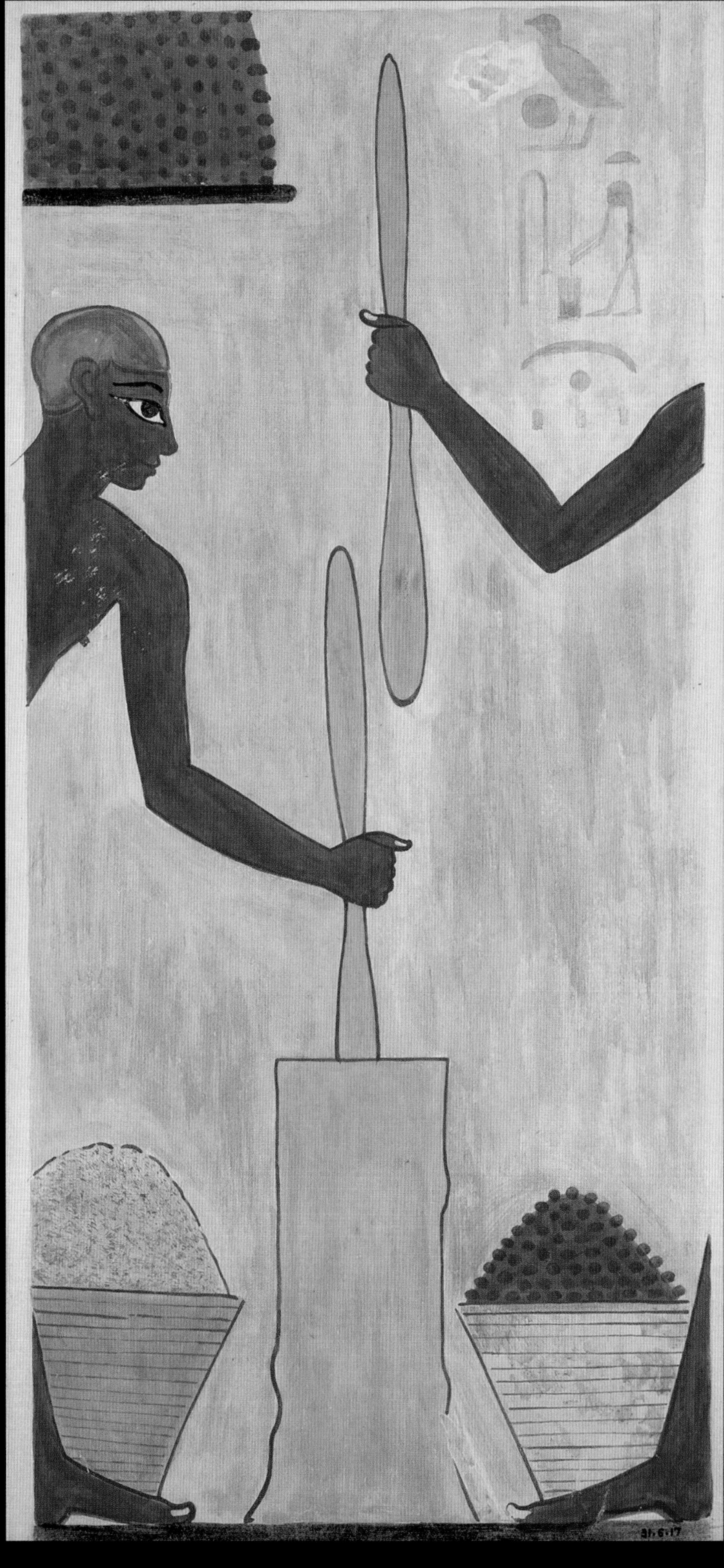

NINA DE GARIS DAVIES
POUNDING MEAL, TOMB OF REKHMIRE, CA. 1504-1425 B.C.
PAPER, TEMPERA PAINT, INK, $17\frac{1}{8}$ x $7\frac{7}{8}$ in.

ROASTED PLANTAIN GELATO

What can't you do with plantain? It's known as the potato of the Caribbean for its versatility and ease of use. Plantain can be used in stews and sauces, roasted, fried, or in this case, as a dessert.

Start with super-ripe plantains. Make sure they're soft to the touch and black on the exterior. If the plantains aren't ripe, you won't get the right balance of sweetness or the right texture for your gelato. When it's finished, the gelato should be creamy and silky smooth. This recipe is soft and sweet, but don't sleep. The flavors will knock you off your feet.

Makes about 1 quart (1 L)

INGREDIENTS

4 very ripe plantains (about 1 pound/455 g), unpeeled
½ cup (125 g) packed dark brown sugar
3 tablespoons (15 g) coconut milk powder
2 teaspoons flaky sea salt
1 large banana (about ½ pound/200 g)
3¾ cups (880 ml) oat milk
1 cup (240 ml) condensed coconut milk

EQUIPMENT

Ice cream maker

PREPARATION

Heat the oven to 350°F (175°C).

Place the unpeeled plantains on a large sheet pan. Bake for 25 to 30 minutes, until the skins turn black. Remove from the oven and allow them to cool slightly.

In a medium bowl, whisk together the brown sugar, coconut milk powder, and salt. Set aside.

When the plantains are cool, peel them and place in a large bowl. Add the banana, oat milk, and condensed coconut milk. Using an immersion blender, blend until smooth. Mix in the dry ingredients and blend on high until smooth and creamy. Cover and refrigerate the gelato base overnight to allow the flavors to incorporate.

The next day, strain the gelato base through a fine-mesh strainer, then transfer it to your ice cream maker and spin, following the manufacturer's instructions. Transfer the gelato to a freezer-safe airtight container and freeze until the gelato sets to your liking, usually 2 to 4 hours, then serve.

LYNETTE YIADOM-BOAKYE
QUORUM, 2020
OIL ON LINEN, $33\frac{1}{2}$ x $39\frac{3}{8}$ in.

SOPHIA-YEMISI ADEYEMO-ROSS
VISIONS OF IRON (ALOE VERA FOR YOUR WOUNDS), 2021
ACRYLIC, WATERCOLOR, PAPER, 30 x 22 in.

THE BRONX TO THE WORLD

DU DIPLO

RAG
MACY

GHETTO
GASTRO
Bronx
GHETTO
GASTRO

We've been about this international vibe. It's been Ghetto Gastro Global from day one. Bronx to the world. From Pelham Bay to Paris, from Dyre Ave to Dakar, our time abroad is a way for us to taste, learn, chill, and soak up game. Sometimes it's about rest and inspiration. Other times we have our cleats in the streets putting in work. Wherever we go, no matter the function, we always show up as ourselves. No code-switching here. For folks used to rocking out in places where they see others who look and sound like them, this can seem like a given. But often we roll to spots where our culture is an outlier. If we do happen to be an anomaly, we aim to kick down the door for those pulling up alongside and behind us. Run it up BX style, ya heard?

Experiencing cultures in different countries can expand, if not clarify, one's sense of national identity. This has long been true for Black Americans who historically have rarely been able to monetize the promises of success in the country that our ancestors built.

Take James Hemings, an eighteenth-century enslaved chef who was brought to Monticello, Thomas Jefferson's Virginia estate, as a young boy. Hemings would eventually accompany Jefferson to France, where the future president was on assignment, as Jefferson's personal chef. Jefferson was a known gourmand and wanted his chef to be trained in the art of French cooking. While in Paris, the cooking sensibility Hemings had displayed stateside shone. He apprenticed for several years and ultimately earned monthly wages while serving as head chef at Jefferson's Paris residence, which operated as an American embassy. The ability to prepare food for statesmen and other dignitaries in a foreign land while still being considered another man's property back home is a dichotomy that's hard to fathom. Hemings must have known how talented he was. Back in the United States, he introduced dishes like meringues, crème brûlée, ice cream, pomme frites, and, famously, a béchamel-based macaroni and cheese. No doubt this taste of creativity and freedom, however limited, affected Hemings's decision to decline Jefferson's invitation to cook for him in Washington once he'd secured the presidency. Hemings had negotiated his freedom after his return to the United States, but it's hard to imagine him enjoying it fully—his family remained enslaved at Monticello.

In more recent times, travel abroad for Black activists, thought leaders, and artists has been integral to shaping their messaging and craft. Sometimes the decision to leave has been transformational. Malcolm X had pivotal experiences in Nigeria, Ghana, Syria, and Egypt, which broadened his understanding of Islam and Pan-African identity. Assata Shakur, a target of ruthless surveillance by the FBI and its COINTELPRO program, escaped prison and fled for Cuba after being convicted in a case that was indicative of the worst police brutality of that time. Performers from Josephine Baker to Nina Simone to Tina Turner looked to Europe as a place they could express themselves fully when American concert venues or radio outlets wouldn't grant them the opportunities they deserved. An interviewer once asked James Baldwin why he chose to go to France. Baldwin, reflecting on the constant deluge of racism, police abuse, and poverty, responded, "It wasn't so much a matter of choosing France—it was a matter of getting out of America. I didn't know what was going to happen to me in France, but I knew what was going to happen to me in New York."

This is not to say the rest of the world is a utopia, even as Black Americans continue to create expat lives in Africa, Europe, and South America, as a few examples. It's odd to be from a country obsessed with maintaining a caste system illustrated by race, while traveling to places that refuse to acknowledge race while operating with similar ideals. A Black person with an American accent in France can be adored, while our French-born siblings descended from the Francophone diaspora—Senegal, Algeria, Togo, Martinique—are often treated disrespectfully. Every society must grapple with its history.

Having a passport doesn't give us a pass to ignore the complexities in life. But like anyone else, Black folks deserve to travel for leisure, too. We deserve to relax. We deserve to trickle these nickels. We deserve to celebrate milestones. And with food as our main event, we're always going to link what's on our plate to who's around us, whether it's an elder tortillera in Oaxaca or a master itamae in Tokyo.

The recipes in this chapter come from our travels mixed with where we're from. Being able to move about freely gives us endless inspiration. Roasted Breadfruit Gnocchi (page 153) merges a mainstay provision of the Caribbean with an Italian dumpling. Our 5th City Karaage (page 148) gets inspiration from a Japanese favorite while we recall the roots of fried chicken on our home turf. And we speak with our friend dream hampton, a filmmaker, writer, and fellow world traveler who drops gems on what it has meant personally and politically to be a product of Black America with the means to globe-trot.

CURRY CHICKPEAS

If you grow up up in the North Bronx, Caribbean cuisine and culture are a part of the tapestry. "Essential" doesn't begin to describe Feroza's Roti Shop, a Trinidadian go-to for West Indian cuisine. We debate our Brooklyn comrades about where the best roti resides, but we hang our hats on Feroza's curry shrimp wrap.

They fill the roti, then hit it with tamarind (and peppa sauce if you nasty). Roti in the Bronx by way of the Caribbean is, of course, the result of merged food influences from African and Indigenous cultures in the islands, and Indian cooking traditions. The latter is a product of the indentured labor the British imported from the subcontinent after slavery was legally abolished. These dishes may not always look like the Indian recipes by the same or similar names (and there are, frankly, countless delicious renditions from that massive mix of cultures), but the combo of flavors consistently create something all their own. Here we have our curry chickpea homage to Feroza's: something a little Trini, a little BX, and a lotta bliss.

CONTINUED

CHEYENNE JULIEN
TRINI SLANGS, 2020
OIL AND ACRYLIC ON CANVAS, 38 x 34 in.

Serves 4

INGREDIENTS

For the curry paste

½ medium yellow onion, diced

1 tablespoon grated fresh ginger (grated on a Microplane)

4 teaspoons curry powder

2 teaspoons white miso paste

1 lemongrass stalk, bruised and chopped

1 Scotch bonnet pepper, seeded and minced

1 teaspoon coconut sugar (optional)

½ teaspoon cumin seeds

For the chickpeas

1 (14-ounce/400 ml) can coconut milk

3 cups (485 g) cooked chickpeas

Flaky sea salt

Store-bought roti or cooked rice, for serving

PREPARATION

Make the curry paste

In a mortar, combine the onion, ginger, curry powder, miso, lemongrass, Scotch bonnet, coconut sugar (if using), and cumin seeds and use the pestle to mash them into a homogeneous paste (pulsing in a blender or food processor will work, too). Set aside. (You can store the curry paste in an airtight container in the refrigerator for up to 1 month or keep it in the freezer even longer.)

Make the chickpeas

Heat a heavy-bottomed medium pot over high heat and add one-quarter of the coconut milk. Allow the liquid to evaporate and let the milk reduce until you see thick bubbles.

Stir in the curry paste and cook until a sauce begins to form. Monitor the heat and lower it as necessary to avoid burning the sauce.

Stir in the chickpeas and the remaining coconut milk. Cover the pot, reduce the heat to medium-low, and simmer, stirring occasionally, for 30 minutes, or until the liquid has reduced by half.

Season with salt to taste. Serve with store-bought roti or with rice, or use as a filling for Dhal Puri Roti (page 132).

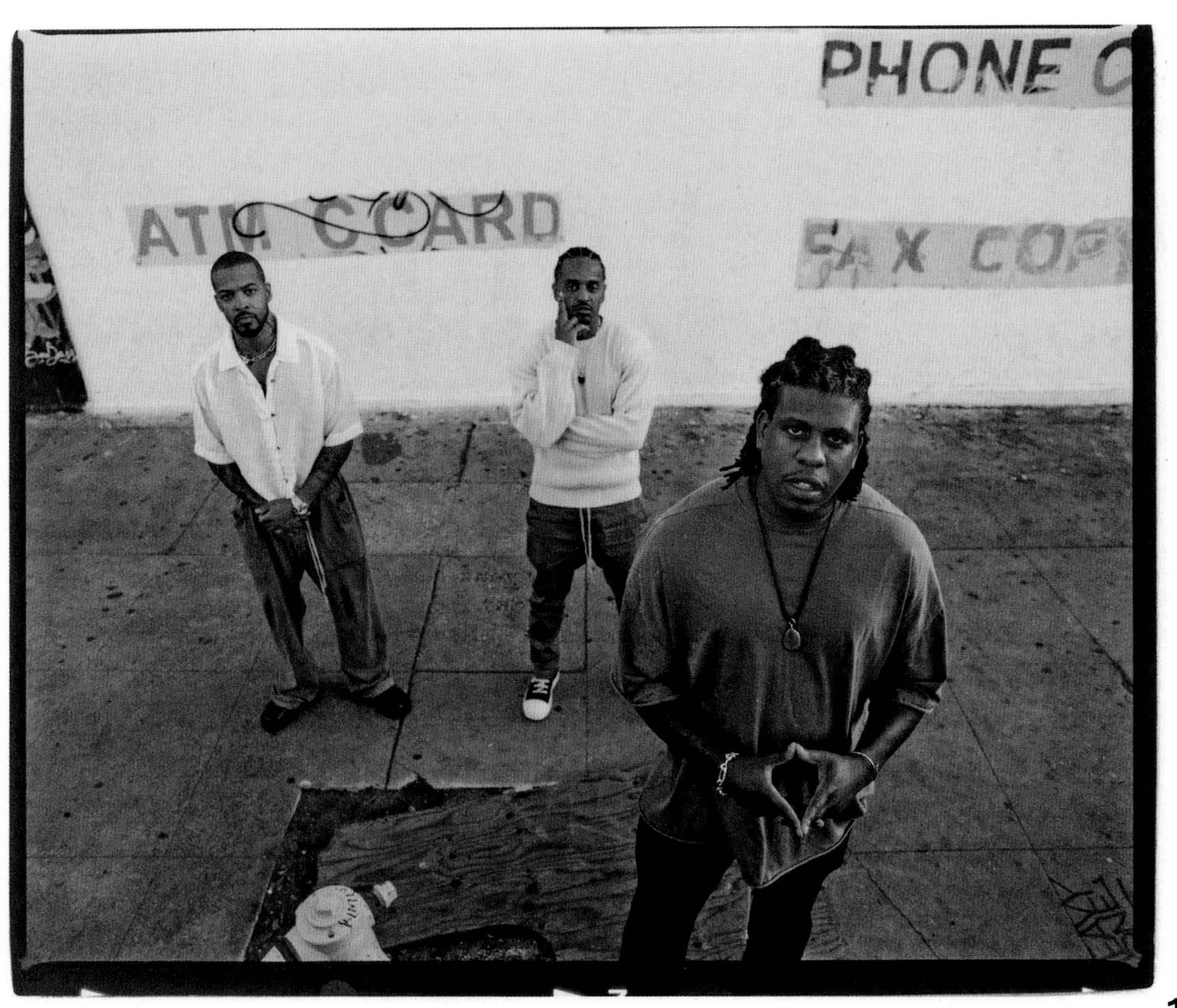

DHAL PURI ROTI

Dhal puri roti is a staple of Trinidad and Tobago and an example of one of the many diverse food cultures available in the BX. Like so many delicious dishes, this is one recipe that gets better as you get used to making it.

There's a rhythm to making the dough, sliding it onto your tawa (a slightly curved griddle pan made precisely for making roti), cooking until it's just right. Don't sweat the steps too much, just go with the flow. If you don't have a tawa, you can use a flat griddle or skillet. The dabla is for flipping the roti, but you can use a flat wooden spoon or spatula instead. Pick up a basting brush to easily coat the dough. This is a pliable dough meant to be filled and rolled, so when it's on the griddle, you're lightly searing it (no browning). You can make the filling in advance and keep it in the refrigerator for 2 to 3 days.

Makes 12 roti

INGREDIENTS

For the filling

1⅓ cups (200 g) yellow split peas, soaked in water to cover for 2 to 3 hours and drained

1 tablespoon Himalayan salt, plus more to taste

1 teaspoon ground turmeric

3 or 4 garlic cloves

1 hot pepper, such as a habanero or Scotch bonnet

3 or 4 fresh cilantro leaves (no stems)

2 teaspoons geera (roasted ground cumin)

1½ tablespoons grapeseed oil

INGREDIENTS CONTINUED

PREPARATION

Make the filling

Fill a large pot with 3 quarts (3 L) water and place over medium heat.

Rinse the soaked split peas, rubbing them between your fingers for a thorough wash, until the water runs clear. Pick through the peas and discard any debris.

Add the split peas to the pot, along with the Himalayan salt and turmeric. Bring to a boil over high heat, then reduce the heat to maintain a simmer and cook for 15 minutes, until the peas are slightly tender but not mushy. Drain.

Transfer one-third of the split peas to a food processor (or food mill) along with the garlic, hot pepper, and cilantro and pulse to

For the dough

4 cups (500 g) all-purpose flour, plus more for dusting
1 tablespoon (13 g) baking powder
2 teaspoons demerara sugar
1 teaspoon flaky sea salt
1¼ cups (300 ml) lukewarm water
¼ cup (60 ml) grapeseed oil
Curry Chickpeas (page 129), for filling

EQUIPMENT

Tawa
Dabla

mince, scraping down the sides of the bowl at intervals to ensure even processing. Do not overprocess into a paste! Transfer to a bowl and repeat with the remaining split peas.

Take the bowl full of ground peas and add the geera and additional salt to taste and mix well to combine.

In a large heavy-bottomed pot, heat the grapeseed oil over high heat. Add the split pea mixture and cook, stirring continuously, for 3 to 5 minutes, until light and grainy.

Make the dough

In a large bowl, stir together the flour, baking powder, sugar, and flaky salt to combine.

Gradually add the lukewarm water and squeeze the dough between your fingers to bring it together. Make sure your water is lukewarm, as this helps bring the dough together. Knead for 3 minutes. You want a soft dough. It's not going to be as shaggy as buss-up-shut, and not as firm as sada roti. Once the dough comes together, rub grapeseed oil all over the dough and place it in a clean bowl. Cover with a clean dish towel and let it rest at room temperature for at least 10 to 15 minutes.

On a clean work surface, divide the dough into about 12 portions (2½ ounces/70 g each). Use some finesse and handle the dough gently. Working with one piece of dough at a time, press and stretch each into a 4-inch (10 cm) disk. Place the disk of dough in one hand and dust with flour. Cupping the dough in your hands to form a bowl, use a tablespoon measure to add about 3 tablespoons of the chickpeas to the dough. The filling should be cooled and dry. Press the dhal into the dough with the back of the spoon. Do not overstuff the dough. Stretch the dough over the filling, pulling the edges up to meet at the top while forming a round ball. Pinch the edges together and rotate to seal the dough. Dust with flour and press all the way around to evenly disperse the filling. Place the filled ball of dough on a floured counter and cover with parchment paper or a clean dish towel. Repeat with the remaining dough. Allow the filled balls of dough to rest, covered, for 15 minutes.

Heat your tawa or a flat-iron griddle over medium-high heat.

Dust the counter and a rolling pin with flour. Use the rolling pin to roll the dough balls into flat rounds and brush with the oil.

When the tawa is hot, add one roti at a time and cook until the dough puffs up, about 30 seconds. Brush the surface generously with oil, then use a dabla or spatula to flip the roti over. Cook for another 30 seconds or so, but avoid cooking so long that the roti develops color. You want it to remain a pliable dough that can be folded. No crispy roti! Repeat with the remaining roti. Serve warm. The roti can be wrapped and refrigerated for up to 2 days; reheat in a skillet on the stovetop over low heat.

DIGGIN IN THE CURRY (D.I.T.C.) WITH CAULIFLOWER RICE

Diggin in the Crates (D.I.T.C. to the ones who know) is a collective of Bronx and Harlem emcees and producers who emerged in the 1990s. The crew that started with Diamond D, Lord Finesse, and Showbiz & A.G. and later brought on Big L, Fat Joe, O.C., and Buckwild is one that has shaped the sound of hip hop. Their approach to sampling jazz, soul, and funk—the music of our early childhoods—inspired countless acts that followed.

A lot of great music hasn't made it to digital streaming platforms, and "digging in the crates" is about combing through vinyl collections, from stacks in parents' basements to chic shops around the world, in search of sounds that defined an era. D.I.T.C. sampled sonic ideas and the orchestration of Black American music's (sometimes underappreciated) masters of composition and arrangements, and used their innovative take on music production, to create different sounds, new access points to music that spoke to a generation. During our travels, we sample cultures, looking for ways to combine flavor and techniques, the way Black hip hop artists dive deep into the archives. We create our own vernacular as an offering: The record needle is the knife, the vinyl is the plateware, the speakers are the spice. Talk to us nice!

In homage to the legends, we named this pistachio plantain curry Diggin in the Curry. It reflects a likkle West Indies in your bowl, by way of Bangkok, with Sicilian vibes. In Bangkok, we visited JJ Market, or formally, Chatuchak Market. With more than eight thousand vendor stalls, this place is a destination. Everything you can think of, have at it. At 1:00 a.m., the night market is bubbling. We had pig's blood noodle soup. We mentioned our love for massaman curry to our guide, Guz. Turns out his mother, Kulasab Jensarikit, makes the most amazing curry. Pierre said, "Word, I wanna cook with her."

The next day, Pierre was in a residential garage an hour and change outside of Bangkok watching Moms cook over hot coals. When Kulasab began, she started with a wok over a big, open flame. As the coals slowly cooled, the heat became more gentle. She first seared some chicken, then cooked down coconut milk and added curry paste into the broth. (Often you see people add the curry paste first, then add liquid.) It was an honor to be in her home, studying how she layered flavors, seeing what the consistency should look like and at what point to add seasonings.

In the United States, stewed dishes from Africa, Asia, and Latin American countries often get described (even dismissed) as simplistic one-pot cooks. This often gets conflated with a "set it and forget it" philosophy that is more about shortcuts and convenience than depth of flavor and intention. But folks like Kulasab, they're not mindlessly throwing ingredients into a pot. This isn't food you ignore while you do other things. It's food you tend to; it takes time and skill, even outside of a professional environment. Khob khun ka to our friends for the lessons.

We eat with our eyes, and folks love the color of this dish. There's something imaginative about a vibrant pot of stewed goodness. The Sicilian pistachios incorporate our time in

Italia and add a nuttiness typically found in curries. Instead of using cashews or peanuts, we're sticking to the color scheme, using that money-green pistachio. Serve the curry with cauliflower rice or a grain of your choice. Once you have an array of flavors and methods in your repertoire, there are no limits. Diamond D rapped something to this effect: *Don't ever rush / The proof is in the pudding so hush!*

Serves 4 to 6

INGREDIENTS

For the curry

1 teaspoon grapeseed oil

4 lemongrass stalks, bruised and minced

1 (1-inch/3 cm) piece fresh ginger, sliced

¾ cup (70 g) sliced leeks (white parts only)

3 large shallots, thinly sliced

2½ tablespoons Madras curry powder

1 tablespoon chickpea miso paste

1½ (14-ounce/400 ml) cans full-fat coconut milk

2 lime leaves

4 serrano peppers, seeded

1 Granny Smith apple, cored and sliced

1 ripe plantain (spotted yellow), peeled and sliced

4 teaspoons fresh flat-leaf parsley leaves

¾ cup (100 g) shelled Bronte pistachios, soaked in cold water to cover for 1 hour and drained

Juice of ½ lime

1 teaspoon flaky sea salt, plus more to taste

Ground Espelette pepper

For the pistachio-coconut gremolata

2 cups tightly packed (50 g) fresh flat-leaf parsley

2 cups tightly packed (50 g) fresh cilantro leaves

1 cup (100 g) unsweetened coconut flakes

½ cup (75 g) shelled Bronte pistachios

1 large shallot

Zest of 1 lemon

1 small bird's-eye chile, minced

½ teaspoon flaky sea salt

For the roasted vegetables

1½ cups (200 g) sliced asparagus (2-inch/5 cm pieces)

2¾ cups (200 g) broccoli florets (2-inch/5 cm pieces)

1 cup (100 g) sliced carrots (2-inch/5 cm pieces)

1 cup (100 g) sliced zucchini (2-inch/5 cm pieces)

¼ cup (60 ml) extra-virgin olive oil

2½ teaspoons Madras curry powder

For the cauliflower rice

1 head cauliflower (about 2 pounds/900 g), cut into florets

3½ tablespoons plant-based butter

PREPARATION

Make the curry

In a heavy-bottomed pot, heat the grapeseed oil over medium heat. Add the lemongrass and ginger and sweat for 2 to 3 minutes. Add the leeks and shallots and sweat until translucent, about 7 minutes.

Add the curry powder and miso and cook for 1 minute. Add the coconut milk and lime leaves and stir to deglaze the pan, using your utensil to scrape up all the good bits from the bottom of the pan. Reduce the heat to low and simmer for 15 minutes. Transfer the mixture to a blender while hot and add the serranos, apple, plantain, parsley, pistachios, lime juice, salt, and Espelette (take care to let the steam escape from the blender as you're blending). Puree until smooth. Set aside.

Make the gremolata

Finely chop the parsley, cilantro, coconut, and pistachios and mince the shallot. Combine in a bowl, then add the lemon zest, chile, and salt. Mix well. Set aside.

Roast the vegetables

Heat the oven to 425°F (220°C).

In a large bowl, toss the vegetables with the olive oil and curry powder until well coated. Spread the vegetables evenly over a sheet pan and roast for 10 to 15 minutes, until they are tender.

Make the cauliflower rice

In a food processor, pulse the cauliflower florets until the texture is fine and grainlike, similar to couscous. Set aside.

In a large pot, bring 4 cups (1 L) water to a boil over high heat. Add the cauliflower rice and cook for about 1 minute, then drain. Place the cauliflower rice in a bowl. Stir in the butter.

Place the roasted vegetables on top of the curry sauce, garnish with the gremolata and cauliflower rice, and serve.

RAELIS VASQUEZ
MEAT AND POTATOES, 2021
OIL AND ACRYLIC ON CANVAS,
60 x 48 in.

ON THE MAP-O

Hong Kong, China, just east of the mainland, is a major hub with a stunning array of cultures. While working on a project there, we had a craving for mapo tofu, a classic dish from Chengdu, the capital of Sichuan Province in southwest China. So we went mobbin for mapo and found just what we needed.

Mapo tofu (traditionally ma po dou fu) gives so many things at once: spicy, salty, funky, lots of texture, and silkiness. It's named after "Old Mother Chen" (Chen Mapo), who, according to legend, had a face marred by smallpox scars. She was known to cook this dish in the late 1800s. Traditionally, it's made with silken tofu and ground pork. The subdued soybean flavor is a delicious counter to the heat and spice.

We replace the pork with a plant-based alternative. A key flavor component of this dish is the doubanjiang, or fermented black bean paste. Look for it in Asian markets (or in the so-called "ethnic" aisle at large grocery stores). The Sichuan peppercorns are also a must; you can't skip or skimp on those. They have a citrusy pop that balances the numbing quality of the heat that is central to Sichuan cuisine. These peppers were once not allowed into the United States, so it's fortunate for us that these restrictions have eased (see Resources, page 295). The heat and aroma add depth—it's not spicy to be spicy. Lastly, reference the Chili Oil recipe on page 292, another layer that adds an irreplaceable kick.

CONTINUED

Serves 6

INGREDIENTS

For the sauce

¼ cup (60 ml) grapeseed oil

1 teaspoon ground Sichuan peppercorns

2 tablespoons minced fresh ginger

2 tablespoons minced garlic

8 ounces (225 g) plant-based ground meat

1 tablespoon doubanjiang (fermented black bean paste)

2 teaspoons Shaoxing wine

2 teaspoons shoyu

⅔ cup (160 ml) Mushroom Dashi (page 292) or vegetable stock

1½ teaspoons red miso paste

1½ teaspoons gochujang (Korean chile paste)

1½ teaspoons taro root flour

For the tofu

Vegetable oil, for frying

3 tablespoons cornstarch

1 pound (455 g) firm tofu, cut into 1-inch (3 cm) cubes, liquid from the container reserved

1 teaspoon Chili Oil (page 292), plus more for serving

4 scallions, finely chopped, white and green parts kept separate

1 long red chile, thinly sliced

1 long green chile, thinly sliced

¼ teaspoon toasted sesame oil

¼ teaspoon raw cane sugar

SOIL (page 291), for garnish

PREPARATION

Make the sauce

In a wok, heat the grapeseed oil over medium heat. Add the Sichuan peppercorns and stir occasionally for 30 seconds. Add the ginger. Cook for 1 minute, then add the garlic. Fry for another minute, then turn up the heat to high and add the plant-based ground meat. Fry the meat, breaking it up as it cooks, until it's cooked through.

Add the doubanjiang, wine, and shoyu to the mixture and stir well. Add the mushroom dashi, miso, and gochujang and stir. Let this simmer for 1 minute or so.

In a small bowl, combine the liquid reserved from the tofu packaging and the taro root flour. You're making a slurry, so keep it a bit runny and mix until thoroughly combined. Add the taro root slurry to your sauce a little at a time and stir. Let the sauce bubble away until it starts to thicken. (Try not to let it get too thick, but if it does, add more dashi.)

Fry the tofu

In a medium pot or separate wok, heat the vegetable oil to deep-fry the tofu (about 4 cups/1 L is a good target) over medium-high heat until it registers 365°F (185°C) on an instant-read thermometer (adjust heat as needed to maintain).

Put the cornstarch in a large bowl. Place the cubed tofu in the bowl and use your fingers or tongs to toss the tofu and coat evenly in the cornstarch. Transfer the dredged tofu to a wire rack. Working in batches, fry the tofu until light golden brown. Use a spider or slotted spoon to remove the tofu from the oil and set aside on a clean wire rack or a sheet pan lined with a paper towel.

Back to your pot/wok of sauce: Add the chili oil, scallion whites, and both chiles. Add the fried tofu and use your spatula to gently toss the tofu in the sauce. Let everything cook for 3 to 5 minutes. Add the sesame oil and sugar along with the scallion greens (reserve some for garnish) and stir until the scallions are just wilted.

Serve garnished with a last sprinkle of scallion greens, some SOIL, and more chili oil.

INTERVIEW WITH

DREAM HAMPTON

A Detroit native, our friend dream hampton made New York her home for half her life. She established herself as a prolific writer and filmmaker, writing for the *Village Voice*, *The Source*, the *New York Times*, and *Vibe*. She filmed road trips to Philly with her neighbor Notorious B.I.G. and videotaped Assata Shakur in hotel rooms in Havana. Her docuseries *Surviving R. Kelly* changed the game. She invited our very own Jon Gray to the *Time* 100 Gala when she was named one of the most influential people of 2019. He was by her side again when she was nominated for an Emmy, and the good friends ended that night at an opening for a Theaster Gates exhibit . She is someone with whom we love to build. She's a master storyteller with wit and style, a fellow lover of art, food, and travel.

Ghetto Gastro: We often talk about wanderlust. When did you begin traveling internationally?

dream hampton: Detroit borders Canada, when you're downtown you can take the tunnel to Windsor. In high school we used to go to Windsor to drink using fake IDs. When we had proper licenses, we would go to Toronto. Toronto felt international to me, and it still does. But when I visited NYU after I'd been accepted, walking around Greenwich Village, I knew right away that city would be my world. At the same time, New York can be quite provincial. When I became friends with actual native New Yorkers, I realized how even in this big city, their small neighborhoods or boroughs would be all they knew. I remember Biggie's first recording session was with Ason Unique, who went by many names, one of them Ol' Dirty Bastard. He was the first person Puff put Big in the studio with, this is before "Party & Bullshit." Big had to meet Ason at this recording studio at 4th and Broadway. I was coming home from the Village, from class, and Big was on Fulton and legit didn't know how to take the train to his session. I was like "Take the C to Jay Street, transfer to the F and go to 4th and Broadway," and he was like "Nah, you coming with us." So I'm back on the train with him. I'd been at his actual first studio session, too, at Daddy-O's house, when he did a verse on Mary's "Real Love" remix. I remember Puff complaining about having to cross the bridge for that session. Puff always acted like Brooklyn was Hong Kong, China, like super far. I remember even when me and Jay-Z were doing *The Black Book*, this book that never came out—I can't believe I'm talking about fucking rappers—

And unprompted!

Ha! But yeah, Jay was talking about how going to the city was a big deal. He won an essay contest in his English class, and they got to see *Annie*. That was a big part of how "Hard Knock Life" happened, because seeing *Annie* was his first play. I say that to say, I landed in New York, this cosmopolitan world city, that in some ways felt very small and very much like home, like Detroit. People live in their neighborhoods, and it's possible to have a small life, even in a big city. But in New York I quickly connected with my lifelong people and they often lived big lives. One of them was Greg Tate, the legendary writer. Along with Vernon Reid from Living Colour and Konda Mason, Greg was a cofounder of the Black Rock Coalition. The BRC was invited to perform in Italy, and Greg invited me. So my first trip abroad was Italy.

Where in Italy did you go?

We went to Rome and to Bari, this seaside town. It was such a revelation to be in a place that felt so old and wasn't America. Months after that, I made my first trip to the continent, to Benin. And then to Côte d'Ivoire.

When was this?

That's '91. Later that year I went to Ghana and was there for a month.

We were just up in Puglia.

I had my first multicourse meal in Rome. One of those nights when you're at a table for three, four hours, leisurely enjoying seven or eight courses. I experienced the same thing in Ghana, but for different reasons. You know how you make a joke, like, *What, y'all going to kill the chicken?* They literally killed the chicken at this one place! I was literally waiting for them to pluck a chicken for the jollof.

My first trip to Jamaica was also 1991, so I guess it was a huge travel year for me. I'm twenty years old going everywhere. I was with Heavy D, Super Cat, and Frankie Paul. What I remember is the food.

Tell us about that.

The diversity of Jamaican food is everything. You have the influence of Rastafarians on the food culture, so unlike in so much of the Caribbean, you get actual leafy greens like callaloo. The escovitch, the curry, the jerk. Jamaican food is so diverse, even as it's so singular. Los Angeles, which has become my favorite food city in the US, is also wildly diverse, even as I mostly eat Asian there.

Speaking of Jamaica, I wonder how you feel about hood tourism? We're both from hoods with codes and one of them is "If you don't have a reason to be in my neighborhood, you shouldn't be here." When I think about places like Kingston and this idea of being curious about another place's hood and going in unescorted, that feels, not code.

It's not.

In Jamaica it becomes clear real quick who's not from there, even before you open your mouth.

How do you process that, being in countries that are predominantly Black, but then realizing that you still stand out because you're an American?

Yeah. It's a thing. I kinda hate it. My political orientation is Pan-Africanism. But traveling to Africa so young, I certainly got sober about any romantic notions I had about, say, the motherland.

I remember landing in Cotonou and maybe I did actually kiss the ground. We were wearing African medallions and reading Biko and Achebe and having study groups about Lumumba and Nkrumah and Mau Mau and I felt like, I'm here! When we got to Côte d'Ivoire I met a brother my age and he invited me out. He took me to his friend's bar and the bar was closed, but there were like five or six people and at least three of them were women. I felt super comfortable. I was staying at this pretty fancy hotel. My hotel had eight pools, on some Dubai-type shit. And when the guy walked me back to my hotel, he basically asked me to pay him for the evening. I'm like, *What?* Like, I'm insulted. I'm like what the fuck, you're charging me an escort fee. I'm right back in the emotion that I had at that moment of being offended. But I also remember being hella sad. He read that and regretted asking me.

I remember thinking, Wow, I'm having this "authentic" African experience and I'm connecting with people my age, but in the end, you know, capitalism is pervasive. I'm not accusing him of being hyper capitalist. I'm saying that I represented money to him. I was a tourist and in his mind, he'd just taken me on a mini tour. This awareness of being perceived as American, which is to be perceived primarily as a resource, has happened throughout my travels. When I'm in Paris, I'm constantly dealing with the attitude of shopkeepers shifting when I open my mouth and they realize I'm not Egyptian or Moroccan. It can get transactional quickly, and it can be heartbreaking and confusing for Black Americans who live with a kind of distance from and dissonance around being an American.

I also understand the many ways we behave like Americans, how we bring a kind of cultural colonialism to these spaces. We got called out about that in South Africa. In the documentary that I made, *Black August*, we were there, supposedly in solidarity, but none of us had really learned about the land issues that were happening post-apartheid. And the assumption is, and it's the right assumption often, that they know about our shit, particularly Black American culture. They know about our artists and our art. Sometimes they know about our politics.

It's this one-way thing. It puts you in the position of white folks in a way.

In that same documentary we made several trips to Cuba. They have these underground restaurants, polancos. Home-based restaurants that operate in the gray space of the black market. I remember feeling incredibly guilty about the kind of buffets that would be at the Hotel Nacional. That bounty was one that the people, because of the rations, which were entirely because of US sanctions, didn't have. Again, here you are as a Black person from America experiencing an equivalent to white guilt. We've got a basket of mangoes at the buffet and this person cooking for tourists in their home gets a monthly ration of two mangoes for their family.

Cuba felt like home. Black people there were like "mi hermano," that kind of vibe.

Cuba feels that way to me, too. Ghetto Gastro, you guys are cultural ambassadors with food as your first offering. Then folks get to know you and get to know the other things that you have to offer. The place that you're representing is the Bronx. And it's so beautiful. But the Bronx then becomes a stand-in for hip hop and the kind of culture that was born out of the Bronx. It becomes a stand-in for every kind of neighborhood in a major city that is disregarded. Like the outer parts of Paris or the south sides of London or the East Side of Detroit.

What does "Black Power Kitchen" mean to you?

I think of literal places. I know that it's an idea and that it's not this brick-and-mortar physical place for you. I think of Harlem and the Senegalese restaurants that are really there for the cab drivers, you're welcome and they'll serve you, but they're legit there for the drivers, when they're off and on their shifts. I think about how much power there is in serving your community in such a specific way.

But then when I think of it more existentially, I think of it as a larger possibility because kitchens aren't just places where food is produced, they are places where ideas are produced. The table is a place to ideate. And not always with some agenda like, "Here tonight, we're going to discuss the possibilities of Black architects reimagining public spaces in our cities." It's the ideation that comes out of a love talk, which is what food induces.

Describe love talk.

There's this way that food is a balm, a healing. It's a comfort, and in a relaxed state, you can be your most loving self. There's a relaxation that happens around food when we can hopefully step into our most authentic selves, an extrovert can take their turn as a listener when they feel safe. They make space for people who may be normally shy, encourage them to tell a story by giving them loving attention. There are times when conversation can be elevated to a place of a love talk, when it's more than what's being said, but by the way the table sets and resets, you know?

5TH CITY KARAAGE

Uptown spots like Kennedy Fried Chicken and Crown Fried Chicken are institutions unto themselves. If you know about the snack box, salute. Fried chicken in Harlem is a product of the Great Migration, when folks like Charles Gabriel moved north and eventually opened the hallmark Charles' Country Pan Fried Chicken. But American fried chicken isn't just delicious—the history gets deep.

The historian Psyche Williams-Forson begins her book *Building Houses Out of Chicken Legs: Black Women, Food & Power* with the waiter carriers of the late nineteenth century. These women in Gordonsville, Virginia, prepared and sold fried chicken and other provisions to travelers passing through the rural town on the railroad. They were poppin up before "pop-ups" existed, supporting themselves and their families as entrepreneurs during and after slavery. What we take away from their legacy is how the cooking and selling of chicken helped many solidify financial stability during the broken promises of Reconstruction, when Black people were supposed to be full citizens but were lawfully restricted from most avenues of free life—particularly, but not solely, in the South. It's no coincidence that Uptown, the phrase "gettin chicken" means securing the bag.

At the risk of oversimplifying a topic that deserves entire books, we can summarize like this: During enslavement, many Black cooks learned their way around kitchens because their lives could depend on having that knowledge and skill. After slavery was abolished, many took to slinging fried chicken (or cooking in general) as one way to make a living. Interestingly, it wasn't until Black folks began navigating their supposed freedoms—applying to schools, looking for paid work, seeking housing—that cartoonish, offensive images of Black folks eagerly consuming chicken or stealing chickens began to appear in essays, comics, advertisements, and postcards, perpetuating a narrative by white society that Black people were subhuman and needed to be controlled, policed, and locked out of mainstream opportunities.

Exacerbated by the deep white resentment of Black people's increasing social and political mobility (this period saw the largest representation of Black people in Congress than any time since), the idea took root that being Black meant that you loved fried chicken so much that you couldn't resist it. This narrative is a painful legacy of slavery that wasn't of our own making and is ironic, given that people all over the world get down with wings and things. But the essence of this stereotype persists.

We know folks who refuse to eat fried chicken around white people, or chefs who don't cook it in their restaurants, because they feel that's the only thing certain diners expect from them. We know younger people who struggle to connect the dots between this history and the sayings they've heard, from late-night stand-up comics to references in Black-centered cinema. We also know how laborious frying chicken could be in preindustrial America, when a cook had to chase and capture the bird, slaughter it, pluck the feathers,

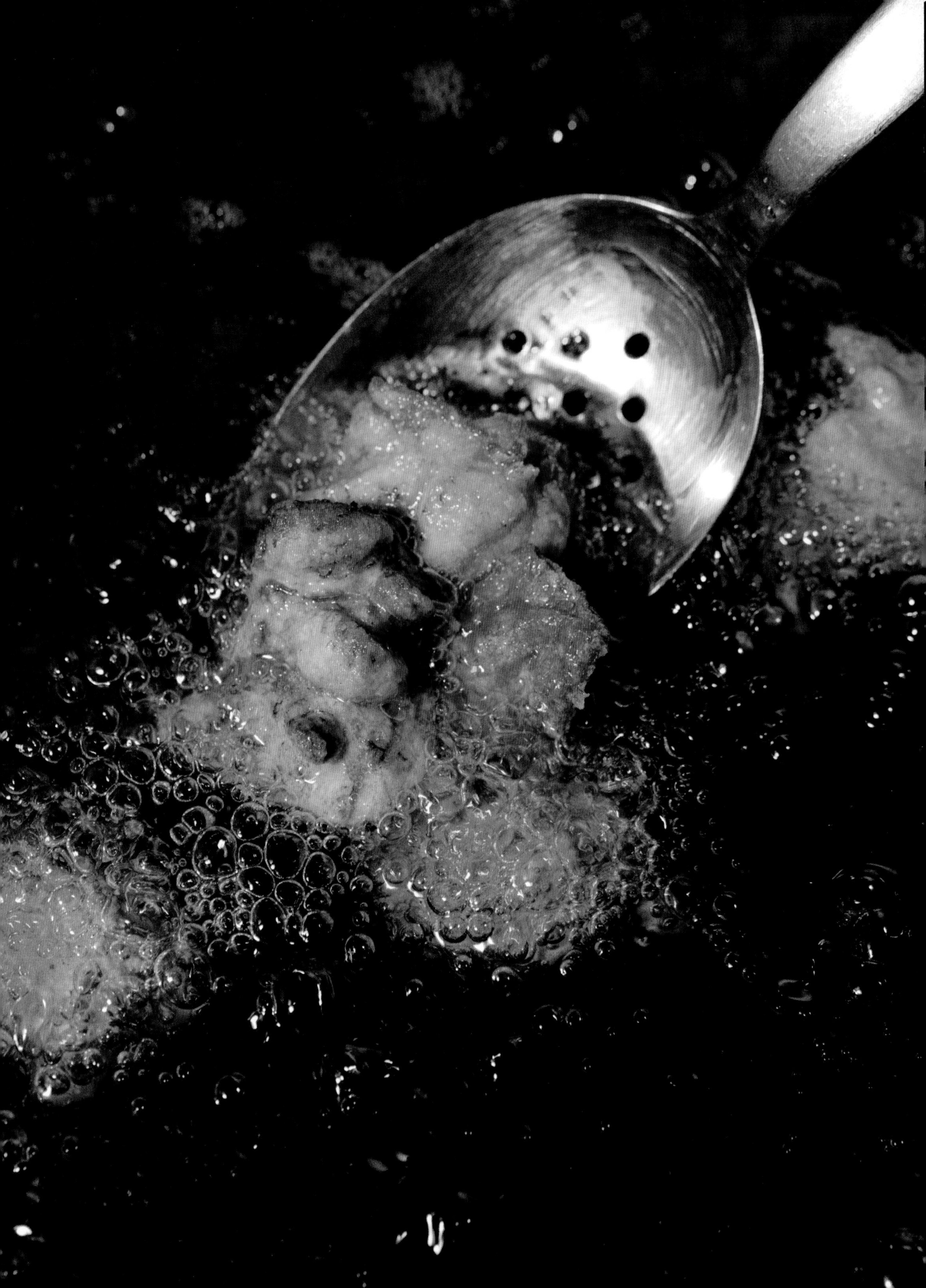

butcher the meat, then batter and fry the pieces. We know that the majority of people working in physically risky, low-wage American poultry and meat plants are Black and brown folks. American fried chicken tastes good. It's also complicated.

In our travels we've learned that some of the best to batter the bird are a long way from Southern-fried secrets or the politics of Nashville hot chicken. Walking down the buzzing streets of Osaka, Japan, is like stepping into an old-school *Tron* video game. Countless bright lights, myriad signs, and underground shops and restaurants—it's a lot to take in.

Japan and Black America have long traded influences, from jazz and hip hop to manga and anime, to name a few examples. The cultural exchange continues with us: the lore of Yasuke, a great African warrior who became a samurai in the 1500s, inspired our specialty carbon-steel knife project, OGÛN. And we're bringing the BX vibes to Burnside, a multiuse dining and lounge space we launched in Tokyo's Harajuku district.

You can get karaage, soy-marinated chicken fried in a coating of potato starch, in many places, but this street eat dates to the post–World War II years, and trust us when we say it's lit. While in Osaka, we enjoy karaage marinated with yuzu, a bright, tart citrus fruit. Our version of the dish is named after Jon and Lester's neighborhood in Co-op City, Section 5, and uses a marinade with lemon and orange. We're bringing the love from Osaka Bay to Baychester.

Serves 4

INGREDIENTS

For the marinade

Juice of ½ lemon

Juice of ½ orange

1 (1-inch/3 cm) piece fresh ginger, peeled and coarsely chopped

3 garlic cloves, minced

1 tablespoon apple cider vinegar

1 tablespoon honey

2 tablespoons shoyu

1 tablespoon vodka

For the chicken

1 pound (455 g) bone-in, skin-on chicken thighs, deboned and cut into cubes about 2 inches (5 cm) wide

4 to 8½ cups (1 to 2 L) vegetable oil, for frying

1 large (50 g) egg, beaten

1 teaspoon onion powder

1 teaspoon sweet paprika

1 teaspoon ground white pepper

½ cup (95 g) potato starch

Aquafaba Aioli (page 290), for serving

PREPARATION

Make the marinade

In a bowl, combine the lemon juice, orange juice, ginger, garlic, vinegar, honey, shoyu, and vodka. Whisk until well combined.

Place the chicken thighs in a large bowl. Pour the marinade over the chicken and massage the liquid into the chicken for about 20 seconds. Cover and refrigerate for 2 to 4 hours.

Fry the chicken

In a large pot or wok, heat the vegetable oil over medium-high heat until it registers 340°F (170°C) on an instant-read thermometer (adjust heat as needed to maintain). Remove the chicken from the refrigerator. Compost or discard the aromatics.

Set up your dredging stations: You're going to have two bowls. Put the beaten egg in the first bowl. In the second bowl, combine the onion powder, paprika, white pepper, and potato starch.

Using one hand for the egg and the other for the dry dredge, coat the chicken in the egg wash, then transfer to the dry mixture. Use a slotted spoon or spider to remove the chicken from the dry dredge and shake loose any excess dredge. Add the coated chicken to the hot oil in small batches and deep-fry until it's golden brown and fully cooked, 5 to 7 minutes. Remove from the oil and transfer to a wire rack. Repeat to fry the remaining chicken.

Serve the fried chicken with aioli on the side for dipping.

CHEYENNE JULIEN
CHICKEN SPOT, 2020
MARKER ON PAPER,
11 x 8½ in.

ROASTED BREADFRUIT GNOCCHI

You'll find breadfruit everywhere in the Caribbean. We can't imagine cuisine from this region without this giant nutrient-rich plant, but it wasn't always that way.

Breadfruit originates in the South Pacific; it's a relative of jackfruit. Its sturdy growth and tendency to bear fruit several times a year made it an attractive resource for European sugar plantation owners who wanted an inexpensive food source for enslaved Africans in the region. They wanted an option that could grow abundantly in the tropical climate but wouldn't encroach on land already dedicated to big money-making sugarcane.

In 1791, English sea captain William Bligh was famously sent to Tahiti to gather breadfruit. After a failed first attempt due to mutiny aboard the ship, the British Admiralty sent him on a second voyage. He and his team took more than two thousand breadfruit plants; just over six hundred made it to Jamaica and Saint Vincent and the Grenadines. The plant's versatile and bounteous nature soon made it ubiquitous in the West Indies. Just as potlikker from stewed collard greens became a necessary source of nutrients for many enslaved Black people in North America who had limited, if any, choice of what food they ate, breadfruit in the Caribbean was first a survival food that became revered for what the ancestors were able to do with it.

Our relationship to food is always political. You'll find breadfruit in Caribbean, African, and Asian markets. It can be boiled, baked, steamed, roasted, or fried. Younger, less-ripe fruit will lend itself to more savory applications, the way you might treat a potato. Ripe breadfruit gets you a bit closer to a sweet taste, similar to ripe plantains. Very mature breadfruit is best for roasting. And in this recipe, roasting over an open flame is what makes this dish special, as the smoke permeates and deepens the breadfruit flavor.

Gnocchi is basically an Italian dumpling, and we see dumplings a lot in Caribbean food (cassava dumplings, as one example). We've spent a lot of time breaking bread in Italy. Even though making the gnocchi is a simple preparation, cooking the breadfruit over an open flame adds a layer of smokiness to the light, fluffy dumpling. Welcome to another stop on the up-in-smoke tour.

CONTINUED

DEAD IN THE MIDDLE OF LITTLE ITALY

Serves 6

INGREDIENTS

1 breadfruit (about 1⅓ pounds/600 g)

About 1¼ cups (150 g) tipo "00" flour (you'll need an amount equal to about one-fourth of the breadfruit weight), plus more for dusting

For the pomodoro

1 cup (240 ml) extra-virgin olive oil

1 large head garlic (12 to 15 cloves), cloves separated and peeled

1 medium yellow onion, sliced

1½ teaspoons red chile flakes

3 sprigs basil

1 (28-ounce/794 g) can San Marzano tomatoes

½ cup (120 ml) water

1½ tablespoons flaky sea salt

1 tablespoon honey

EQUIPMENT

Outdoor grill, preferably charcoal

PREPARATION

Roasting over an open-flame charcoal grill, cook the whole breadfruit over the charcoal until the skin becomes black and charred, 30 to 40 minutes, depending on the size of the breadfruit. When it's fully black with gray spots (it should look like a hot coal), it's done cooking. Allow the breadfruit to cool slightly—be careful with the hot ashes.

Wearing gloves, use a knife to carefully cut away the blackened exterior of the breadfruit, leaving you with the interior. Separate the core and mash the breadfruit in a mortar using a pestle, or transfer to a bowl and use a potato masher. (Alternatively, you can split the breadfruit in half, remove the fibrous core, then scoop out the interior.)

On a clean surface, knead the mashed breadfruit and flour together until a smooth dough forms. Separate the dough into 4 equal portions and roll each into a long log, 18 to 24 inches (46 to 61 cm) in length. Apply consistent pressure and roll outward to ensure the dough is evenly distributed.

Using a pastry cutter or dough scraper, divide each log of dough into pieces about 1 inch (3 cm) wide. Set aside on a sheet pan lightly dusted with flour.

Make the pomodoro

In a large, heavy saucepan, warm the olive oil over medium-low heat. Add the garlic and cook until it softens and begins to caramelize to a golden color, about 3 minutes.

Add the onion, chile flakes, and basil and cook until the onion is translucent, but be careful to avoid browning it.

Stir in the tomatoes and water. Raise the heat to medium, bring the mixture to a simmer, and cook, stirring occasionally, until the flavors have melded and the sauce has thickened slightly, about 30 minutes.

Remove from the heat and add the salt and honey. Using an immersion blender, blend the sauce until smooth. Taste and adjust the seasoning as desired, but remember that the pasta water will also add more seasoning.

Bring a large pot of salted water to a boil. Remove the gnocchi from the refrigerator. Reheat the tomato sauce in a sauté pan over low heat.

Add the gnocchi to the boiling water in small batches; cook until they float to the top, 1 to 2 minutes. Using a slotted spoon, transfer the cooked gnocchi to the sauce. Repeat with the remaining gnocchi. When all the gnocchi have been added to the sauce, bring the sauce to a simmer, cook for 1 minute, then serve immediately.

SALTFISH TAKOYAKI

We can't get enough of the street food scene in Japan. One of our favorite snacks is takoyaki, a fritter-like ball made from diced octopus cooked in a seasoned batter. We immediately connected takoyaki to conch fritters in the Bahamas and fish cakes in Barbados.

Like breadfruit, saltfish (salted cod) was preserved and imported to the Caribbean as a food source for the enslaved. Today it's a celebrated part of many cuisines, and Jamaica boasts ackee and saltfish as its national dish.

To make this recipe, soak your saltfish one day ahead. While some boil the saltfish to reduce the salinity borne out of the preservation process, we prefer to soak it overnight. The intense heat of boiling dries out the fish. If you want to speed the process, you can soak the fish in milk. Either way, be sure to change out the liquid once during the soak to discard the extracted salt.

You'll need a takoyaki pan to make these balls, and if you're looking for bonus points, cop a couple of takoyaki pin sticks or skewers. The pin sticks are worthwhile to help you turn and rotate the takoyaki. As a backup, you can use toothpicks, but don't use chopsticks; they're too large for the task. The pan looks like a circular muffin tin, and it's a must for the ease of cooking and uniformity of the takoyaki. These are meant to be a shareable snack or appetizer. Ball till you fall, takoyaki papis and mamis.

CONTINUED

Serves 10

INGREDIENTS

For the saltfish

1⅓ pounds (600 g) boneless, skinless salted cod

4 garlic cloves, crushed

4 scallions, sliced on an angle

1½ teaspoons finely chopped fresh marjoram leaves

1 habanero chile, finely chopped

For the takoyaki batter

2 cups (240 g) tipo "00" flour

1 teaspoon flaky sea salt

8 large eggs, separated (see Note)

1 cup (240 ml) coconut milk or oat milk, warmed

9 tablespoons (4½ ounces/125 g) plant-based butter, melted

8 large (250 g) egg whites

2 tablespoons cane sugar

¼ cup (60 ml) vegetable oil, for the pan

Chive powder, for serving

Aquafaba Aioli (page 290), for serving

EQUIPMENT

Takoyaki pan

2 takoyaki pin sticks or skewers

Note: *You'll need to separate 8 eggs total to get the egg whites you need for this recipe, but you'll only use 2 of the yolks.*

PREPARATION

Prepare the saltfish

The day before you want to eat the takoyaki, place the salted cod in a bowl and cover with cold water. Refrigerate for 24 hours. Change the water once to remove excess salt.

Drain the fish and place it in a saucepan. Add enough cold water to cover the fish. Bring to a boil over high heat. Reduce the heat to low and simmer for 8 to 10 minutes; it will firm up a bit. Drain the fish and set aside until cool enough to handle, then, using a fork, shred the fish into small flakes. (If you want to uniformly finesse your flakes, transfer the cooled fish to the bowl of a stand mixer fitted with the paddle attachment and beat on medium speed to break it into flakes.)

Transfer the flaked fish to a large bowl and add the garlic, scallions, marjoram, and habanero. Mix well and set aside.

Make the takoyaki batter

When you're ready to cook the fish, in a medium bowl, mix the flour and salt. In a separate bowl, whisk together 2 egg yolks, the coconut milk, and melted butter. Pour the wet ingredients into the dry ingredients and mix.

In the bowl of a stand mixer fitted with the whisk attachment, whip the egg whites and sugar on medium-high speed until well combined, about 3 minutes. Gently fold the whipped egg whites into the batter.

Add the batter to the bowl with the fish mixture and mix well.

Before you start cooking, make sure you have everything at the ready: your takoyaki pan, a small dish of oil for coating the pan, pin sticks to flip the takoyaki, and a serving plate.

Heat the takoyaki pan over medium heat. Using a brush or paper towel, generously coat the pan with oil. Give the fish batter a quick whisk, then spoon it into the individual sections of the pan until all are filled. Fill each section all the way up to the top. It's okay if they overflow a bit.

The takoyaki can take 3 to 5 minutes to cook. Move and rotate each ball as it cooks. When the edges start to look more solid and opaque, it's time to flip them. Use your pin sticks to rotate the takoyaki 90 degrees, then pour in a bit more batter. If they don't move easily, they need more time to crisp up.

Let cook, stuffing in any excess batter that's outside the ball, and turn again. Cook until the balls are crispy and brown, moving them around in their section of the pan to evenly cook them. As the balls crisp up, it will be easier to flip them.

Transfer to a serving plate and finish with chive powder and aioli.

LIMONADA DE COCO

On a trip to Cartagena, Colombia, a group of Afro Colombian women welcomed us in the square with a beautiful ceremony featuring traditional dancing and freshly made limonada de coco, a nonalcoholic lime-and-coconut smoothie.

San Basilio de Palenque has a stunning history. Africans who escaped enslavement from the Spanish established the town in the early 1600s, making it the first independent community in the Americas. Isolated by geography (Palenque is inland from Cartagena by about an hour and tucked in a mountainous region), the Africans retained parts of their Bantu-Congo language, creating a Creole that is still spoken there. But freedom without resources isn't sustainable, and this growing community had to find ways to support itself. The Palenqueras, free Black women, established trade of the local produce along with handwoven baskets that they sold in Cartagena. This tradition has evolved into the Palenqueras posing in their traditional dress for tourists, showing off the striking beauty of the culture.

We want to drink limonada de coco more than water, it's that good. It's a perfect beverage for large groups, and kids love it, too (it's not too sweet). Enjoy it on a summer day, or when you're in the mood for something tropical.

Serves 4

INGREDIENTS

1 (14-ounce/400 ml) can full-fat coconut milk, unshaken

¼ cup (60 ml) fresh lime juice (from about 5 limes), plus more if needed

3 tablespoons agave syrup, plus more if needed

1½ cups (360 ml) ice cubes

Coconut water or water, if needed

PREPARATION

In a blender, combine the coconut milk, lime juice, agave, and ice. Blend on high until very smooth. Taste and adjust the amount of lime juice or agave to your liking.

If the mixture is too thick, adjust with coconut water or water. Drink expeditiously.

KERRY JAMES MARSHALL,
UNTITLED (CLUB COUPLE), 2014

43
KODAK PORTRA

WATERMELON AND PRIMETIME GINGER LIME

One of the best parts of traveling is the collection of aromas and flavors we've acquired, each place, each dish, expanding our palates. These experiences influence not just how we eat but what we choose to add to a dish. We're creating our own flavor playlists.

Summertime Uptown means watermelon trucks, jam-packed with fresh-picked melons from Georgia and South Carolina, find their way to the streets of the Bronx and Harlem. Folks come from all over to call dibs on the sweet red or yellow black-seeded watermelons that vendors like the Black Seed Brothers take pride in selling. Ain't nothing wrong with enjoying melon on its own, but finesse can go a long way.

In this recipe, in addition to the watermelon flesh, we pickle the rinds to use as much of the fruit as possible and to pack a little bite in the salad. Coriander, star anise, and cardamom in the pickling liquid give the flavor a warming boost. We candy pepitas for a crunchy balance to the soft fruit. The dressing is citrusy with a burst of ginger. This isn't the watermelon we grew up eating, but it's a pleasure, especially in that summer weather.

CONTINUED

RENELL MEDRANO
SEEDED, HARLEM WORLD RBG, 2019

HANK WILLIS THOMAS
THIS AIN'T AMERICA, YOU CAN'T FOOL ME, 2020
HAND-GLAZED PORCELAIN, 9 x 15 x 6 in.

Serves 4

INGREDIENTS

For the pickled watermelon rind

8 ounces (225 g) watermelon rind (from a 1-pound/455 g watermelon)

1 cup (240 ml) rice vinegar

1 cup (240 ml) spring water

½ cup (150 g) palm sugar

2 tablespoons coarsely chopped fresh ginger

4 teaspoons flaky sea salt

1 teaspoon red pepper flakes

1 teaspoon coriander seeds, toasted

1 teaspoon whole green cardamom, toasted

1 lime leaf

1 star anise pod

For the ginger-lime dressing

1 shallot, unpeeled

1 tablespoon extra-virgin olive oil, plus more as needed

Flaky sea salt

2 tablespoons minced fresh ginger

½ cup (120 ml) fresh lime juice (from 4 limes)

¼ cup (60 ml) fresh orange juice

Pinch of ground white pepper

For the melon salad

3 cups (455 g) cubed or balled watermelon

3 or 4 fresh mint leaves, torn

Candied Pepitas (page 291), for serving

Micro basil, for garnish

Pinch of flaky sea salt, to taste

Pinch of Aleppo pepper, to taste

Lime zest, for garnish

PREPARATION

Pickle the watermelon rind

Using a sharp peeler, remove and discard the exterior green portion of the watermelon rind. You should have a rind that is mostly white, with a little bit of pink or red on one side. With the peeler, create 3-inch (8 cm) ribbons of rind.

In a 2-quart (2 L) saucepan, combine the vinegar, water, palm sugar, ginger, salt, pepper flakes, coriander, cardamom, lime leaf, and star anise. Bring to a boil over medium-high heat and hold at a boil for 1 minute, then carefully add the watermelon rind. Return to a boil, then remove the pan from the heat and allow to cool for 30 minutes.

Using a canning funnel and a ladle, transfer the watermelon rind to a 2-quart (2 L) jar. Pour in as much of the pickling liquid as possible. Cover the jar and leave at room temperature for 90 minutes. Refrigerate the pickled rinds overnight before using. (They can be stored in the refrigerator for up to 1 month.)

Make the dressing

Heat the oven to 375°F (190°C). Place the whole shallot on a sheet of aluminum foil and drizzle with olive oil and a pinch of salt. Wrap the shallot in the foil and roast it for about 20 minutes. Allow it to cool for about 30 minutes in the refrigerator, then peel.

In a blender, combine the roasted shallot, ginger, lime juice, orange juice, and salt and white pepper to taste. Blend for about 1 minute. With the motor running, slowly add the olive oil and blend until the dressing is fully emulsified.

Prepare the melon salad

Place the cubed watermelon, 5 pieces of pickled watermelon rind, and the mint in a large bowl. Drizzle the dressing over the melon mixture and toss to coat. Sprinkle with additional olive oil, the candied pepitas, micro basil, salt, Aleppo, and lime zest and serve immediately.

COCONUT CEVICHE

In Havana, Cuba, we feel at home, like we're in another motherland. Cuba has deep African roots. You can hear Africa in the call-and-response of Cuba's salsa and rumba music—often referencing the Yoruba names of the Orishas. You can hear Africa in the sound of the Batá drummers, their precise rhythms an expression of Santeria that originates from the Yoruba of modern-day Nigeria.

You can see it in the faces of people as you walk the streets of the capital, many of whom look like us. What's also remarkable to us as visiting Black Americans is how so many African customs were retained throughout slavery (in the 1800s, Cuba became the largest colony of enslaved people in Latin America, a result of consolidated efforts to continue forced work on the island after abolition in the United States). The official word is that Cuba is a color-blind society, owing to its leaders' ideas of nationalism. But in its food, music, fashion, and art, Cuba, while certainly a mix of cultures, is a very Black country.

Wifredo Lam was an Afro Cuban artist of African, Spanish, and Chinese heritage. He is best known for merging the imagery of his homeland and specifically African artistry with European techniques. Lam studied and lived in Madrid and Paris during much of his career. He is counted among the finest artists of the surrealist and cubist traditions. His work often features references to African masks and Santeria, including figures that mythically merge human and animal form. He painted references to the injustices of war (his early years as an artist coincided with World War I) and the reach of slavery and its connection to sugar production in his home country. He also painted images that celebrated the beauty of Black people and their history.

This coconut ceviche with plantain chips is inspired by Lam and his paintings. We serve the coconut meat and broth inside a charred coconut, but if you don't have a blowtorch, don't let that stop you from catching a tropical vibe. A regular coconut shell or bowl will still give you a taste of paraíso.

CONTINUED

Serves 6

INGREDIENTS

For the coconut broth

4 cups (1 L) coconut water
2 cups (480 ml) coconut milk
4 to 6 fresh lime leaves

For the plantain chips

2 green plantains, peeled and thinly sliced lengthwise
¼ cup (60 ml) coconut oil

For the coconut ceviche

3 young coconuts (1½ to 3⅓ pounds/680 g to 1.5 kg each)
Fruit from 3 finger limes
2 habanero chiles, thinly sliced
1 scallion, green part only, sliced
2 tablespoons Lemongrass Oil (page 293)
Chili Oil (page 292), for garnish

PREPARATION

Make the coconut broth

In a saucepan, combine the coconut water, coconut milk, and lime leaves. Bring to a simmer and simmer for 10 minutes. Remove from the heat and allow the broth to cool, then place in a covered container and refrigerate overnight.

Make the plantain chips

Heat the oven to 300°F (150°C). Line a sheet pan with parchment paper.

Place the sliced plantain strips on the prepared pan. Brush both sides with coconut oil. Add another sheet of parchment on top of the plantain. Layer a second sheet pan on top of the parchment-covered plantain slices, then apply pressure with a heavy oven-safe dish like a cast-iron skillet.

Transfer the stacked sheet pans to the oven and bake the plantain chips for 30 minutes, rotating the stack every 10 minutes so they cook evenly. When they're ready, the plantain chips will have a tanned look, but they won't be brown.

Make the coconut ceviche

Carefully slice the young coconuts in half. Use a spoon to scoop out the coconut meat and set aside. Reserve the shells, being sure to remove any meat remnants.

In a large bowl, combine the coconut meat, finger lime flesh, habanero slices, scallion greens, and lemongrass oil. Mix well.

Line the bottom of the reserved coconut shells with a serving of the coconut ceviche. Garnish with chili oil.

LARISSA DE JESÚS NEGRÓN
THE PERSISTENCE OF LABOR, 2019
ACRYLIC AND OIL PAINTING ON
CANVAS, 16 x 20 in.

CO
CO
RICO
Dieta

REBELS
WITH A
CAUSE

OASA DuVERNEY
A NURTURED WAVE SANKOFA, 2021
GRAPHITE ON PAPER, 16 x 18 in.

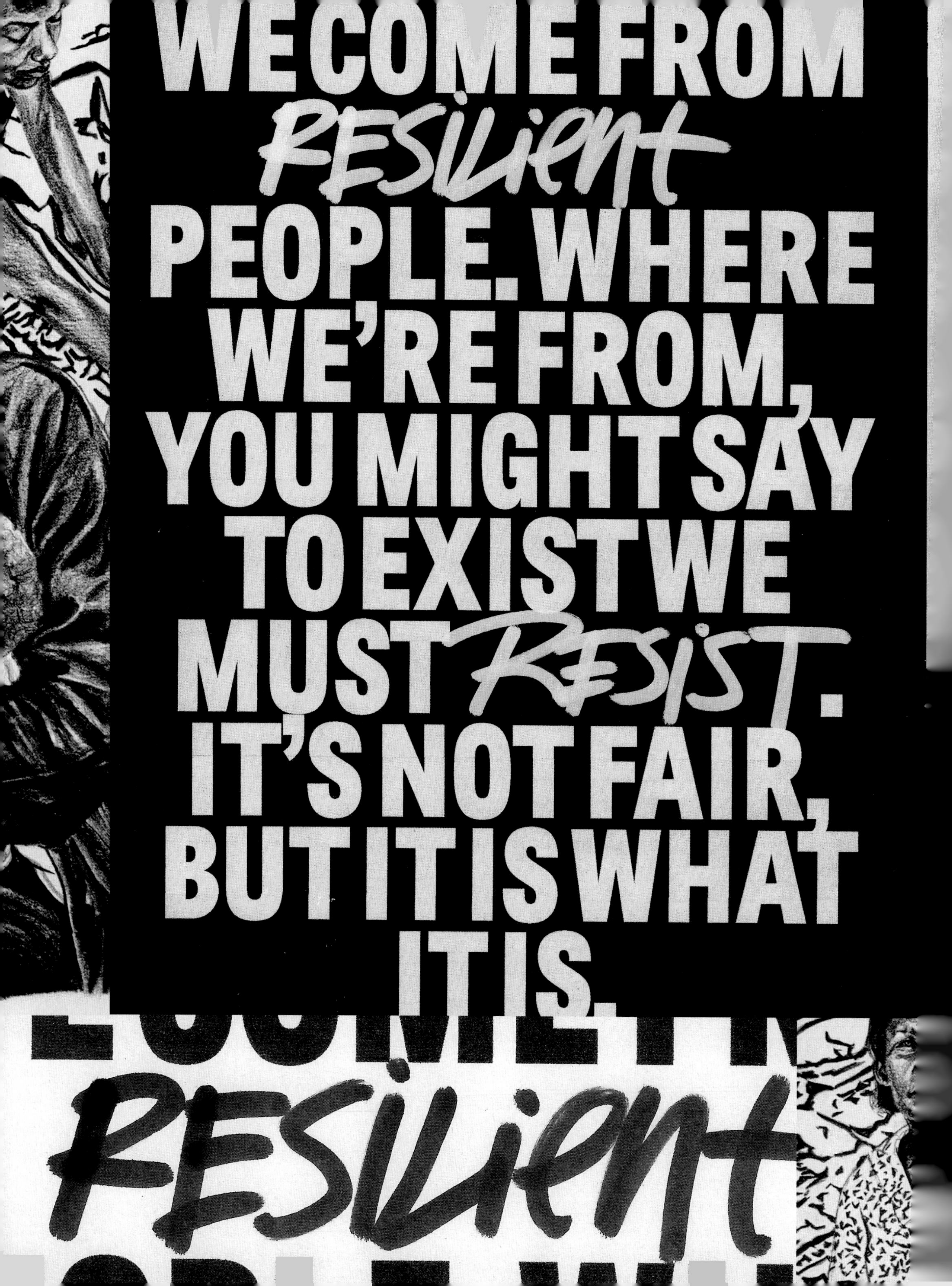
WE COME FROM
RESILIENT
PEOPLE. WHERE
WE'RE FROM,
YOU MIGHT SAY
TO EXIST WE
MUST RESIST.
IT'S NOT FAIR,
BUT IT IS WHAT
IT IS.
RESILIENT

We come from resilient people. Where we're from, you might say to exist we must resist. It's not fair, but it is what it is. Ghettonomics—which we define as a system of neglect that has disinvested from and poisoned Black neighborhoods—has affected the three of us in different ways. Many people in the Bronx, a borough of diverse communities, have felt the weight of these systemic issues personally.

We came of age in the midst of the AIDS epidemic, the emergence of crack block by block, the failed War on Drugs, and the harm of trickle-down Reaganomics. We had joy in our lives, but we also were constantly aware of a cycle of pain, prison, and poverty, with no exit ramp. Decades later, the headlines seem fresh, but in reality, the story feels all too familiar.

The police remain a constant threat. In New York, many essential workers who pushed through the pandemic live in the Bronx. COVID-19 transformed their day-to-day, taking thousands of lives in a short period of time. A willfully ignorant government ignored AIDS at its peak, and the same was true for the coronavirus. Both affected folks who are often overlooked.

We come from resilient people, even if many of us are tired of needing to be resilient. We are descendants of people who learn the game, adapt, and when the time is right, flip it. In 2020, we started working with La Morada, the South Bronx Oaxacan restaurant that has been a pillar since they opened in 2009. Husband-and-wife team Natalia Mendez and Antonio Saavedra were farmers in San Miguel Ahuehuetitlán, in northwestern Oaxaca, before migrating to New York. They've been a crucial resource in the community, supporting refugees and the undocumented. When we collaborated with nonprofit Rethink Food NYC at the onset of the pandemic, our initial goal was to get food to those made most vulnerable by a system of neglect: families with lower household incomes, seniors, the formerly incarcerated. When the uprisings began in response to ongoing police brutality, we felt it was our duty to feed as many of the protesters as we could. The lack of access to food is and has been a race issue. It's food apartheid. We don't use the term "food deserts," because that implies a natural occurrence. The systemic inaccessibility of healthy, affordable food sources for so many people of color and those living in poverty is anything but nature made. La Morada offered their kitchen and resources, and with Rethink, we collectively fed tens of thousands of people.

The collaboration with our friends at La Morada is influenced by the Black Panther Party (BPP), who many still predominantly associate with violence, or as the federal government called them, domestic terrorists. But a fairer interpretation of the Panthers also considers their circumstances, many of them young victims of long-standing police abuse fed up with such attacks, who wished to protect themselves and their neighbors (history has taught us that a few European settlers in the "New World" started a whole revolution with the British over similar complaints).

In 1969, the Oakland chapter of the BPP launched a free breakfast program for schoolchildren. Members and volunteers sought donations from grocers and received guidance on healthy meals. The impact on the kids was immediately noticeable by school officials, who saw that students were more focused and energetic because they weren't hungry. The initiative spread to other chapters, and soon the BPP was feeding thousands of children per day nationwide. This positive approach conflicted with the militant depiction of the group in the media. Under the leadership of J. Edgar Hoover, who considered the BPP a serious threat, the FBI discredited the program and its intent. The free breakfast program was eventually disbanded, but not before the BPP had successfully demonstrated the power of ensuring hungry mouths got fed. In part due to pressure from communities who'd seen the results of the Panthers' work, the federal government permanently adopted its own school breakfast program in 1975.

Our medium is primarily food. But social justice is deeply embedded in what we cook, who we serve, where we direct funds, and the efforts we make toward building a society that has a place for us and our people.

Resistance and rebellion are important tools in an ongoing effort to see Black people truly liberated. Resistance can be everyday actions that work toward creating equity, like abolishing prisons and ICE. Rebellion is often the protests that help catalyze political transformation, like the demonstrations in response to the police murders of Black people.

The recipes in this chapter all touch on an aspect of Black resistance and rebellion: For example, Ghetto Griot (page 176) speaks to Haiti's historic independence that upended ideas about the longevity of slavery, and the Black Power Waffle (page 208), one of our iconic dishes, leans on coconut and cocoa and the story of a people's identity. We sit down with Emory Douglas, the former minister of culture for the Black Panther Party, whose groundbreaking art and design gave a movement its visual language.

We sustain ourselves with nourishing food, being in community with our peers, and learning ways to upend complex systems to create healthier, enriching futures. Through resistance and rebellion, we can see change through action. We invest in ourselves, and we reinvest in our community, and we hope to inspire others to do the same.

GHETTO GRIOT WITH QUIKLIZ

Haitian (and Haitian American) culture has been prominent in New York City for generations, but its impact has been global. Just think of Jean-Michel Basquiat, the second-generation Haitian and 1980s graffiti artist turned painter whose style still resonates in art and fashion today. We see Basquiat's influence on the historic Black fashion brand Pyer Moss, founded by another Brooklyn-born Haitian son, Kerby Jean-Raymond.

You're more likely to find clusters of bomb Haitian food spots in Brooklyn, specifically in Flatbush, than in the BX. But the Haitian influence on Black identity everywhere has been centuries in progress. When we think of resistance in the Americas, we must show respect to what Haiti has meant and what it continues to signify.

Enslaved Africans had a history of rebelling against owners in Saint-Domingue, a colony on the island of Hispaniola ruled by the French from the seventeenth century. (Rebellions against slavery were constant wherever the institution was in place, even as consequences for quelled uprisings imposed by white colonizers were barbaric.) But the overseas tensions created by the French Revolution generated new political weaknesses to exploit on the island. Under the leadership of formerly enslaved generals Toussaint Louverture and his successor Jean-Jacques Dessalines, the Black enslaved led the fight to end slavery and took their independence from the French. Renamed Haiti in 1804, the former colony became the first Black-governed nation in the Americas, and only the second sovereign nation in the hemisphere, after the United States. We're inspired by their hard-won, historic victory.

Griot ("griyo" in Haitian Creole) is a classic pork dish served with a side of pikliz, a spicy "slaw" or pickled veggie mix. The meat is cut into chunks, braised in its own marinade, then fried. The result is a flavorful, tender center and a crisp exterior. We use jackfruit in this recipe for a plant-based take, echoing a common practice in Caribbean households to cook with savory fruits. If jackfruit is new to you, look for its spiky green exterior in the produce section, with prepared fruits, or it might be pre-cut and plastic-wrapped, hanging with the tofu and alternative proteins. Fresh and whole is best, if you can get it. Jackfruit can have a faint sour or funky scent to it, and the flesh can remind you of banana or mango. It's really its own thing, and this recipe sets off its sweetness.

CONTINUED

Serves 4

INGREDIENTS

For the quikliz

2 cups (140 g) thinly sliced savoy cabbage

½ red onion, thinly sliced

1 medium jicama, peeled and julienned

7 medium green, red, or yellow ají dulce, or 2 bell peppers

3 scallions, thinly sliced

4 Scotch bonnet peppers or habanero chiles, seeded and thinly sliced

4 garlic cloves, grated on a Microplane

1¼ teaspoons flaky sea salt

12 whole black peppercorns, toasted

4 whole cloves, toasted

1½ cups (360 ml) coconut vinegar or white vinegar

Juice of ½ lime

For the dry dredge

1¾ cups (220 g) all-purpose flour

¼ cup (50 g) potato starch

3½ tablespoons smoked paprika

3 tablespoons ground white pepper

2 tablespoons garlic powder

1 tablespoon celery salt

1 tablespoon freshly ground black pepper

1 tablespoon dry mustard

1 tablespoon ground coriander

1 tablespoon ground ginger

1½ teaspoons ground dried thyme

1½ teaspoons dried basil

1½ teaspoons dried oregano

2 teaspoons flaky sea salt

For the jackfruit griot

5 cups (1.2 L) grapeseed oil

2 tablespoons coconut oil, melted, or olive oil, plus more as needed

2 pounds (900 g) jackfruit

Flaky sea salt, to taste

Cooked rice, for serving

¼ cup (15 g) chopped fresh flat-leaf parsley

PREPARATION

Make the quikliz

In a large bowl, combine the cabbage, onion, jicama, ají dulce, scallions, hot peppers, garlic, salt, peppercorns, and cloves. Toss well.

Pack the vegetables into a 1-quart (1 L) mason jar. Pour the vinegar and lime juice over the vegetables. Gently press down on the vegetables until they're completely submerged in the pickling liquid. Cover the jar with a lid and refrigerate for at least 3 days before opening. (The quikliz will keep in the refrigerator for up to 2 months.)

Make the dry dredge

In a medium bowl, mix the flour, potato starch, paprika, white pepper, garlic powder, celery salt, black pepper, dry mustard, coriander, ginger, thyme, basil, oregano, and salt until well combined.

Make the jackfruit griot

In a Dutch oven or skillet, combine the grapeseed oil and coconut oil, and heat over medium-high heat until it registers 370°F (190°C) on an instant-read thermometer (adjust heat as needed to maintain).

Clean the jackfruit, cut it into 1½-inch (4 cm) chunks, then coat it in the dry dredge. Working in small batches, fry the dredged jackfruit in the hot oil until it's evenly browned, 5 to 10 minutes. You want it nicely browned in spots, but not so brown that it dries out. Transfer the cooked jackfruit to a wire rack or a sheet pan lined with a paper towel and season with salt.

Serve the jackfruit griot on a bed of steamed rice with a side of quikliz, garnished with the parsley.

ALVIN ARMSTRONG
THE GRASS IS ALWAYS GREENER, 2021
ACRYLIC ON CANVAS, 48 x 72 in.

TOUSSAINT

Clairin is a clear cane spirit made from indigenous sugarcane juice in Haiti. Rhum agricole from Martinique and Guadeloupe is distilled from sugarcane juice as well, which is why clairin often gets compared to them. (Most rum is distilled from molasses; clairin is often categorized as rum.)

Because of the distinct terroir that clairin develops from the rural, wild fermentation process and old production methods, some experts say a comparison to mezcal from Mexico is more accurate. We like to think that this product expands oversimplified, commercialized perceptions of rum in the United States, just as Haiti is much more than what it is reduced to in dominant American media narratives.

Unfiltered and fermented in open air with wild yeasts, clairin can be zesty, floral, herbaceous, tangy, or even vegetal and funky. It's often described as "the people's rum," owing to its history of being made in small batches in the outskirts. More than five hundred small distillers from the coastline to the jungles use homemade stills to make the spirit. We dig the clairin from distiller Michel Sajous for its earthy flavor and lingering finish.

We named this drink in reference to Toussaint Louverture, the leader of the Haitian Revolution. Haiti was one of many "sugar islands" in the Caribbean where enslaved Africans were brought to farm the infamously laborious crop, generating unseen wealth for European colonizers. It's exciting to see Haiti's clairin become more widely available, a drink for and by the people, and full of revolutionary spirit.

Makes 1 cocktail

INGREDIENTS

2 ounces (60 ml) Clairin Sajous
¼ ounce (7.5 ml) falernum
½ ounce (15 ml) lime juice
½ ounce (15 ml) simple syrup
Lime wedge, for garnish

PREPARATION

In a cocktail shaker filled with ice, combine the clairin, falernum, lime juice, and simple syrup. Shake vigorously until chilled. Strain into a chilled glass and garnish with the lime wedge.

EMMANUEL MASSILLON
DISTORTED VALUES, 2021
SUNFLOWER SEEDS, ACRYLIC PAINT, RESIN, JET INK PRINTS ON CANVAS,
40 x 40 in.

EMMANUEL MASSILLON
PUNISHED FOR REBELLION, 2021
WOOD, METAL NAILS, PIGMENT, RUBBER, FEATHERS, AND RESIN,
68 x 16 x 16 in.

MOSS BOSS

Wild sea moss grows in many places, but it's especially important in Caribbean cultures, where the dried seaweed is soaked and then blended into an edible, nutrient-dense gel.

Sometimes referred to as Irish moss (which is similar, but from a different geographical area), sea moss in the Caribbean has been getting the trendy superfood treatment. But it's been integral to natural medicinal practices for ages, thanks to its containing 92 of the 102 essential minerals the human body needs.

Brother Roy's Green Garden, our juice bar in the Bronx, features sea moss–based drinks on their menu, bringing a staple ingredient in many Caribbean homes to a wider audience. (Peep Resources, page 295, for where to buy it.) In a neighborhood that's been dominated by corporate fast-food chains and media messaging that makes unhealthy, industrialized foods cheaper and more accessible than fresh, organic ones, it's an expression of resistance (and sometimes, one of privilege) to choose personal health over convenience. Sea moss belongs right up there as an elemental ingredient in Black food. This Moss Boss smoothie taps into a long tradition of self-care in our communities. It's filling without being heavy and will fortify you for the day ahead.

Serves 2

INGREDIENTS

2 cups (480 ml) oat milk

1 cup (240 ml) ice

2 bananas, peeled and frozen

2 tablespoons plus 1 teaspoon peanut butter or almond butter

1 tablespoon agave syrup

1 heaping tablespoon sea moss gel (preferably purple and organic)

2 tablespoons raw oats

1 teaspoon ground cinnamon

1 teaspoon vanilla extract

PREPARATION

In a blender, combine the oat milk, ice, bananas, peanut butter, agave, sea moss gel, oats, cinnamon, and vanilla. Blend on high until combined and smooth. Enjoy immediately.

CHILI LIME LIBERATION PASTA

Black August commemorates the Black organizers, freedom fighters, activists, revolutionaries, and political prisoners who've been detained, imprisoned, or killed in their efforts to challenge American systemic racism. Many know that figures like Malcolm X, Angela Davis, and Martin Luther King Jr. were imprisoned at various points in their lives. And many, like civil rights activist Medgar Evers and Black Panther Fred Hampton, were murdered. Still countless others with less or no public recognition have been affected by the same vicious process of policing and mass incarceration.

Imprisoned organizers began the Black August tradition to mourn, honor, and reflect on the deaths of Khatari Gaulden and George Jackson. Jackson, who became an activist while locked up, died in August 1971 during an escape attempt from San Quentin State Prison in Northern California. Years later, in August 1978, Gaulden also died at San Quentin after suffering a head injury while playing touch football in the prison yard. While other imprisoned men begged facility guards to get Gaulden urgent medical attention, the guards instead searched those present. Gaulden bled out.

Echoing aspects of the Muslim holiday Ramadan (many Black Americans practice Islam, and there's a long history of Black people converting to Islam while incarcerated), Black August became a secular time during which observers fast until sundown, focus on personal wellness, study and teach political history, and advocate for humane treatment within the prison system. It has become more widely known as activists and organizations continue to fight for and educate about creating an abolitionist state.

Our Chili Lime Liberation Pasta features ingredients that are generally available on the prison commissary list. In addition to the physical limitations that make incarceration so brutal, nurturing a healthy mental state in spaces where positive outlets are limited, if offered at all, can be impossible. Finding ways to be creative with limited means no matter where you live is something many can relate to, and this dish takes something simple, basic even, and makes it pop. Lester whipped up a version of this dish as part of our segment in the Black National Convention in August 2020, a livestreamed event to build solidarity and mobilize Black-led organizations and communities in the weeks after the uprisings in response to George Floyd's murder.

Pasta itself isn't a pathway to freedom. We do believe that knowledge is one step forward in that noble pursuit.

CONTINUED

Serves 4

INGREDIENTS

3 cups (720 ml) grapeseed oil

1 (16-ounce) box angel hair pasta

2 tablespoons extra-virgin olive oil, plus more for garnish

1 tablespoon minced garlic

1 yellow onion, minced

1 seasoning packet from a package of hot chili ramen, or 3 g ground Espelette pepper

1 yellow bell pepper, thinly sliced; reserve ends of the pepper for the sauce

4½ tablespoons (65 g) plant-based butter

Zest of 1 lime

Flaky sea salt

SOIL (page 291), for garnish

PREPARATION

In a large skillet, bring the grapeseed oil to 375°F (190°C). Line a sheet pan with paper towels.

Fry the dried pasta until it's golden in color. As soon as caramelization occurs, quickly pull the pasta out of the pan to prevent overcooking. Use delicate tongs or tweezers to avoid breaking the thin pasta. This step will indeed require some finesse! You got it. Lay the fried pasta on the prepared pan and set aside.

Pour the olive oil into the same skillet and heat over medium-high heat. Add the garlic, onion, and chili seasoning. Let the dry seasoning bloom in the oil for about 20 seconds. Add the sliced bell pepper and reduce the heat to low.

Bring a pot of salted water to a boil. Add the bell pepper ends and cook for about 3 minutes. Remove the pepper ends with a slotted spoon or small strainer and set aside.

Add the fried pasta to the same pot of boiling water and cook for about 90 seconds, until the pasta is cooked al dente, or just to the point that it has a bite. Be gentle when stirring. Turn off the heat and reserve 1 cup (240 ml) of the pasta water. Use a slotted spoon or skimmer to remove the pasta from the pot and add it to your skillet with the aromatics. Toss to coat the pasta in the seasoning.

In a blender, combine the bell pepper ends with the butter and reserved 1 cup (240 ml) pasta water and blend until smooth. Add this sauce to your skillet. Toss lightly to coat the pasta and transfer to a serving bowl. Garnish with olive oil, lime zest, flaky salt, and SOIL, then serve.

RENELL MEDRANO
UNTITLED, 2019

JACK MACK

The Hunts Point Peninsula in the South Bronx is home to the Hunts Point Food Distribution Center, which includes massive wholesale meat, fish, and produce markets, plus independent leasing to private vendors. It sits on more than 300 acres, sees up to $3 billion in annual sales, and is accountable for 60 percent of produce sales in New York City alone.

But the center's wholesale focus limits the access Hunts Point residents have to it. Nearly half the residents of Hunts Point live below the federal poverty level and have inadequate options for healthy, affordable foods. This community earns among the lowest incomes in New York City, and they experience high rates of diabetes and obesity. The traffic generated by the busy center on the Sheridan Expressway contributes to bad air quality in the area—Hunts Point sees systemically high incidences of childhood asthma and related hospitalizations. These people, predominantly from Hispanic, Black, and Asian backgrounds, take the brunt of the impact of a commercial hub dedicated to food, but they don't reap the benefits.

About a mile away from the distribution center, across from the Rikers Island jail complex on the East River, is a floating hell officially known as the Vernon C. Bain Center. The City of New York opened the jail in 1992, a reported temporary fix to absorb the impact of mass arrests in the wake of the crack epidemic. Thirty years later, the quick-fix ship is still sailing, and has become an intake processing facility for Bronx detainees while housing medium- to maximum-security prisoners. At 625 feet long, the vessel looks more like it houses supplies than humans, though about eight hundred people are said to be incarcerated there at any given time.

We once rolled up to the fish market at Hunts Point in preparation for a Kwanzaa feast. Three Black men in a car? NYPD pulled us over on our way home that evening, shining flashlights into the vehicle. "What'd you get? What kind of fish?" the officer asked.

Here's olive oil–poached Spanish mackerel, amped up with sofrito and chili oil. It's an ode to the tinned mackerel that they serve in prison. Inside, they call it Jack Mack. When we serve this dish, we plate it up in the can. It's a small way to remember those locked away. Note that for this recipe, we're using a tomato-based Portuguese- or Spanish-inspired sofrito. It differs from sofrito recipes you'll see from Puerto Rico, which use a lot more fresh herbs.

CONTINUED

Serves 4

INGREDIENTS

For the sofrito

¼ cup (60 ml) extra-virgin olive oil

5 garlic cloves, minced

1 large yellow onion, finely chopped

2 tablespoons smoked paprika

2 bay leaves

1 sprig thyme

3 ounces (80 g) fresh tomato, peeled, seeded, and chopped

2 tablespoons canned crushed tomatoes

Flaky sea salt

For the mackerel

4 skin-on Spanish mackerel fillets, sliced in half lengthwise

2½ cups (600 ml) extra-virgin olive oil

Pinch of flaky sea salt, to taste

2 garlic cloves, peeled

1 fresh chile (like a Fresno chile or Espelette pepper)

1 bunch lemon thyme

Chili Oil (page 292), for serving

Grilled bread, such as a bâtard, for serving

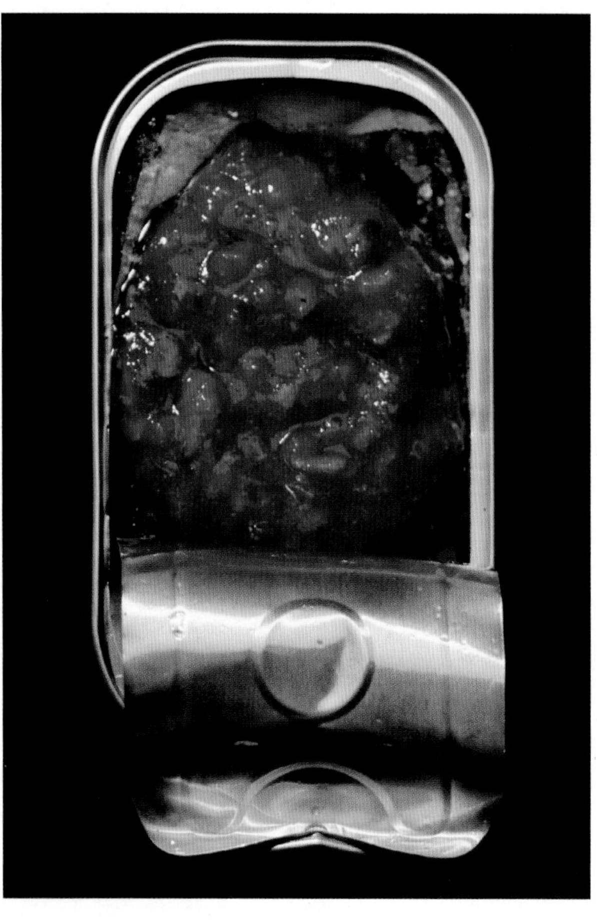

PREPARATION

Make the sofrito

In a medium saucepan, combine the olive oil and garlic and cook over low heat for 1 to 2 minutes, until the garlic becomes fragrant but doesn't start browning.

Add the onion, paprika, bay leaves, and thyme and cook, stirring occasionally to avoid burning, for 30 minutes, or until the onion browns.

Add the fresh tomato to the pan and cook for about 5 minutes, until the tomato breaks down. Low and slow gets big, developed flavors. Add the crushed tomatoes and cook for another 40 minutes, stirring occasionally. Season with salt and remove from the heat.

Prepare the fish

Heat the oven to 275°F (135°C).

In a shallow, oven-safe casserole dish or skillet, place the fish in a single layer and cover with olive oil. Season with salt and add the garlic, chile, and lemon thyme.

Bake for 25 to 30 minutes, basting often, until the fish is cooked through; it should feel a bit firm to the touch.

To serve, place the poached fish in a shallow bowl, then cover with a healthy serving of sofrito. Add 1 to 2 tablespoons of the poaching liquid over the top. Finish with a light drizzle of chili oil. Serve with grilled bread.

RETURN OF THE MACK

STATE GREENS

The food options generally made available in jail and prison are dismal. High in sugar, carbs, and sodium, and often composed of expired or rotten ingredients, the makings of a prison meal are among the clearest examples of food apartheid in our nation.

Fresh fruits and vegetables are usually nonexistent. Diabetes and heart disease diagnoses are rampant, especially for an aging population with no opportunity for parole due to exaggerated prison terms that mostly affect Black and brown folks sentenced during the racist War on Drugs.

It's the rare institution that creates educational opportunities for incarcerated people to garden and learn about food science and nutrition, or have access to healthy vegetables in meal prep. When these programs and policies are in place, less food ends up in the garbage, composted food can help reduce spending, and more important, people are more emotionally and psychologically stable because they are eating as they should. This creates a safer environment for everyone, including staff. And for those leaving prison one day, as most incarcerated people will do, they can potentially return to their communities with increased knowledge and skill. The idea that healthy food is only a reward for people with higher incomes is pervasive in our society, and the opposite end of the spectrum is no more obvious than behind bars.

If food can be a love language, it's hard to beat a simmering pot of collard greens. But we make a raw take that comes pretty close. We call this collard green salad State Greens, in rejection of the nutrient-deficient foods that end up on the prison plate. This recipe allows you to enjoy the greens' deep natural flavor, a basic joy any living being deserves to experience. Don't skimp on the massage step. That's where you'll gently break down the fibrous leaf to create a texture that goes down real easy.

Serves 4

INGREDIENTS

1½ pounds (680 g) collard greens, leaves stemmed and thinly sliced

1 tablespoon Bragg Liquid Aminos

3 tablespoons toasted sesame oil

1 tablespoon manuka honey

1 teaspoon diced shallot

1 garlic clove, minced

1½ teaspoons minced fresh ginger

2 scallions, thinly sliced, white and green parts separated

1 tablespoon extra-virgin olive oil

⅓ cup (30 g) thinly sliced yellow bell pepper

Flaky sea salt

SOIL (page 291), for garnish

PREPARATION

Place the greens in a large bowl.

In a small bowl or glass measuring cup, combine the liquid aminos, sesame oil, honey, shallot, garlic, ginger, and scallion whites. Mix until well combined. Pour the marinade over the collard greens, then drizzle the olive oil over the greens mixture.

Using clean hands, gently massage the collards for 2 to 3 minutes. The greens will soften and begin to feel almost wilted. Give the greens and marinade a good stir, then cover and place in the refrigerator for about 2 hours.

Remove from the refrigerator and fold in the bell peppers and scallion greens. Season with salt to taste. Place the salad in a bowl and garnish with SOIL. Serve immediately.

INMATE

HANK WILLIS THOMAS
CAPITAL (GREEN), 2021
MIXED MEDIA INCLUDING US PRISON
UNIFORMS, 54 x 87 in.

INMATE

INTERVIEW WITH

EMOR

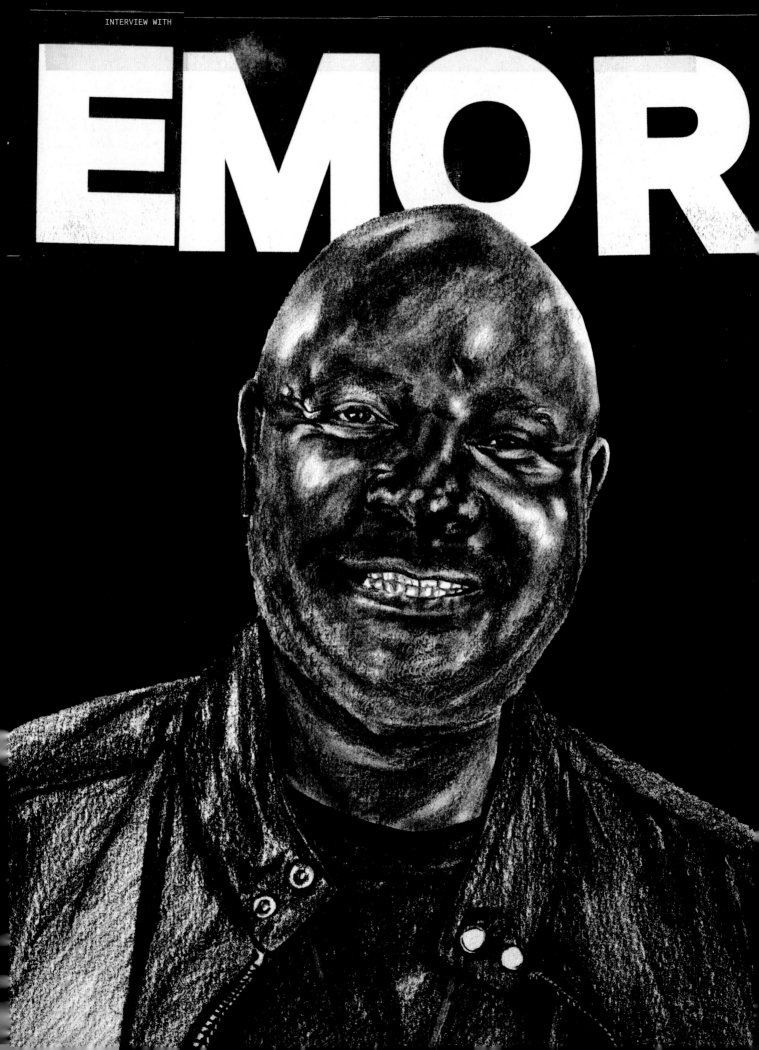

Beginning as the revolutionary artist for the Black Panther Party in 1967, Emory Douglas later became the party's minister of culture. He was responsible for the design and production of their newspaper, which had a nationwide circulation in the hundreds of thousands. His artistic choices brought visual urgency to the experiences of Black communities throughout the country, who were being over-policed, harassed, and surveilled. Using applications like silk screen and collage, he defined a visual language of protest that feels timely today. Emory grew up in the Bay Area after his family moved there from Grand Rapids, Michigan. He studied commercial art at City College of San Francisco.

The Black Panther Party for Self Defense was founded in Oakland, California, in 1966, by Huey Newton and Bobby Seale, with Eldridge Cleaver joining soon after (Stokely Carmichael, later named Kwame Ture, also had a leadership role). They eventually had offices in Seattle, Los Angeles, Chicago, Philadelphia, and New York. The group's structure and mission were influenced by international revolutionaries and the Nation of Islam. Their Ten-Point Program demanded that Black people get fair employment and housing, and education. It pressed for an end to police brutality, state-sanctioned murder. And it stated plainly that Black people deserve restitution in the form of land and money for generations of enslaved labor.

Ghetto Gastro: How did you come to be involved with the Black Panther Party?

Emory Douglas: This was during the period of the Black Consciousness Movement in the country, 1965, '66, '67. I was in the Black Arts Movement and I was going to City College of San Francisco. This was during a time when in universities, we were changing the colonial names of the "Negro" student unions to the "Black Student Union" or "African Student Union."

All these new ways of identifying were going on within the young Black community in relation to how we define ourselves, who we were as African Americans, African, Black people. All those debates were going on, and this was at a height of police injustice in this country. Just like it is now. Young folks were trying to figure out what we could do in relationship to dealing with those issues. What happened is that being in the Black Arts Movement, there were some brothers and sisters who were planning to bring Malcolm X's widow, Sister Betty Shabazz, to the Bay Area. One of the brothers came and told me that they wanted me to do a simple poster to promote that event.

I went to this meeting to prepare for the event; we were discussing security and those things. Huey Newton and Bobby Seale were there. This was maybe early January or February 1967, about three and a half months after the organization had started. I knew that's what I wanted to be a part of.

I didn't have a car. I lived in San Francisco at that time, and I used to catch the bus over to Huey's house. He showed me around the neighborhood and then we went by Bobby Seale's house. That was my beginning of joining the Black Panther Party. By April that year we'd been organizing, hanging out, going on patrols, observing what was going on with the police and these stops, which could be highly intense. The police would be harassing and intimidating young folks, and we'd be letting them know their legal rights, standing a legal distance away to not be involved with the arrest. We were telling youngsters all they had to do was give a name, address, and phone number, or take the Fifth Amendment, and that we would try and bail them out. That's why I started. There was urgency. Point number seven of the Ten-Point Program: "We Want an Immediate End to Police Brutality and the Murder of Black People."

There was a place called the Black House in San Francisco where a lot of cultural events used to go on. A sidebar: Huey Newton and Bobby Seale had heard of Eldridge Cleaver but had not known how to get in touch with him. When the group was trying to get Sister Betty Shabazz to come to the Bay Area, they weren't initially getting a response. Someone said there was this brother who just got out of prison, who was staying at his lawyer's house in San Francisco, and that he was a follower of Malcolm X in prison. They said, we may go ask him. I went with them to the house and that person was Eldridge Cleaver. Eldridge wrote a letter to Betty Shabazz to invite her, and that's when she came. Huey Newton was one of the brothers who agreed to do security for the event—they went to the airport, escorted her off the plane, and the first place she wanted to go was to North Beach to connect with Eldridge. That's how that link comes together when I talk about the Black House.

Downstairs [in the Black House] there'd be cultural events and folks like Sonia Sanchez, Ed Bullins, the playwright, Amiri Baraka. All them used to come through there, but Eldridge lived upstairs. During that time, Eldridge worked as a reporter for *Ramparts* magazine. It was a pretty progressive liberal magazine, which allowed him to cover the Panthers and not be in violation of his parole and risk being sent back to prison.

Even when there were cultural events going on downstairs, Huey and them would always go upstairs to pick Eldridge's mind. It happens that one day I went by there, wasn't nothing happening. Eldridge, Bobby, and Huey were downstairs, just talking. And when I came in, I seen Bobby was working on this legal-size sheet of paper on a typewriter, which became the first paper of the Black Panthers, volume one. They were writing about a young brother named Denzil Dowell, who had been unarmed and murdered by sheriffs in north Richmond. Other activists felt that they could help the Dowell family and got Huey and Bobby in touch with them. [Dowell had been shot in the back and head in 1967. The coroner found more shots than the police said they fired. Dowell was said to have jumped a fence in fleeing, but his family maintained that a prior injury would have made that impossible. The media reported that the killing was a justifiable homicide before the verdict was delivered. A predominantly white jury cleared the officers of wrongdoing; later it was learned that the jury foreman was illiterate.]

Bobby Seale was working on telling the story, on doing the head with the markers for the masthead of the paper. I seen them doing that when I came in. I said, "I can help you improve that," because I had materials from studying commercial art at City College. I went home, got my stuff, and came back and they said, "Well, we're finished with this, but you seem to be committed because you've been coming around." And I had been, since late January or February. He said, "We're going to start our paper and it's going to be about telling our story from our perspective."

A large segment of the community wasn't reading at the time, so they learned through observation and participation. We wanted to have photographs, captions, and illustrations for those who were not going to read the articles, but still get the gist. My first title was Revolutionary Artist and later I became the Minister of Culture.

What did that involve?

I worked on the newspaper production, made sure it got out on time, putting it together was my responsibility. Then as we grew, teaching folks who worked with me the same things that I was doing. We were creating culture. We were creating revolutionary culture as it evolved. We began to focus more around the artwork and particularly the pig drawings—that took on a life of its own. You see, it transcended the African American experience, or just the Black Panther Party. It became a universal symbol for repression.

You were instrumental in defining a visual language of rebellion and protest. Decades later, visual representation of Black people's fight for equity and full representation is still necessary. Your mural REPARATIONS (2007/2021) addresses this. What does reparations mean to you and why is it important?

The struggle continues. It's still police murders being justified, unemployment, indecent housing, inferior education; these things continue to exist today. Fifty years later, sixty years later, as much as things may change, some things stay the same. That means that there is the need to continue with art that speaks to those issues, that illustrates those issues. Art is a way to communicate.

Ghetto Gastro has been deeply influenced by the Black Panther Party. Thinking about food sovereignty, food being used as a weapon of oppression, but it's also understanding that our liberation lies within the soil and having sovereignty. We're inspired by the BPP's breakfast program, which started as a way to serve Black children, but ultimately influenced federal policy to ensure any student in need didn't go to school hungry. How did that get going?

A lot of people don't know that when the party started, Huey Newton and Bobby Seale had an advisory committee, several middle-class Black folks in the Bay Area that they knew. There was Ron Dellums, who was then the state representative before he became a congressman for twenty-seven years, and other locals like the first Black mayor [in Oakland], Lionel Wilson.

There was a sister named Ruth Beckford who was a dancer and performed with Katharine Dunham back in the day. Huey used to bring her by when we were talking about working on the newspaper, before we had the central headquarters in San Francisco in Eldridge Cleaver's studio apartment. [Due to Cleaver being previously incarcerated and affiliated with other groups considered radical by the government, his movements were highly restricted and monitored. He was not legally permitted to cross the Bay Bridge from San Francisco to Oakland, and his involvement with the BPP would have been a parole violation. His role with the Panthers was not made public and he anonymously signed his writings in the BPP newspaper as the Minister of Information.]

The breakfast program developed after Eldridge came on board, first beginning with a few churches that opened their doors, to community centers, and even folks' homes. Ruth said we could use her minister's church, which was in the hood, and that became a launching pad for breakfast offerings in the community. We had this letterhead that stated the people who were on the advisory committee. We used that to take to the food vendors and let them know what we were doing. This was legit in the context of asking them for donations for the programs.

The Panthers, along with people in the community, would get up at two or three in the morning and fix breakfast for the kids before they went to school. The whole idea behind the program was because we understood that low-income, poor families had to make hard choices between paying the rent, the PG&E [utility] bill, or feeding their kids and then be in crisis in the context of maybe not having paid your rent or being in crisis by not having enough to eat. Kids were going to school hungry. That means that they couldn't focus on the lesson. All those kinds of things came into play. That was the reason the program started, so kids could go to school not being malnourished.

At the same time, our work was pointing out the contradictions of what the United States government wasn't doing in relationship to the needs in the community. Back then the treasurer of the State of California was in a more powerful position than the governor. His name was Jesse Unruh, and he said the Black Panther Party was feeding more hungry children than the government. That went all over the place; they played that all day long on the news. It had a great impact. And then you started to have the breakfast programs, free lunch programs in many schools, and parents began to demand that. We were leading by example, putting into practice things that the community could see that they could take up for themselves and began to demand.

The government had already positioned the Panthers as a threat, but it seemed that they became more fearful of the Panthers once the community involvement became more widely known. There was so much surveillance and pressure on the organization, but do you feel like it got worse once you all became known for feeding people?

Well, of course. You could actually see it, because of the support. People were beginning to become more supportive and making demands around quality-of-life issues. This was a youth movement, and you had a lot of young people gravitating to it, being inspired by what we were saying. No matter where they were in the world, they were inspired by us. They could see our work in the context of what they were going through in their lives and wanting to be about change as well.

It's wild that the breakfast program brought even more heat down from J. Edgar Hoover.

The breakfast program was called public enemy number one, because it had such broad appeal, by J. Edgar Hoover. That's documented. The first thing they destroyed when they attacked the office was the eggs, all the stuff that we had for the breakfast meals. That was in Chicago. They destroyed the food. Took the milk, poured it all out, destroyed all the eggs.

In our work, we pay homage to ancestral traditions. Looking to our health, building the body to be ready for the revolution. Like, you gotta take care of the temple. Tell us about your journey toward eating plant-based.

I started in 1980, but in the Black Panther Party we began to look at how pork is bad for you, even though that came from what the Nation [of Islam] was talking about back then. Others were talking about it as well. Everything we made in the breakfast program was vegetarian for the kids, you know? I recall what happened is that my comrades gave me a cookbook. It was this hippie cookbook that dealt with nothing but soybeans. Everything from pies to noodles. It opened up a whole new world because with the recipes, from that, I was able to begin to evolve and develop different eating habits.

What's your favorite go-to thing to make?

A lot of lentils. I like millet and amaranth greens. Quinoa, primarily quinoa. And the adzuki beans. I'll eat those quite a bit.

When you think about moving toward the future, inspiring future generations like you've inspired us, what do you hear when we say "Black Power Kitchen"?

The dynamics are different today. 'Cause you know, the whole landscape, no kind of support systems, all types of sophistication in the repression today, in more ways than we can probably think of. You got all that shit you're dealing with, confronted with. I think of self-determination. It means the power to determine your destiny. The Ten-Point Program, it wasn't about hating someone else, or hating other cultures, it was about respecting oneself, self-empowerment.

PLANTAIN MOLE WITH ROASTED SQUASH

As we mentioned on page 175, our friends at the Bronx restaurant La Morada have been ardent advocates for the undocumented, using their Oaxacan restaurant as a place not only to feed people but also to provide refuge. But beyond the important activism and education, Natalia is renowned for her various moles. We are inspired by moles, and the way peppers and fruits work together to create a sweet, savory base. We're not using chocolate in this recipe, but the mole has depth from the dates, and the chiles and tomatoes bring out a nice umami in the sauce.

Serves 4

INGREDIENTS

For the plantain mole

2 tablespoons extra-virgin olive oil
½ white onion, diced
1 garlic clove, diced
5 cups (1.2 L) water
1 plum tomato, diced
2 to 3 yellow plantains, thinly sliced
½ Golden Delicious apple, cored and diced
¾ cup (100 g) roasted peanuts
3 chipotle chiles in adobo sauce
3 tablespoons chopped dates
2 tablespoons demerara sugar
1 teaspoon flaky sea salt
2 sprigs thyme

INGREDIENTS CONTINUED

PREPARATION

Make the plantain mole

In a large pot, combine the olive oil, onion, and garlic and place over medium-high heat. Let the onion sweat for 2 to 3 minutes, until it becomes translucent.

Reduce the heat to low and add the water, tomato, yellow plantains, apple, peanuts, chiles, dates, sugar, flaky salt, and thyme to the pot. Simmer for 3 hours. Transfer the mixture to a blender and blend on high until smooth. Strain the sauce through a sieve and set it aside.

Prepare the squash

Heat the oven to 425°F (220°C). Line two baking sheets with parchment paper.

In a saucepan, melt the butter over low heat. Remove from the heat. Using an immersion blender, whip in the honey until emulsified and smooth.

CONTINUED

For the roasted squash

11 tablespoons (5¼ ounces/150 g) plant-based butter

½ cup (170 g) honey

1 medium kabocha squash (10½ ounces/300 g), peeled, seeded, and sliced into 2-inch-thick (5 cm) crescent-shaped wedges

1 green plantain, thinly sliced on a mandoline

¼ cup (60 ml) grapeseed oil, for brushing

Smoked salt

Put the squash slices in a large bowl and pour in the honey-butter emulsion. Toss to coat, then transfer to one of the prepared pans, arranging the slices in an even layer. Bake for 25 minutes, until the squash is well caramelized—it should look browned on the bottom. Remove from the oven and set aside, but do not turn off the oven.

Brush the green plantain slices on both sides with the grapeseed oil. Place the plantain on the other prepared pan. Cover the plantain slices with another sheet of parchment, then set an empty sheet pan on top to apply pressure to the plantain chips. It might seem like you're doing the most, but it's worth it for the evenness in cooking. Place the stacked pans in the oven and bake the plantain for 15 minutes, until crispy.

To plate your dish, start with the mole at the bottom. Layer the squash on top and garnish with the plantain chips. Serve with a sprinkling of smoked salt. Any remaining mole sauce can be stored in an airtight container in the freezer for up to 3 months.

AYA BROWN
"NATALIA MENDEZ" LA MORADA, COVID-19
ESSENTIAL WORKERS COMMISSION, 2020
COLOR PENCIL ON BROWN KRAFT PAPER,
9 x 12 in.

IBRAHEM HASAN
CROWN FRIED, 2019

BLACK POWER WAFFLE

This velvety waffle is named for the rallying cry "Black Power," coined by the militant leader Stokely Carmichael, who later changed his name to Kwame Ture (a reference to Kwame Nkrumah and Sékou Touré, the first presidents of Ghana and Guinea, respectively).

The native Trinidadian came to the South Bronx as a teen. He would eventually become the leader of the Student Nonviolent Coordinating Committee (SNCC), formed from the sit-in protests that fought to desegregate dining spaces in the South. He then became prime minister of the Black Panther Party, but he had used the term "Black Power" before then. We pay homage to the Black Panther Party's groundbreaking community-based free breakfast program, which inspired the federally run version launched in the 1970s and still in place throughout the country today. Ture eventually separated from the Black American groups he had helped form and became a Pan-Africanist. He lived in Guinea for the last three decades of his life, convinced that the United States was incapable of structurally creating equity for Black people, but his thinking shaped the modern era of political organizing and civil rights and has been a model for antiracist activists of myriad cultural backgrounds.

In our efforts to explore dairy-free ingredients in a base, we love how the mix of cocoa powder and coconut creates a slightly nutty, mild flavor. It's not too rich or sweet and makes a moist waffle.

CONTINUED

Makes 4 to 6 waffles

INGREDIENTS

2 cups (240 g) pastry flour or all-purpose flour

1 cup (120 g) unsweetened black cocoa powder (preferably King Arthur)

1 cup (70 g) unsweetened shredded coconut

¼ cup (50 g) cane sugar

¾ teaspoon kosher salt

¼ teaspoon (1 g) baking soda

1 (14-ounce/400 ml) can coconut milk

½ cup (120 ml) coconut oil

2¼ teaspoons (9 g) active dry yeast

2 large (100 g) eggs

½ cup (120 ml) chocolate syrup or sauce

½ to 1 teaspoon black food gel (optional)

½ cup (120 ml) warm water

Plant-based butter, sorghum syrup, sliced banana, or vanilla or coconut ice cream, for serving

PREPARATION

In a large bowl, whisk together the flour, cocoa powder, shredded coconut, sugar, salt, and baking soda. Make a well in the center. Set aside.

In a medium saucepan, warm the coconut milk and coconut oil over low heat, until the oil is melted and the temperature reaches 110°F (45°C). Remove from the heat and whisk in the yeast. Allow the yeast to bloom for 10 minutes. The mixture should be bubbling on the surface.

Add the eggs, chocolate syrup, and food gel (if using) and whisk thoroughly for about 30 seconds, until the mixture has thickened slightly.

Pour the coconut milk mixture into the well in the flour mixture. Whisk together to make a smooth batter, switching to a rubber spatula as the mixture thickens, if needed. Add the warm water and mix in.

Allow the mixture to sit at room temperature for 15 to 30 minutes. (The longer the batter rests, the fluffier the waffles will be.)

Prep a waffle iron according to the manufacturer's instructions. Make the waffles according to the iron's specifications. Stack the waffles as you make them on a plate and cover with a clean, dry dish towel to keep them warm. Serve with your preferred butter, sorghum syrup, banana, or vanilla or coconut ice cream (or any combination that rocks your world).

ARTHUR JAFA
LeRAGE, 2017

AMERIKKKAN APPLE PIE

Deconstructing the apple pie symbolizes a more truthful telling of the American story. And as the saying goes, What's more American than apple pie? To that we answer, the state-sanctioned killing of Black people. Food as a venue for artistic expression can make some uncomfortable. But nothing is more discomfiting to us than ignoring the truth of our community's existence, in plain sight.

Like many Black folks in our country and around the world, every single day we navigate a complex web of systems that try to convince us we're unworthy of life's pleasures. They say we're dangerous for others to be around. In this recipe, we reject notions that Black people lack humanity. We embrace instead a belief that to make something whole, we must all understand the disparate parts.

This is an ambitious preparation for beginner cooks, but that "traditional" apple pie isn't who we are. Remixing the apple pie challenges who gets to write the official American narrative. It's also a beautiful dessert that can provide a sense of comfort. Eat up.

CONTINUED

Serves 6

INGREDIENTS

For the pickled apples

½ cup (120 ml) ginger juice
½ cup (120 ml) water
¼ cup (60 ml) fresh lemon juice
¼ cup (60 ml) agave syrup
1 star anise pod
1 whole clove
1 cinnamon stick
1 Granny Smith apple, cored and thinly sliced

For the apple compote

2 Gala apples, peeled, cored, and diced
1 teaspoon ground cinnamon
¼ cup (60 ml) apple cider
2 tablespoons fresh lemon juice
2 tablespoons organic cane sugar

For the ginger crumble

4 cups (540 g) all-purpose flour
½ cup (100 g) dark brown sugar
½ cup (100 g) organic cane sugar
2 tablespoons ground ginger
1½ teaspoons flaky sea salt
1 tablespoon ground cinnamon
9 ounces (2¼ sticks/250 g) unsalted butter
2 tablespoons honey
⅓ cup (80 ml) molasses

For the poached apples

⅔ cup (160 ml) apple cider
1½ teaspoons agave syrup
1 cinnamon stick
½ vanilla bean, split lengthwise and seeds scraped from the pod
2 or 3 green cardamom pods
1 Macoun or Gala apple, scooped into balls with a melon baller
Vanilla ice cream, for serving

PREPARATION

Make the pickled apples

In a medium bowl, whisk together the ginger juice, water, lemon juice, and agave to combine. Add the star anise, clove, and cinnamon stick. Put the apple slices in an airtight container, then pour in the liquid. Cover and set aside at room temperature for 8 hours before serving.

Make the apple compote

In a small saucepot, combine the diced apples, cinnamon, apple cider, lemon juice, and sugar. Bring to a boil, then immediately reduce the heat to maintain a simmer and cook for 8 to 10 minutes. The liquid should reduce and thicken like a syrup. The apples should be soft but not mushy. Remove from the heat and let cool. Cover and refrigerate until you're ready to assemble the pie. (The compote can be stored in an airtight container in the refrigerator for up to 1 week.)

Make the ginger crumble

Heat the oven to 350°F (175°C). Line a sheet pan with parchment paper (do not use aluminum foil; doing so will brown your crumble before it cooks evenly).

In a large bowl, mix together the flour, both sugars, ginger, salt, and cinnamon. In a medium saucepan, combine the butter, honey, and molasses and heat over medium heat, just until the butter has melted. Pour the butter mixture over the dry ingredients. Using gloved hands or a mixing spoon, incorporate the ingredients until the dough comes together. Don't overwork it—it should look crumbly. Cover the bowl and chill in the refrigerator for 15 minutes. Crumble the chilled dough onto the prepared sheet pan. Bake for 30 minutes, until it looks golden brown.

Make the poached apples

Pour the apple cider and agave into a medium saucepan. Add the cinnamon stick, vanilla seeds and pod, and cardamom. Bring to a boil. Remove from the heat and cover the pan. Allow to steep for 30 minutes. Strain the liquid through a fine-mesh strainer into a clean medium pot (discard the solids).

Place the pot over low heat, add the apple balls, and cook for 7 to 10 minutes, until the apple is just tender (you can test with a fork if you're not sure). Remove the poached apple balls from the liquid and cool.

To assemble the pie, place a couple of spoonfuls of the crumble on each of six plates. Arrange the pickled apple, apple compote, and poached apples around the crumble on each plate, dividing them evenly. Add a scoop of vanilla ice cream on top of the crumble. Serve immediately.

LARISSA DE JESÚS NEGRÓN
PHILOSOPHICAL MEDITATION, 2020
ACRYLIC AND OIL PAINTING ON CANVAS,
16 x 20 in.

IBRAHEM HASAN
SCORCHED CORE, 2019

Dear Mama

Amazing grace personified. The cinematic, vibrant pop of Easter Sunday church hats. The up-tempo, high-note call-and-response of the Black sorority. Making leftovers look like gourmet dishes. The riffs that soar from Etta James, Josephine Baker, or Beyoncé. What magic can't be attributed to Black women?

Amazing grace personified. The cinematic, vibrant pop of Easter Sunday church hats. The up-tempo, high-tone call-and-response of the Black sorority. Making leftovers look like gourmet dishes. The riffs that soar from Etta James, Josephine Baker, or Beyoncé. What magic can't be attributed to Black women?

Black women are the creators. They are foundational to all Black liberation. From the earliest days of this nation through today, Black women have been on the front line, even if often forced behind the scenes, in the various movements for Black equity. We come from families with powerful matriarchs: mothers, aunties, and grandmothers who raised families, built careers, and nourished their communities. Black women do all this in an environment of great difficulty. Policy decisions and media messaging constantly say that they don't matter. These women matter to us. Black women matter.

From a culinary perspective, the United States owes Black women a great debt. They are arguably the architects of American cuisine, which draws much of its core identity from the skilled contributions of enslaved Africans and their descendants. Their foundational role in the cultivation, harvest, butchering, baking, preparation, and service in and beyond the American South helped spark new flavors, dishes, and cooking traditions that encompassed the best of what the African continent had to offer with the resourceful innovations of displaced people figuring out how to make themselves at home.

Black women have safeguarded and shepherded our food history in this nation. The once overlooked expertise of a matriarch like Edna Lewis; the innovations of Georgia Gilmore and Leah Chase, who both literally nourished activists in the civil rights movement; the editorial vision of Toni Tipton-Martin; the scholarship of Jessica B. Harris. These women and many like them paved the way for us to do what we do, which is to use food to build community and tell our own stories. These women are the mothers of our collective food history.

We say food is a weapon, which is another way to say that food is a means of protest, but good food can also be a tool of liberation. No matter what's going on around you, a great meal provides a sense of comfort; it can offer a personal, if only temporary, sense of freedom. When we think about the origins of this country and the essential role that Black women continue to play in our food system today, it's easy to see how the reach of Black women extends far past the kitchen. We can't separate this influence from the painful and brutal history of chattel slavery that commodified the fertility of Black women, generating an unpaid, primarily agriculture-focused labor force, by means of birth. This legacy affects our communities today. Maternal health data for Black women in the United States reflects an uncaring system leaving them up to six times more likely to die during childbirth, regardless of class. In our recognition of Black women's resilience, we cannot overlook how too many are being failed. These gaps challenge us to contribute to systems that cultivate well-being for all.

We are influenced by ancestors whose names we don't know and the ones that we do. Women like Fannie Lou Hamer from the Mississippi Delta, who in the 1960s advocated for the rights of Black sharecroppers to vote and founded the Freedom Farm Cooperative in 1969. She bought 40 acres of land in the Delta, where families planted vegetables, soybeans, and cotton. The organization started a pig bank to support the families but was never able to achieve the financial backing it needed to sustain itself. Hamer's outlook on food sovereignty inspires us to think about how we can subvert existing systems so that Black people and other systemically oppressed communities can access healthy food, which is their birthright. We aren't alone in this effort.

Yemi Amu is a farmer and the founder and director of Oko Urban Farms in Brooklyn, where she established New York City's first outdoor and only publicly accessible aquaponics farm. In Yoruba, Yemi's ethnic group and language, "oko" means "farm," and also references the orisha Oko, a deity of agriculture and fertility. Yemi is highly sought throughout the city for her skills as an educator, and her work uses farming to arm New Yorkers with food security and knowledge. The aquaponics method allows her team to sustainably cultivate fresh vegetables, which Oko sells at farmers' markets. The organization has expanded to multiple sites in Brooklyn.

Leah Penniman and her colleagues at 80-acre Soul Fire Farm in Petersburg, New York, are reclaiming a relationship to the land, working to empower Black and brown people to gain agency within an unjust food system. Centered in their work is the fundamental acknowledgment that the American food system was built on genocide and exploitation of Indigenous, Black, and brown people, and obstacles like the generational loss of Black-owned farming land due to government discrimination and racial intimidation. Leah and her colleagues approach the land with a communal relationship in mind, using Afro-indigenous farming techniques and ancestral, regenerative practices. They distribute naturally grown products to communities facing food apartheid and provide the ingredients for thousands of meals. Education is a key aspect of Soul Fire Farm, where people come from far distances to learn methods they can take home. We're inspired by the transformative widespread impact these Black women–led organizations are having, in our own backyard.

The recipes in this chapter reflect a few of the countless ways Black women close to us have contributed to our nourishment and well-being. We talk with—who else?—our mothers: Denise Lee (Jon's mom), Roxanne Serrao (Pierre's mom), and Elizabeth Walker (Lester's mom). The recipes are simple, delicious dishes just like the ones we grew up with, just like many of the Black women we know who make magic daily.

OVERNIGHT COCONUT OATS WITH DATE SYRUP

New York's winters can be biting cold. Before Lester headed out for school as a young'un, his mom would slather a thick coat of Vaseline across his face to protect his skin from icy wind, then send him on to wait for the bus.

Truth be told, no Black mama needs cold weather as an excuse to make sure their kid's face stays moisturized. (Shout out to all our shea butter babies out there.) Nourishment comes in many forms, and a comforting breakfast that can take you through the day is a beautiful way to care for yourself and others.

This ain't that instant oatmeal business. We soak the oats overnight so that the granules absorb the water and significantly reduce cook time. Growing up, Lester used to hear "Hold you down, like steel," a turn of phrase that defies definition, but nods to folks getting what they need from where they need it. This bowl will hit you with its creamy richness, thanks to the combo of coconut milk and plant-based butter. The steel-cut oats in this recipe will hold you down and get your day started right, even when there's no snow on the ground.

CONTINUED

Serves 4

INGREDIENTS

1 cup (160 g) steel-cut Irish oats

1 (14-ounce/400 ml) can coconut milk

1 vanilla bean, split lengthwise and seeds scraped from the pod

½ teaspoon ground green cardamom

2 tablespoons raw cane sugar

Pinch of flaky sea salt

2 tablespoons plant-based butter, plus more for serving

¼ cup (60 ml) date syrup (store-bought)

Blueberries

Sliced banana

Ground cinnamon

Candied Pepitas (page 291; optional)

Chia seeds (optional)

PREPARATION

In a large bowl, cover the oats with 3 cups (720 ml) water and let soak overnight.

The next day, drain the oats and transfer to a saucepan. Add the coconut milk, vanilla seeds and pod, cardamom, sugar, and salt and cook over medium-low heat, stirring occasionally to avoid lumps, until the mixture has thickened and the oats are fully cooked, about 20 minutes. Add the butter and stir gently. Remove from the heat.

Spoon the oats into bowls for serving. Drizzle the date syrup on top of the oats and top as you like with more butter, blueberries, banana, and cinnamon. Candied pepitas or chia seeds are a good look here, too.

MARTINE SYMS
MY MOTHER IS AN ANGEL, 2022

TOYIN OJIH ODUTOLA
WHAT HER DAUGHTER SEES, 2018
PASTEL, CHARCOAL, AND PENCIL ON PAPER,
57¾ x 42 in.

HASH HOUSE

Far too often, sweet potatoes are relegated to holiday dishes like sweet potato casserole and pie. But the naturally sweet orange flesh of this tuber is a year-round staple that can make a play during any course. Our take on potato hash centers bright, warming elements like ginger, a hint of coriander, and cinnamon. You can curve the ketchup for our Aquafaba Aioli.

Serves 2

INGREDIENTS

3⅓ cups (800 ml) grapeseed oil
1 pound (455 g) sweet potatoes, peeled and cubed
3 tablespoons olive oil
½ cup (85 g) oyster mushrooms
2 garlic cloves, chopped or grated
1 tablespoon minced or grated fresh ginger
¼ sweet onion, chopped
3 scallions, sliced, white and green parts kept separate
½ red bell pepper, chopped
½ green bell pepper, chopped
½ teaspoon sea salt
½ teaspoon paprika
½ teaspoon ground cinnamon
¼ teaspoon freshly ground black pepper
⅛ teaspoon cayenne pepper
⅛ teaspoon ground coriander
Aquafaba Aioli (page 290), for serving
Fresh dill sprigs, for garnish

PREPARATION

Heat a cast-iron skillet over medium heat. We'll come back to it.

In a medium saucepan, heat the grapeseed oil over medium heat until it registers 365°F (185°C) on an instant-read thermometer. Line a sheet pan with paper towels and set it nearby. Add the sweet potato cubes to the hot oil and fry for about 6 minutes, stirring occasionally. The exterior of the cubes should look a bit blistered. Using a slotted spoon, remove the sweet potatoes from the oil and transfer them to the lined sheet pan to drain.

Return to your hot cast-iron skillet. Add the olive oil and the oyster mushrooms. Pan roast the oyster mushrooms until they develop a brown color and their moisture evaporates, about 8 minutes. Add the garlic, ginger, onion, scallion whites, bell peppers, salt, paprika, cinnamon, black pepper, cayenne, and coriander. Stir well to incorporate the spices. Cook over medium-high heat for 8 to 10 minutes, then add the fried sweet potatoes and scallion greens. Stir to combine and remove from the heat.

Drizzle the hash with the aioli. Garnish with fresh dill sprigs. Serve immediately.

GREENBACKS

Making stewed greens can be a family affair. Stripping the collards from their stems, washing them thoroughly (Moms says do it twice), and slicing them into even ribbons that will cook down to dark rivulets can all be distributed throughout the household.

A pot of collard greens meant a satisfying meal was on deck. While a must-have for the holiday spread, collards could pop up any time. Traditional collard recipes have used seasoning meats like neckbone or ham hock for the rich broth, known as potlikker. Ours uses a hit of Aunt Millie's sofrito, bright with peppers, aromatics, and garlic. Champagne vinegar lends a touch of acidity, and the white miso adds umami.

Serves 4

INGREDIENTS

5 tablespoons (75 ml) extra-virgin olive oil

⅓ cup (145 g) diced yellow onion

2 teaspoons minced garlic

2 tablespoons Aunt Millie's Green Sofrito (page 290)

2 cups (480 ml) vegetable stock

1 bunch (1 pound 2 ounces/500 g) collard greens, washed and sliced

2 teaspoons flaky sea salt

⅓ teaspoon smoked paprika

¼ teaspoon red chile flakes

2½ teaspoons champagne vinegar

1 tablespoon honey

1 heaping teaspoon white miso paste

PREPARATION

In a large skillet, combine 3 tablespoons of the olive oil, the onion, and the garlic. Cover and cook over medium-low heat for about 10 minutes, until the onion develops a slight caramelization.

In a stockpot, heat the remaining 2 tablespoons olive oil over medium heat. Add the sofrito and cook for about 5 minutes. Add the stock, collard greens, salt, paprika, chile flakes, vinegar, honey, and miso and stir. Raise the heat to high and bring to a boil, then reduce the heat to maintain a simmer and cook, stirring occasionally, for 90 minutes, or until the greens are tender. Spoon into individual serving bowls and eat immediately.

MOM'S SPAGHETTI

Lester's mom, Elizabeth, made a version of this spaghetti. She would get the ingredients from the bodega nearby. Ground turkey was her protein, but we use plant-based protein here. When spaghetti is on the stove, the scent drifts throughout the house. (For Lester, it signaled Mom was in a good mood.)

Spaghetti was bonding food. Everyone goes back for seconds and thirds, lots of talking around the table or in front of the TV. Elizabeth's finesse is a touch of sugar to make sure the tomato sauce isn't too acidic. These days, we might add a bit more pepper to bring some heat. Older kids practicing their knife skills can get in on the prep work and help get those bell peppers, garlic, and onions ready for the pot, chop-chop. Leftover spaghetti is great, too. Let the oils seep into the pasta, or put the next-day sauce between two slices of garlic bread. If you don't have Espelette, you can use red chile flakes or cayenne pepper.

CONTINUED

Serves 4

INGREDIENTS

¼ cup (60 ml) extra-virgin olive oil, plus more for serving

½ sweet yellow onion, minced

3 garlic cloves, minced

10 ounces (285 g) plant-based ground meat

3 large vine tomatoes, diced

1½ tablespoons double-concentrated San Marzano tomato paste

1 cup (240 ml) vegetable stock, plus more as needed

1 tablespoon flaky sea salt

1 tablespoon cane sugar

1 tablespoon ground Espelette pepper

1 tablespoon chopped fresh oregano

2 tablespoons chopped fresh basil

1 teaspoon chopped fresh thyme

2 tablespoons plant-based butter

1 (17.5-ounce/500 g) box of spaghetti (such as from Rustichella d'Abruzzo)

Micro basil, for garnish (optional)

PREPARATION

In a large pot or Dutch oven, combine half the olive oil, the onion, and the garlic. Cook over medium heat for about 5 minutes, until the onion is slightly caramelized and aromatic. Add the rest of the olive oil and the plant-based ground meat. Cook for about 20 minutes, stirring regularly so the meat is crumbly and develops a brown color. Be sure to break up any clumps of meat.

Add the diced tomatoes, tomato paste, stock, salt, sugar, Espelette, and half the fresh oregano, basil, and thyme. Stir and cook until the mixture is well combined, 15 to 20 minutes. (You can add more stock depending on how saucy you like your ragù, but be careful to add it in small increments. If you overdo it, keep the sauce going on the heat with the lid off for a bit longer so the excess liquid can evaporate.)

Add the butter and the remaining fresh herbs and simmer for about 10 minutes more.

Meanwhile, bring a large pot of generously salted water to a boil (think about 2 tablespoons of salt for every pound/455 g of pasta, you know the vibes; we like the flaky sea salt). Add the spaghetti and cook according to the package instructions. You want the pasta to cook until it's al dente, so it has a little bite to it.

Drain the pasta and add it to the sauce. You can hit it with a bit of olive oil, then stir again to combine. Plate and serve with fresh micro basil on top, if desired. Eat immediately.

STRONG BACK STEW

We're obviously big fans of plantain. Its nutritional value and versatility make it one of our favorite ingredients. The bodegas always have plantains on deck. Pierre's Bajan grandmother called her version of this dish "strong man soup." She made it with cassava, pumpkin, and other ground provisions and served it to her kids every Wednesday. It was filling enough to satisfy them all day, and Pierre's father, Andrew, says her rendition would make them feel invincible. This lentil stew marries Latin American and Caribbean influences.

CONTINUED

Serves 6

INGREDIENTS

For the stew

4 tablespoons coconut oil
6 scallions, white parts only, chopped
1 yellow bell pepper, diced
2 shallots, diced
2 tablespoons minced fresh ginger
2 celery stalks, diced
2 garlic cloves, finely chopped
½ teaspoon ground cloves
1 teaspoon ground turmeric
1 teaspoon smoked paprika
6 cups (1.5 L) vegetable stock
1 (14-ounce/400 ml) can coconut milk
1 cup (150 g) dried split yellow peas, soaked overnight, then drained
1 Scotch bonnet pepper, halved and seeded
4 sprigs thyme
2 tablespoons finely chopped fresh sage
1 bay leaf
1 cup (150 g) diced peeled sweet plantain
1¾ cups (250 g) diced carrots
Flaky sea salt

For the dumplings

1⅓ cups (200 g) plantain flour
1½ teaspoons (7 g) baking powder
1 teaspoon ground white pepper
1 tablespoon flaky sea salt
1 tablespoon chopped fresh chives
½ cup (120 ml) coconut milk, stirred well
2 tablespoons plant-based butter, melted

For garnish (optional)

SOIL (page 291)
Lemongrass Oil (page 293)

PREPARATION

Make the stew

In a large stockpot, heat 2 tablespoons of the coconut oil over medium heat. Add the scallion whites, bell pepper, shallots, ginger, celery, and garlic. Cook until the vegetables soften, about 5 minutes. Add the cloves, turmeric, and paprika and allow the spices to bloom for 2 minutes.

Add the stock, coconut milk, split peas, Scotch bonnet, thyme, sage, and bay leaf. Bring to a boil, then reduce the heat to maintain a simmer, cover, and cook until the peas are tender, about 2 hours.

Remove and discard the thyme sprigs and bay leaf. Using a ladle, transfer half the soup to a blender, then puree. Pour the blended soup back into the pot and stir to combine. This step gives the soup a texture that's not too chunky and not too smooth.

In a medium saucepan, heat the remaining 2 tablespoons coconut oil over medium heat. Add the sweet plantains and cook until they're just caramelized brown, about 5 minutes. Here we aren't frying them to doneness, we're adding another layer of flavor before transferring them to the soup. Using a slotted spoon, lift the fried plantains out of the pan so the oil drains off, add them to the soup pot, and stir.

Make the dumplings

In a medium bowl, mix the plantain flour, baking powder, white pepper, salt, and chives. Pour in the coconut milk and melted butter and use a fork to incorporate the ingredients. Once the dough starts to come together, you can use your hands to form it into a sticky ball.

Leave the dough ball in the bowl and cover with a clean, dry dish towel. Set aside to rest at room temperature for about 15 minutes. The dough won't change in size, but you do want to give the ingredients a few minutes to bond. Using a bench scraper (dough scraper), cut the ball in half, then cut each half in half. Keep doing this until you have 32 (1-inch/3 cm) dumplings. (This is more or less a guide; don't stress on an exact count. You just want them to cook uniformly and look appetizing.)

Add the carrots and dumplings to the pot. Simmer for 1 hour, or until the dumplings are fully cooked and a bit on the fluffy side. You want these to be really bathing in the stew, soaking up all that goodness.

Taste the soup and add salt to your preference. When ready to serve, garnish with SOIL and lemongrass oil, if you like.

SUNDIAL
TRADITIONAL
AFRICAN MANBACK
IF IT'S ITAL IT'S VITAL

INTERVIEW WITH

DENISE LEE, ROXANNE SERRAO, ELIZABETH WALKER

THE SOURCE

To know any of us is to know who our mothers are.

Denise Lee studied and worked as a speech therapist—it's no wonder Jon has a way with words.

Roxanne Serrao was baking cakes and pies as her hustle while raising four kids. For Pierre, cooking several meals a day both to feed his family and for work is a true labor of love.

Elizabeth Walker and her son Lester are cut from the same cloth—the expression was coined for mother and son. Strong-willed and tough, no games played, she kept Lester on his pivot at all times.

Thanks to these women, our mothers, we learned to appreciate, and wanted to offer to others, the exchange of serving food and being well fed.

Ghetto Gastro: What were your early impressions of how food came to the table in your household growing up?

DENISE LEE: From my grandmother's kitchen. She came to New York from Pittsburgh to study dietetics. Food—nutritious food—has always been a part of our legacy. I don't know if anybody else was in the kitchen with her. I know I was there. She would have me set the table. My grandmother believed in setting the table and she always had pretty china, flatware, and there was a dish for every selection, you know, especially during the holidays.

I was always in the kitchen with her, chopping the onions and the celery, whatever needed to be done. My introduction to the renowned cookbook *Joy of Cooking* came through my grandmother's kitchen as well. I learned by just watching my grandmother, and then even as an adult, I would call her and ask her how to cook certain things. Scratch cooking was on holidays, but during the week we did a lot of freezer stuff.

ROXANNE SERRAO: My dad was a gardener. He had multiple gardens all across the city and he would bring home the collard greens, the tomatoes, green or red—everything was fresh.

My mom believed in scratch cooking. There was nothing from the box. We had to peel the potatoes. We had to grate the pickles in order to make relish, even though relish was clearly available in the store. We'd say, "Ma, can you pick up some relish when you're at the store?"

She says, "I'll have your dad bring some pickles from the garden."

"Ma, they're not pickles when he brings them, they're cucumbers!"

"He'll make them into pickles."

So we would try, it would fail. And then we would skirt around and try to find another way to get our relish. But everything had to be made fresh. That's my early days. I remember the milkman bringing fresh milk. He would bring milk, eggs, and cheese, leave it at the door. Mom would make homemade ice cream. Everything was from scratch.

This was in Hartford?

SERRAO: In Hartford, Connecticut, that's right. We lived in the projects.

ELIZABETH WALKER: Mine was from Thanksgiving. My mother and my great-grandmother, they did most of the cooking. I remember being so happy. At the time—they still do it now—they give out big turkeys. And there was so many of us that my mother had this gigantic turkey. It was so big. Oh my God. Then the stuffing inside the turkey and the smell of everything together. Smelling wonderful. Powerful.

People just took their time. They didn't have food processors. They chopped everything up, buttered everything up. Putting it together was so amazing. If my mother had taken us to restaurants, it woulda been nice. But we had that in our apartment buildings. We had Asians, we had Spanish, we had Black, we had Indian, we had all cultures growing up in my community. They had great pantries. When you come out the building, people will whisper—*Ohhh Ms. Richardson is frying some chicken! You better go over there and get some of that.*

Did your relationships to food—eating, preparing, or ordering out—change once you became pregnant or after you became a parent?

LEE: My ideas didn't change at all. I tend to cook fresh food, but by the time I became pregnant with Jon, I was working in the beauty industry. I was working for John Atchison, who was one of the first Black celebrity [hair]stylists in New York City. Because I was in the heart of the city, I had access to fresh fruit, even fresher food, actually, because of all the fruit carts. They were on every corner. In addition to that, I had expanded my palate by being in that area, 55th Street and Fifth Avenue, right in the heart of one of the entertainment districts. We worked around the corner from CBS, a few blocks away was Rockefeller Center.

One block over was the shopping area with the high-end department stores. Henri Bendel was right around the corner, Bloomingdale's a couple of steps away. So I was eating better and fresher but also more eclectic food. One of my favorites at that time was La Bonne Soupe, which was a French café right next to the salon. I would go there for lunch. I might go across the street and have some Sichuan. So I had access to this variety of foods, and it was fresher than what I was used to eating in our neighborhood. That's how my food experience began to expand. Once Jon was born, I was cooking from scratch.

SERRAO: I would say "my shift," I never really did change. I do take shortcuts. Understand that. Shortcuts are key sometimes. However, when I went to college, that was when my palate changed, because [the food I grew up eating] wasn't just coming to the table. You had to go to *it*, ha! Sometimes it was in somebody else's dorm. You got food the way you could get it when you're on a college campus.

WALKER: When I was pregnant with Lester, I craved burgers and Italian ices. I baked apple pies. I baked an apple pie almost every other day. But when I was pregnant, I tried to be health-conscious about what I put in my body. And I can't say how other people feel when they're pregnant, but once you have a baby and your kids come out and then your shape is gone, I don't know about for other people, but for me—I really didn't enjoy having to take that weight off because I love to eat so much.

Some kids resist new foods. How did you think about exposing us to different ingredients or cuisines?

SERRAO: I told them everything was chicken. *Everything* was chicken. It didn't matter what it was and they would try it and be like, "Ooh, that tastes good!" Okay! They were eating lamb. But it didn't matter with Pierre. Pierre was an eater. He ate everything, so I could tell him what it really was and he would eat it. But the other ones? No. They didn't want to hear it. So that was my trick.

For the vegetables, I told them everything would make them strong. "You want to be the strongest one in school? You better eat that broccoli! You want to be the strongest one? You better eat it!" They got the message and they would have competitions on who could eat the most. Oh yeah. I played a lot of mind games to get them to eat and participate in the kitchen.

LEE: I was in school a lot during Jon's younger years, like from age two. I was pursuing my bachelor's, then my master's, and on and on. We ate out a couple of times a week. I think that's when he got introduced to eating a lot of different foods, because we lived at that time on 100th Street. Again, close proximity to areas that had better food selections. We were eating Indian food, we were eating Chinese food. Soul food, because we were close to Harlem. He got an opportunity to pick what he wanted. And this when he was really young.

WALKER: Lester wasn't picky. My other son, Chad, he was picky. But if they smelled it and they tasted and they liked it, they would eat it.

Roxanne, what was dining out like as you were raising Pierre and his siblings?

SERRAO: My husband is very ritualistic. Every month we took the kids out to a different restaurant. That was our exposure to different foods, and every month we went someplace different.

It was more about behavior, more about grooming. Learning how to eat with a knife and fork, wiping your mouth between bites, chewing silently, not slurping while you're drinking. And pretty much not talking while you're eating, all that stuff. That was where the education took place—in the restaurant. Right. 'Cause at home you can, you know, you can do the old smack or that Mama's look across the table, you know? You give 'em that *[Roxanne exaggerates one eye looking pointedly across from her]*. Letting them know something is not good etiquette. They would get it *real* quick!

WALKER: We didn't go out a lot to eat. But they already knew before we even went out, I just had a look, 'cause I have that look like my mother. So if I look at you and you're not doing what you know that you supposed to do . . . it's just a look. I know if I'm going to take them somewhere, they're going to order what they're going to eat, and then they're going to eat what they order. Even if it took an hour to make their order. I hate to waste food.

We did take a lot of vacations. We did go on cruises. We did go to California a lot. Lester was the one that was interested in different tastes, he always tried new things.

Do you think about food as it relates to your political identity or as an expression of your political beliefs in this country? The farming, purchasing, eating, the community in food?

WALKER: Yeah, for me, growing up, we didn't really have experiences going out to eat. When I grew up, it was only one Chinese restaurant in my neighborhood, and everyone would go to it. This was on 106th Street and next door to my Catholic school. It was between Third and Second. That would be a special treat.

But where I grew up, the projects I grew up in, it was so cultural—people didn't need to go to restaurants because at the time everyone ate from everyone's apartment. We didn't eat pork because my mother had high blood pressure, she didn't cook like that. But my great-grandmother was sneaking pickled pig's feet and would say we couldn't eat it 'cause it was after eleven o'clock. I'd sneak and try to taste it. But yeah, you could tell Ray's mother on the eighth floor was cooking chitlins on the holidays. Or Lucy down the hallway. If you had food and you were cooking, you could just knock on somebody's door and say you got extra. A lot of people had a lot of children.

LEE: I think food is very political. And I knew that without *knowing* it was political as a youngster. Once the supermarkets came in, the mom-and-pop stores dried up. I remember going to the fruit and vegetable stand. I remember going to the fish market. And once white flight came, well, I was witness to that as well. I saw my neighborhood change from having a few white people to being mostly Black and Hispanic people.

And when the white people left, they took their goods with them. They closed up their stores. They closed the corner store, the candy store, the shoe store. They closed up the fish market and the fruit and vegetable stands. And then I saw supermarkets come in, but then everything wasn't as fresh. It was like, when white people left the neighborhood, so goes the best food, and when they return, you see a return of the fresh markets and things of that nature. Of course, with the absence of fresh food, there's a decline in health. And what we had access to was the bodegas and the Chinese restaurants. There was one Chinese restaurant in my neighborhood that sold fabulous food. And we were friendly with them because I think they also had the Chinese laundry where we used to launder our linen, back in the day. You would take your shirts and sheets to be professionally laundered at the Chinese laundry. We had a relationship.

But once these entities began to flee, you no longer had a relationship with your local purveyors. The relationship was suddenly hostile. You go into a market and they just assume that you're going to steal. You go into a bodega, they're watching you like a hawk, assuming that you're going to steal. The relationship changed and of course, you know, food is energy. The food that we're buying has no energy, it has no information. People are now consuming a lot of lifeless food.

But as Elizabeth said, there was a sharing of food. And it's the sharing of food that knits us together as a community. I've experienced that through the church because my grandfather was a pastor. After church, there was always food available. The Black restaurants sustain that community. When we own something, then it's sustenance. If we don't own it, then you see a decline of the socioeconomic status of our people. That was my experience coming up, how access to food reveals the socioeconomics of a neighborhood, or just how you're treated in connection with food. Like, people who aren't necessarily from the neighborhood but are supplying the neighborhood with goods and services? Don't respect you! But they'll take your money.

WALKER: We didn't have money to go out, but when we were kids, our special treat was candy. Because our mother didn't give us candy. When we had a dollar, the *whole house*, 'cause it was like six of us, we were like, *Oh, I'm your best friend! I'm your best friend!* Because a dollar would get you a hundred pieces of candy. Period!

Ha. Penny candy.

WALKER: That's my fondest memory of food, something that went in your mouth that you loved. I don't think y'all ever grew up with a penny dollar store. I mean penny, penny candies.

[Jon] I had penny candy when I was living in Metro North in Harlem.

[Lester] Ma, and they had penny candies at Polo Grounds on 55th! They had the candy shack. It's where they used to sell newspapers and all that, but it was just straight candy, penny caaaaaandy!

WALKER: Right! Yes, yes.

And people don't talk about that as much, I guess, because of the [sugar] and diabetes. But it was so much fun. We was like, "You know, I got this bag right here." We had the brown bag full of candies. You used to shake the bag like *chh chhh chhh chh!*

Say you get a dollar from a cousin or uncle or somebody—you saved your dollar until the next week, because you could get a hundred candies, like, *Ehhh! Where you get those candies from?* So that was my fun. If you had a bag of penny candies, you was good.

What does "Black Power Kitchen" mean to you?

LEE: It means legacy and passing on not only the power of good food, nutritious food, but how you can use food to uplift you spiritually, emotionally, and socially. Because food is information and energy.

If you're eating a diet that's robust in vegetables and quality foods, then you're going to feel better. And when you feel better, you interact better. You treat people better when you feel better.

WALKER: Black Power—it's power, baby, in them pots! Power! Love in your heart for that food! It draws people who want to get into this—it's our culture. Black Power is a culture. Period. Everyone wants a bite of it. When I hear "Black Power," I hear growth, enlightenment, the desire to get fed. Once your stomach is full, you start feeling good. You want to communicate. You want to love. I hear love in those pots. That's why our people say, "It was like you put your foot in that food!" You put your whole *life* in that food.

SERRAO: That toe in it!

WALKER: Sounds like it should be some powerful food coming out that kitchen. Hopefully.

SERRAO: When I hear "Black Power Kitchen," the first word that comes to me is "power."

WALKER: Exactly.

SERRAO: To me [it] is to take control. Take control of your life, of your well-being, of your health. Bring it in the kitchen and do it together with your family. Everybody coming together, putting their toe in it.

WALKER: Yes! Hallelujah!

SERRAO: That is some rejoicing happening in that kitchen. It's being blessed with love, and happy people make happy food. I'm convinced of that. It always focuses around food. Good food. Elizabeth said that community was important and people were able to eat at other people's houses. That's how I grew up. When my dad came from his garden, he didn't only stop at our house and drop vegetables off to us. He brought them to anybody in his passing. It didn't matter if they was sitting outside on the doorstep. Which is what we did. He would drop off collard greens, green beans, to everybody. They'd get corn. Sometimes, he come home with an empty bag and we'd be like, "Dad, where's our vegetables!"

"Oh, I gave them to so-and-so and so-and-so when so-and-so." We would go down to their house and that's where we ate that night, because we knew where the good food was. We can bring it back. Bring it back into the kitchen and handle it with the power that we have as Black people. I love it.

WHAT IS THIS, VELVET?

You can find red velvet cake in most Black neighborhoods, especially in Harlem. It's often a capstone to celebratory Juneteenth meals, as are many red foods (red drink, watermelon, hot links) that symbolize Black people's sacrifice and enduring quest for freedom.

While historians of Black foodways haven't traced the origins of the dish to Black people, we grew up seeing and aspiring to have red velvet cake all the time. As a kid, Jon tried to avoid going to church on Sundays, but if a trip to Amy Ruth's on 116th was on the agenda, he was gonna pull up for that red slice. Their version tasted homemade, was super moist and not too sweet, with beautiful pecans along the icing. Our version gets its color from freeze-dried raspberries, which you'll find in the dried fruit section of the grocery store. Crush them into a fine powder using a mortar and pestle to give your cake its vivid hue.

CONTINUED

Serves 12

INGREDIENTS

For the cake

Nonstick spray or melted butter

2¾ cups (550 g) cane sugar

4¼ cups (420 g) cake flour

¾ cup (65 g) freeze-dried raspberries, crushed into a fine powder

1 tablespoon kosher salt

1 tablespoon (17 g) baking soda

1 tablespoon (13 g) baking powder

½ cup (120 ml) grapeseed oil

½ cup (120 ml) buttermilk

4 teaspoons fresh lemon juice

3 large (150 g) eggs

2 teaspoons vanilla extract

1½ cups (340 g) boiling water

For the frosting

4 cups plus 2½ tablespoons (500 g) confectioners' sugar

14 ounces (400 g) cream cheese

10½ ounces (2⅔ sticks/300 g) unsalted butter

¼ cup plus 2½ tablespoons (100 g) sour cream

½ teaspoon vanilla extract

5 tablespoons (40 g) crushed candied pecans, for garnish

1½ tablespoons raspberry powder, for garnish

PREPARATION

Make the cake

Heat the oven to 350°F (175°C). Line three 9-inch (23 cm) round cake pans with rounds of parchment paper cut to fit and grease with nonstick spray (or you can use just enough melted butter to coat the bottom and sides).

In a large bowl, whisk together the cane sugar, flour, raspberries, salt, baking soda, and baking powder, then sift the mixture into another bowl and set aside.

In the bowl of a stand mixer fitted with the paddle attachment, combine the grapeseed oil, buttermilk, lemon juice, eggs, and vanilla. Mix on low speed until you get a homogeneous liquid, 2 to 3 minutes. With the mixer running on low, add the dry ingredients, one large spoonful at a time, and mix until just combined; do not overmix.

With the mixer still on low, add the boiling water in a slow stream. Pouring slowly will gradually increase the temperature of the batter—this way, the eggs won't cook. You want the water to be hot to help emulsify the batter and create a smoother, more velvety cake. Aim for a final batter texture that's thin like brownie batter.

Divide the batter evenly among the three prepared cake pans. Bake the cakes on the center rack for 40 minutes. Don't move them around while baking or they will collapse. Remove the cakes from the oven and let them cool completely.

Make the frosting

In the bowl of the stand mixer fitted with the paddle attachment, combine the confectioners' sugar, cream cheese, butter, sour cream, and vanilla. Begin mixing on low speed and gradually work up to high, making sure to scrape down the sides and bottom of the bowl. Mix thoroughly, ensuring there are no lumps.

Remove the cakes from their pans. Place one cake layer on a cake plate. Spread an even layer of the cream cheese frosting on top. Repeat with the second and third layers, ensuring an even layer of frosting between each layer. Finally, frost the top and sides of the cake. Sprinkle the top with crushed candied pecans and raspberry powder. Slice and enjoy. Leftover cake will keep for 3 to 5 days, wrapped or in a container.

AWOL ERIZKU
632, 2021

GINGER ME

Ginger beer is nonalcoholic, spicy, and straightforward, made with fermented ginger, sugar, water, lime or lemon, and what you might call a little island time.

Don't confuse ginger beer with ginger ale. The latter has a flavor that offers a hint of ginger, while ginger beer is not shy at all about the root flavor. Many ginger beers use other spices and aromatics, but this recipe keeps it simple and lets the evolving ginger do the work. To get your brew going, you'll need a starter culture, or bug. The combo of ginger and sugar will feed naturally occurring yeasts, which gets the fermentation process started.

We learned this recipe from Jon's mom, Denise, who taught us about the drink's probiotic benefits. This one's got a burn on the finish. We like our ginger beer to leave a little stinger! You can brew the tea as strong as you would like, using anywhere from a thumb to an entire hand of ginger.

CONTINUED

Makes 1 gallon (4 L)

INGREDIENTS

For the bug

1 (1-inch/3 cm) piece fresh ginger, plus additional to feed your bug

2 teaspoons organic cane sugar, plus additional to feed your bug

1 cup (240 ml) filtered water

For the ginger tea

4 quarts (4 L) cold water

1 hand of ginger (you can use less, but the Gs like it spicy)

1¼ cups (250 g) organic cane sugar

Juice of 2 lemons

PREPARATION

Make the bug

Grate the ginger into a mason jar. Add the sugar and the filtered water, then stir.

Cover the jar with a cheesecloth and rest it on the counter away from sunlight, but in a warm space. Each day, feed the bug by adding the same amount of sugar and ginger.

After 2 to 3 days, it will begin to bubble. When the bug becomes vigorously bubbly, it's ready to mix with the tea.

Brew the ginger tea

Fill a pot with 2 quarts (2 L) of the cold water and bring to a boil. Grate the ginger into the water and add the sugar; stir to dissolve. Bring to a boil, then simmer for 30 minutes to infuse the ginger into the water. Remove from the heat and allow the mixture to cool to room temperature and the tea to infuse for 1 more hour. Strain the ginger tea. Add the lemon juice.

Strain the ginger bug and add that liquid to the cooled tea. (When you add the probiotic juice from the ginger bug to the ginger tea, you're adding the beneficial bacteria and yeasts so the brew will begin fermenting.) Add the remaining 2 quarts (2 L) cold water to the combined ginger liquid.

Sanitize clean clamp-top bottles. Place a small funnel at the mouth of each clean bottle, one by one, and fill each bottle up to within 1 inch (3 cm) of the top. Clamp the bottles shut and leave them in a warm, dark place for 10 to 14 days.

As the yeasts and bacteria in the ginger tea begin to digest the sugar, the by-product they generate is carbon dioxide (CO_2). The CO_2 means your ginger beer is carbonating. The longer it ferments, the bubblier it becomes. Pierre recommends that first-timers use a plastic soda bottle for at least one serving of the ginger beer. As the carbonation increases, the plastic bottle will become firmer and harder to the touch, giving you a reliable way to keep tabs on the developing carbonation. Alternatively, just crack open one of the bottles periodically to gauge the developing pressure. Make sure to check its progress every day after the first 5 days.

Once the ginger beer has reached the carbonation level you desire, put the bottles in the fridge and keep them cold until ready to serve.

To serve, simply drink up!

I'M THE COLOR PURPLE

Concord grape juice is so familiar to us, from the juice boxes we drank as kids to Biggie Smalls's famous shout-out. The name of this recipe is also a nod to the pivotal book by Alice Walker and the culture-shifting movie starring Whoopi Goldberg and Oprah Winfrey that followed it.

Even before the days of constantly streaming TV, in a lot of our households there was always a Black-led movie on repeat, the kind of vibe where everyone has seen or heard the dialogue so often, you and your friends can quote the lines. This drink can be served without booze or add the rum for a pop of grown-folks kick.

Makes one 10-ounce (300 ml) drink

INGREDIENTS

4 ounces (120 ml) ginger beer (store-bought or see page 243)

2 ounces (60 ml) aged rum (such as Mount Gay XO; optional)

2 ounces (60 ml) soda water

2 ounces (60 ml) freshly pressed Concord grape juice (or store-bought organic, not from concentrate)

1 ounce (30 ml) fresh lime juice

Crushed ice, for serving

1 or 2 Concord grapes, for garnish

1 or 2 pieces candied ginger, for garnish

PREPARATION

In a mixing glass filled with ice cubes, stir together the ginger beer, rum (if using), soda water, grape juice, and lime juice. Strain into a highball glass filled with crushed ice. Add the grapes and candied ginger to garnish.

Eyes on the Prize

WANGECHI MUTU
THE SEATED I, 2019
BRONZE, $79\frac{13}{16}$ x $33\frac{3}{4}$ in., AN EDITION OF 3

It's been said that Black folks are exceptionally good at looking toward the future because the past has been so hard to endure. Our collective memory is filled with images that predate most of our lives by decades—images of resistance, fighting back, or taking a stand. These elements of our past are important, but that's not a holistic reflection of who we are as a culture, nor where we're going. Some of the most beautiful historical images we've seen are those of Black folks in states of joy, ease, and rest, like everyday workers taking a load off to iconic figures photographed outside of their typical element.

Fundamentally, we are entrepreneurs and nonconformists and as such, we have adapted to a culture that pushes hustling and grinding. But we've seen what nonstop work does to people. We've experienced burnout. It's all fun and games until it's not. At some point, you've got to take stock of what matters. We have ambitious goals and, as Black men, we're working against a social construct that makes everyday life unbelievably hard sometimes. But we've got our community—our families, our friends, our collaborators. We believe that if we continue to build alongside one another with intention, we can create healthy, nurturing relationships and practices.

It's not common for Black men to openly speak this way, not where we're from. In the streets, patriarchy can have sudden and permanent consequences (patriarchy is real everywhere, but it does not impact everyone the same). Standing out for the wrong reasons can cost you. We learned this really young. We're also socially discouraged from sitting with ourselves in states of rest, and this is true for pretty much anyone who's set foot on US soil. What does it mean to think of our bodies not solely as a means to stack green, which our communities seriously need, but as beings who have the right to simply exist, undefined by a job or wage? We've heard the phrase "Put the oxygen mask on yourself first," but that can be difficult to model in practice. Especially when there aren't too many examples preceding you.

REGINALD O'NEAL
SPRING IS HERE, 2021
OIL ON CANVAS, 44 x 52 in.

GARRETT BRADLEY
AKA, 2019
SINGLE-CHANNEL HD VIDEO (COLOR, SOUND), 8:17 min.

DEREK FORDJOUR
VOLLEY FOLLEY, 2020
ACRYLIC, CHARCOAL, CARDBOARD, OIL PASTEL, AND FOIL ON NEWSPAPER MOUNTED ON CANVAS, 90 x 72 in.

One way we've learned to process our fast-paced lifestyle and professional demands is to incorporate practices of well-being and self-discipline. We meditate, exercise regularly, and read (or do the audiobooks!). We realized that living in a constant state of alert and always being on edge was not sustainable, and more than that, it didn't feel good. We want to be able to eat well, move around the world safely, and build lives in aesthetically pleasing spaces that support our needs. You should not have to be a trillionaire to do that in this country, but for so many that dream isn't actionable. We take steps where we can. We check in on our loved ones. We keep our eyes on the prize. We have moments where we look at each other like, yo, we need to pause and catch up. Sometimes we do this collectively as a group, other times we go off in our different directions. When we come back, we're restored and feel more alive.

In this last chapter, we're slowing it down. These recipes are meant to sustain and nourish for the future we want to experience, with some levity and play. Greens make a strong appearance. Garden Greens (page 258) features a generous serving from the farmers' market, and Ginger Garlic Spinach (page 262) is a fast and easy dish. Show love for your people with Stewy Newton (page 254), a big pot of feijoada-inspired richness. And we close it out with fruit-focused treats, because no culinary journey is complete without a dose of somethin sweet. We sit down with artist Theaster Gates, who shares ideas of space making and archiving Black history, and curator-writer Kimberly Drew, who brings us back to our bodies and how we honor them.

DERRICK ADAMS
FLOATER 107, 2020
MIXED MEDIA, 50 x 72 in.

COGNITION

Sometimes we need a little help harnessing energy and focus. Our ancestors and melanated people throughout the world have been using ingredients from plants to support our cognitive awareness and facilitate restoration.

In recent years, such ingredients have inspired new generations of health and wellness enthusiasts. Cognition is an adaptogenic morning milk to give your day a smooth and gentle boost. The piperine from the black pepper helps amplify the properties of turmeric, while the cocoa butter acts as a mood protector with a little caffeine. Lion's mane and ashwagandha help with clarity.

Serves 2

INGREDIENTS

¾ cup (180 ml) plain, unsweetened oat milk
½ cup (120 ml) coconut milk
1½ teaspoons agave syrup, plus more to taste
1½ teaspoons cocoa butter
1 teaspoon ground turmeric
1 cinnamon stick or ½ teaspoon ground cinnamon
½ teaspoon lion's mane powder
½ teaspoon ashwagandha
Pinch of freshly ground black pepper
Pinch of grated fresh ginger

PREPARATION

In a small saucepan, whisk together the oat milk, coconut milk, agave, cocoa butter, turmeric, cinnamon, lion's mane, ashwagandha, pepper, and ginger to combine, then warm over medium heat until hot to the touch but not boiling, 3 to 4 minutes. Whisk continuously the whole time.

Turn off the heat and taste. Adjust the sweetness level to your preference. Remove the cinnamon stick if you used one. If you prefer a super-smooth texture, you can strain the milk to remove the grated ginger. Serve hot.

STEWY NEWTON

This is our take on the dish feijoada, perhaps most popularly associated with Brazil but also found in Cape Verde, Angola, and Mozambique—all former colonies of the Portuguese empire.

Feijoada is a bean stew cooked with salt pork, smoked sausage, and beef. It has many variations, including those that feature ground provisions or hearty greens like kale. It's traditionally credited as a creation by the enslaved Africans of modern-day Brazil.

For centuries feijoada has been served as a meal among families or large groups, a weekend affair, thanks to the long cook required. Today the stew is a hallmark of leisure with loved ones and slow, easy meals. It's Brazil's national dish, soul soothing in its richness, and one that inspires us to take stock of what we have and to enjoy our friends and family.

Our version uses black beans, mushrooms (note that we call for hen of the woods mushrooms, not chicken of the woods—they're not the same), and plant-based sausage. Give yourself a day to soak the dry beans and let the stew come into its own. Have your people over, dish it up, and kick back.

CONTINUED

Serves 12

INGREDIENTS

½ pound (226 g) dried black beans

½ cup plus 2 tablespoons (180 g) flaky sea salt

3 or 4 bay leaves

¾ cup plus 1 tablespoon (190 ml) extra-virgin olive oil

1 head garlic, cloves separated and peeled

2 sprigs thyme

1 pound (455 g) oyster mushrooms, cut into chunks

1 pound (455 g) hen of the woods (maitake) mushrooms, cut into chunks

8 ounces (225 g) plant-based hot sausage links, sliced about 1 inch (3 cm) thick

8 ounces (225 g) okra, chopped into ½-inch-thick (1 cm) rounds

1 teaspoon smoked paprika

1 teaspoon ground Espelette pepper, plus more if desired

1 teaspoon smoked sea salt

6 scallions, white and green parts kept separate, thinly sliced

½ large white onion, diced

12½ ounces (350 g) kabocha squash or pumpkin, cut into large dice

10 ounces (285 g) white yam, diced

2 tablespoons red miso paste

¼ cup (55 g) dates, minced

½ teaspoon onion powder

1 (14.5-ounce/411 g) can crushed tomatoes

2 tablespoons tomato powder

3 cups (720 ml) Mushroom Dashi (page 292)

Cooked rice or ancestral grain such as fonio, for serving

Orange zest, for garnish

PREPARATION

Put the black beans in a large bowl and add enough water to fully submerge the beans. Add 5 tablespoons (90 g) of the flaky salt, cover the bowl, and refrigerate overnight or for about 8 hours.

Drain the soaked beans, transfer to a large pot, and cover them with fresh water, then add the remaining 5 tablespoons (90 g) salt and the bay leaves. Cover with a lid and cook the beans over medium-low heat for 4 hours. (You can continue onward with the other elements of the dish while the beans are doing their thing.) Around the 4-hour mark, taste the beans. At this point, they should be tender and easy to chew but not mushy. Strain the beans' cooking liquid into a large bowl and set aside. Return the beans to their pot.

Heat the oven to 350°F (175°C).

Pour 6 tablespoons (90 ml) of the olive oil into a small (about 6-inch/15 cm) roasting pan, then add the garlic cloves and 1 sprig of thyme. You want to keep the pan very small so the garlic is submerged in oil and cooks as a confit. This step is also seasoning the oil, which you'll use to roast the mushrooms in a moment. Cover with foil and bake for 15 minutes, or until the garlic turns light brown. Remove from the oven and raise the oven temperature to 375°F (190°C).

Discard the thyme and use a slotted spoon to transfer the garlic to a cutting board; set the oil aside. Mince the roasted garlic until it's near paste consistency and set aside.

Place a large cast-iron skillet on the stovetop over medium-high heat and add half the garlic-thyme seasoned oil. Be careful—the roasting pan is still hot. Working in batches so you don't crowd the skillet, add all of the mushrooms and a pinch each of flaky salt and Espelette pepper, if you like, and cook for 10 minutes, until the mushrooms begin to brown and caramelize. Use a slotted spoon to remove the mushrooms and transfer them to a wire rack or a paper towel–lined sheet pan.

In a Dutch oven or large pot, heat ¼ cup (60 ml) of the olive oil over medium heat. Add the plant-based sausage and brown it for 10 to 15 minutes.

While sausage is browning, line a sheet pan with foil. In a large bowl, combine the okra, paprika, Espelette, smoked salt, and remaining 3 tablespoons olive oil. Use a spoon to mix thoroughly, then transfer the seasoned okra to the lined sheet pan. Roast for 20 to 25 minutes. The okra will brown, but be careful to not burn it.

Back to your Dutch oven: Add the mushrooms, garlic, roasted okra, remaining thyme sprig, scallion whites, onion, squash, yam, miso, dates, onion powder, crushed tomatoes, and tomato powder to the pot with the sausage. Add the cooked beans and 3 cups (720 ml) of their cooking liquid. Add the mushroom dashi. Stir well. Cook over medium-low heat, stirring occasionally, for 90 minutes.

Remove from the heat and stir in the scallion greens. Serve with rice or an ancestral grain. Garnish with orange zest.

GARDEN GREENS

We need and love the greens. Whether we're catching our favorite vendor at Saturday's farmers' market or picking a small haul from the community garden, we constantly crave the assortment of flavorful, nutritious, and versatile green leaves.

If you're able, try to venture out to a local, independent market, sign on to get a box of veggies from a local farmer, or if you have the space, maybe try your hand at a container garden to get into different tastes.

Experiment with leaves that you haven't seen before. Talk to the shop attendants or farmers about how to use different herbs and leaves. The unexpected combination of sweet and bitter, soft and sturdy, can truly expand your idea of what a green salad can be. When you're eating seasonal leafy veggies, you're going to get a fulfilling mix of flavors that's truly of your own local terroir. And don't sleep on our vinaigrette, either. Whisk, whisk, whisk to get it emulsified for a nice, even, not-soupy coat to the greens. Do it up.

CONTINUED

Serves 4

INGREDIENTS

For the coconut vinaigrette

2 tablespoons coconut vinegar

2 teaspoons Dijon mustard

2 teaspoons coconut nectar

Pinch of flaky sea salt, to taste

¼ cup (60 ml) grapeseed oil

For the salad

About 6 cups (220 g) micro lettuces (such as mesclun, pea tendrils, sunflower sprouts, or amaranth)

2 rainbow radishes, thinly sliced

1 small carrot, thinly sliced

1 Persian cucumber, thinly sliced

¼ cup (50 g) pepitas, toasted

Assorted fresh herbs (such as chervil, flat-leaf parsley, cilantro, and amaranth)

6 to 8 edible flowers (look in the produce section at the grocery store; optional)

PREPARATION

Make the vinaigrette

In a small bowl, whisk together the vinegar, mustard, coconut nectar, and salt. While whisking, slowly stream in the oil and whisk to combine. (If not using immediately, store in an airtight container in the refrigerator for up to 1 week.)

Make the salad

Wash the greens. Transfer the greens to a bowl and add the radishes, carrot, cucumber, pepitas, herbs, and flowers (if using). Toss the salad with the coconut vinaigrette. Enjoy immediately.

TOYIN OJIH ODUTOLA
PICNIC ON THE GROUNDS, 2017–2018
PASTEL, CHARCOAL, AND PENCIL ON PAPER,
$74\frac{1}{2}$ x 50 in.

GINGER GARLIC SPINACH

This quick sauté puts just enough heat on your spinach to wilt the leaves and incorporate the aromatics. You can also use this template for other greens you might have on hand, like kale, Swiss chard, escarole, or the mild leaves of gai lan (Chinese broccoli).

Serves 4

INGREDIENTS

2 tablespoons extra-virgin olive oil
2 tablespoons minced shallot
2 garlic cloves, minced
1 teaspoon minced fresh ginger
1 pound (455 g) baby spinach
Flaky sea salt
Coarsely ground white pepper
SOIL (page 291), for garnish

PREPARATION

In a large saucepan, heat the olive oil over medium-high heat. Add the shallot, garlic, and ginger and cook for about 30 seconds, just until translucent. No browning!

Add the baby spinach to the pan. It will seem like a lot at first, but don't trip; the leaves will wilt quickly. Just gently rotate the spinach around the pan with tongs. Tell them babies everything's gonna be all right. Cook until the leaves have all wilted and reduced in volume, about 5 minutes.

Season with salt and pepper to taste, then serve. The kicker is the SOIL for garnish, so don't forget it. Enjoy immediately.

Who plays
of heart
skill
you it was Just my Imagina-ation running awayy
Imagina-ation running awayy

KERRY JAMES MARSHALL
PAST TIMES, 1997
ACRYLIC AND COLLAGE ON CANVAS
$108\frac{1}{4}$ by 157 in.

INTERVIEW WITH

THEASTER

Theaster Gates is Chi-Town all day, with family roots in Mississippi. His work as an artist spans sculpture, performance, and song, archiving, and vividly, the use of land and what he calls Black space to allow for a reclaiming of culture. In *New Egypt*, he built a large, towering structure inspired by African architecture, composed of the entire *Ebony* magazine archive—seventy-one years of Black stories bound in red, black, and green covers (a reference to the Black Power movement). Decked in prestige, he's been awarded the French Légion d'honneur, the Nasher Prize for sculpture, and many other honors. His exhibitions have shown around the world, including in Venice, Paris, London, and Milan.

Ghetto Gastro: What does it look like for you to care for yourself through food?

Theaster Gates: I think of the ways in which Black people have transmitted information to the kitchen. It was palpable for me as a young person, either watching my mom and my grandmother in Mississippi or watching my eight sisters and my mom transfer knowledge. My mom would give my sisters information and then my sisters would give it back to my mom. Like my mom's dressing got better because my sister Robin Gates—we call her Robbie—followed her instructions. And then she'd be like, "Oh, Mom, what if we took the celery out and we added bok choy?" or whatever. Those moments of transmission were one of the things that gave me pleasure, because I found I was seeking knowledge as a young kid. I was looking forward at church, looking forward with the homies. And then at home, it was happening in the kitchen. You could hear how my mom would deal with problems and help my sisters work out their problems. But all of that was happening while they were cooking, while they were battering chicken or cleaning greens.

There are these two kinds of nourishments: eating the food, then what happens when you have the pleasure of being present while food is being cooked and while food's being thought about. We're nine siblings. Food was ongoing, it didn't stop. All day you were preparing for the next meal, or you were cleaning from the last meal, or you were putting things away, talking about the next meal, talking about grocery lists.

It was a way of understanding how to live. That gave me a tremendous amount of pleasure. Like even before we sat down, there was already pleasure. But I think what's happened in my lifestyle was the foods of my family or the foods of Black people weren't always the foods that were made tangible or present as my sphere grew. Part of what I had to learn was how to embrace the foods of Black people in this larger sphere of cultural activity. In a white world when I was in school in Iowa, the foods that were native to the Iowans were different.

[In college] we would have to then figure out how to get to Suzanne Henderson's crib because she could cook greens. She was a soprano in the choir, and we would end up at her crib after church in college. We were constantly trying to bring the food forward. In a way, food was a radical act, because it was a way of maintaining one's sense of identity in the company of others. For me, the sustainability, or the sustained possibility, has more to do with how do you understand the truth that food was acting as an emotional and spiritual anchor? In the same way, I was trying to figure out how to grapple with language and how to grapple with mannerisms and ways of being Black. I also had to grapple with how to maintain a connection to my mom and my grandma, and that was primarily happening through food. That gave me pleasure.

When you started seeking out, re-creating, or evolving those meals or practices outside of your childhood home, did you understand that as a reflection of your identity, or was it more about comfort and incorporating what you missed?

At the time it didn't feel like I was proving something as much as I was missing something. It's like, *Man, it would be nice on a Saturday morning if I had some grits, but they don't even sell grits at the local store.*

For the middle part of my adulthood, there were moments where I had longing and desire for Black foods when I was away from them or when I was in a different country or environment. In that sense, I think I was subconsciously trying to construct those things that were familiar, and food was a big part of that reconstruction. It wasn't an aggressive act of like, you know, *Let me cook some chitlins on the third floor of my residence hall.* It was like, *I miss my mom and I miss my family, I wish I had our foods.* Like, *I haven't had neckbones in a long time* and then, *Oh wow, nobody could throw down neckbones like my mom.* Or even the idea of sucking that bone and getting to meat and my mom teaching me how to eat it. All those things were kinds of love and transmissions as I was sucking that neckbone. And so the neckbone is actually a device that triggers good emotions. It was an affect of love.

You can see in the public discourse, we're still learning how to accurately frame Black food culture in the US—much of it has come from struggle and sacrifice, but so much comes from our cultural expressions of love and celebration. What does it look like to nurture yourself and to create spaces where your community feels that nurturing?

Yeah. I've been having an ongoing conversation with Leslie Hewitt, she's an important visual artist to me. And she's one of the great young philosophers of this moment. Leslie and I always talk about how we carry the archive—in this case, the Black archive, how we carry that in our bodies. For a long time, the big trauma of Black people, especially those coming from the transatlantic experience, is that we didn't have the right to own things and to root in a place. That rootlessness had to become a way of understanding ourselves.

My practice initially was about trying to counteract this idea of rootlessness by owning land and by digging so deeply in a place that those who carry the archives in their body could then have a place of repository where their bodies might rest and their archives might unfurl.

The ability to recall a set of experiences and then materialize those experiences—those experiences may have been memories, thoughts, laughter, joy, trauma, maybe—but finding ways to materialize those things and then put them in a place so that other people could have an experience with those memories without my body needing to be present, right? I would say in part, that's what art is. One part is, what happens when you reflect on civil rights? You think about these moments that happened in Birmingham and Selma and Cicero, Illinois; Tulsa, Oklahoma. You think about these moments and then you conjure a device that helps people remember that something bad happened or something good happened or Black people were resilient. I feel like I got that part. But a thing that started to happen almost impulsively or intuitively was that I also had the sense that I was part of the psychic team that was meant to try to deepen the rootfulness of our experience. And I was doing that by making space and then making program.

The making of those spaces was a way of dealing with the trauma in my own life. The state took my parents' land in Mississippi. They didn't have good lawyers that could fight this. The Army Corps of Engineers needed to build a dam, and they flooded a portion of our land in Mississippi.

How can I use those truths to then in Chicago have the team that I need that could fight for us and ensure that the space I was making for myself and others, that that space would be there for a very long time? In a way, nurturing myself was about participating in the building of a nation and feeling like I was an active member of a squad that could restore things that were taken from us and allow others to benefit from the land piece.

As I say to Ghetto Gastro all the time, it's one thing to make a dinner happen. It's another thing to make a dinner happen *on your land.* And for people to know into the future, that dinners will continue to happen here, or great times of reflection will continue to happen here, or wealth could be created here, et cetera. I've kind of made it my mantra to show varying ways that we could be involved in creating the devices that would house our body archives.

So much of Black Americans' relationship to land, as you said, is about a sense of historic rootlessness, but also a sense of trauma and also an expectation of labor when it comes to that land. The flip side of that labor is rest, which, while deserved, is also beyond the imagination for many folks. How do you rest? How do you think about rest as another aspect of nurturing and feeling rooted?

That's a beautiful question. I'm still figuring out how to rest. One of the things that I saw historically with my mom and dad was that every summer when we would go to Mississippi, the family reunion, or that time together in the summer, wasn't just about making sure that the kids knew their cousins in the South. It was also, my dad could go fishing and my mom could spend time with her mom, who didn't come to Chicago.

Part of the reason that I talk about retreat and have a Black artist retreat is because I feel like the act of going somewhere else, or going back to a place and pausing and taking time, is so absolutely necessary and critical to our well-being. Pulling out from the world and giving yourself time and space to be made strong again, before going back into the world. This is the way I talk about retreat. Humphreys County [Mississippi], which is where my mom was from and where our land is, was a different kind of labor, because my family owned that land. The output of labor was not benefiting someone else.

It meant that we could eat, and then my uncle could sell or give away bushels of corn in Clarksdale, Mississippi, in Indianola, or Isola, or whenever we were moving through small towns or on our way to the auction sale. He would sell his big hogs and get little hogs and feed them, all those processes were ways in which we were using labor to sustain ourselves. The rest from that labor was knowing that the labor was doing multiple works. It wasn't going out to boss man. It was passing down the traditions around farming and providing a necessary income that allowed my uncle to manage. My uncle and my other family members, they were managing 800 acres of farmland in Mississippi.

I like working hard, but I don't like working hard from a traumatic place, like I don't have a choice in working hard. I work hard so that the retreat, that drive to Mississippi or that desire to be around my homies—I feel so absolutely within my right to pause. You know what I mean? Because I know that I put in my time. In some ways I feel like a Black Calvinist; there's probably a way in which a work feels like a reward or a duty. But I know that in nation building, for those who sleep all day, it's hard to help the nation.

While I don't use words like "self-care"—it's not the language that I grew up with—what I believe is that when you work hard, you should rest. I'm learning how to rest. Resting is also reading these books that I have around me or, on the artistic side, taking time to be inspired. I'm waiting on the word so that all these processes and processing and synthesizing, those things ultimately lead to new manifested ideas, new ways of using my time and labor to do great things. In that sense, yeah, self-care is about what you do when you've committed yourself to great things.

Is it possible to imagine what work and rest can provide outside of being a conduit to more work? It's difficult for many Black folks to even allow themselves to imagine what that can feel like. To imagine what freedom looks like inside of the system that is white supremacist, capitalist, and that is fundamentally saying you exist to work, and much Black liberation thought leadership refutes this. How do you progress in a society that demands that of you while understanding, at the same time, that it's not a game you can win?

It's a super-important question. For some reason, I was just thinking about conversations with Sabina Bokhari. She's a colleague and a friend. I realized [that] for years we worked together, and we talked about work and we would every once in a while pass a casual "How are things, how are your people?" But when we gave ourselves permission to have a full conversation about our lives, I found that Sabina was rich in spirit in ways that I couldn't have imagined, because we never talked about the rest of our lives. We only talked about work. One way of thinking about your question, is it possible that there are some parts of Black liberation that one can't get to when they're preoccupied with a kind of task-based activity? And then, are there other kinds of conversations that we can have when we're not preoccupied with those tasks? I believe that there are important conversations to have about liberation. So, creating the preconditions where you can be without the burden of work tasks, and it's in a space where you said, *Hey, it's okay for us to think about the health of the rest of our lives*, and then see what that conversation is.

So when you think about love as a sacred act within Black liberation and love being a thing that needs to happen outside of labor, or a certain kind of labor, and it may mean that the radical act is that one would have to give up time from the fields to be somewhere else so that you can have time to be in love. And for me, love is at the beginning. This is bell hooks, love is at the root of a certain kind of liberatory practice. And I'm learning to make time for that.

When you think of Ghetto Gastro and Black Power Kitchen, what does that mean to you?

What Ghetto Gastro has been able to do is capture the physical and emotional space of Black joy and use this dinner platform or this food platform as a way of amplifying the importance of our conviviality, of our being together and kicking it.

It also may be the hype—there's a little bit of this that's about hype, right? It's about hyping up the importance of being together. There's the dinner that we just had, our "Friendsgiving" dinner here in Chicago [that] you led. What was beautiful about that is that because your platform preexisted, people came with high expectations of what the night might be. How do you create a platform where people are excited about meeting strangers, excited about eating new foods, excited about being challenged? Because this was a racially diverse group of people, but all those things are happening under the auspices of Black leadership and Black culinary intention, which means that there might also be a Black ideology. Hosting in a beautiful space, intentionally having a nonlinear feel to the night, having great music and good vibes. It felt like Black space. And that space was then demonstrating that because of the intelligence in Black sociality, it was reaffirming other forms of philosophical, spiritual, Black intelligences.

I felt reaffirmed that sometimes kicking it is the best way to show how fly we are, how smart we are, how kind we can be to each other. No other agenda, just kicking it. So maybe some of my words are different. I don't use the term "Black liberation" in my daily life, but when I think about the ability to kick it and not be preoccupied with others, other outsiders, I feel like I'm into a kind of postcolonial fifth, sixth level. I'm like, I don't even think about them. I don't even think about them when they present. I'm thinking about us. I'm thinking about the us-ness. Now we have our own spaces where we can convene, and we don't have to tell nobody.

I was thinking, with Ghetto Gastro, how do you continue to reaffirm the power that we have and not have to hype it up? You just deepen those connections because sometimes mugs don't need to know what you do. Right? So it's like, all right, let's have our public-facing Ghetto Gastro. Then let's have a dinner that helps our nephews heal, that helps us have hard conversations where we could be better than we were, because somebody can really speak truth to us, you know? I'm very, very excited that we have a platform. And I think the next move in the platform is the slow-and-low dinner. The one that affirms us, even when no one else knows that dinner happens.

MOFONGONES

Traditional mofongo hails from Puerto Rico, a delicious mash-up of fried green plantain, garlic, and chicharrón.

The plantain is fried then pounded in a mortar and pestle with the pork rinds and garlic. As a side dish served with broth, meat, or seafood, it bears resemblance to fufu, a pounded starch, often yam, from West Africa that's served with stews. Tostones can be found throughout Latin America, twice-fried green plantains that have a distinctive crunch. Our creation, mofongones are a combination of the interior texture of mofongo with the exterior texture of a tostone. To be clear, mofongo and tostone are both holistic recipes that are solid on their own. Much respect, we're not trying to improve anybody's tradition. But mixing the best of both? That's fire. Enjoy these mofongones as a snack, or serve with dishes like Twerk n Jerk (page 103) or Stewy Newton (page 254).

BONY RAMIREZ
EL PLATANERO, 2020
ACRYLIC, COLOR PENCIL, OIL PASTEL, HOBBY KNIFE BLADES; PAPER ON WOOD PANEL, 36 x 48 in.

CONTINUED

Serves 2

INGREDIENTS

½ cup (110 g) Aquafaba Aioli (page 290)
1 teaspoon Aunt Millie's Green Sofrito (page 290)
1 pound (455 g) green plantain, peeled and chopped
3 teaspoons flaky sea salt
3 cups (720 ml) grapeseed oil
4 garlic cloves
Lime zest

EQUIPMENT

Large mortar and pestle

PREPARATION

Combine the aioli and sofrito in a small bowl and stir until fully incorporated. Cover and refrigerate for 1 hour so the sofrito can properly bloom in the aioli and the sauce has time to chill and meld flavors by the time the plantain is ready to rock.

In a medium pot, combine 3 cups (720 ml) water, the plantain, and 1 teaspoon of the salt and bring to a boil over medium heat. Cook for 20 minutes, until fork-tender.

In a small saucepan, combine 1 cup (240 ml) of the grapeseed oil and the garlic cloves. Cook over low heat for 10 to 15 minutes, until the garlic is tender and light brown in color. Use a slotted spoon to remove the garlic from the oil and place in a large mortar. Reserve the seasoned garlic oil.

Use a slotted spoon or spider to remove the plantain from the pot and transfer to the mortar. Add 1 teaspoon of the salt. Pound with the pestle until the ingredients are fully incorporated and the mixture is smooth and pliable.

Line a sheet pan or large plate with parchment paper. Use your hands to shape and form the plantain mixture into about 8 patties, each approximately 2 inches (5 cm) wide and weighing approximately 2 ounces (50 to 60 g) each. Transfer the patties to the lined pan as you form them. Set aside.

In a cast-iron skillet, combine the reserved garlic oil with the remaining 2 cups (480 ml) grapeseed oil and heat over medium-high heat until a thermometer registers 355°F (180°C), adjusting heat as needed to maintain. Working in batches, shallow-fry the plantain patties for about 10 minutes, flipping them halfway through. They should look brown and have a delicious crispy texture. Remove the mofongones and place on your lined sheet pan. Finish with a sprinkle of the last teaspoon of salt immediately after you remove the patties from the skillet.

When you're all done frying, hit the mofongones with lime zest. Serve with the sofrito aioli for dipping. Eat hot!

CHEYENNE JULIEN
BLACK OUT, 2020
ACRYLIC ON CANVAS, 60 x 48 in.

PURPLE HAZE PIE

Jon's grandfather, Howard, learned to cook in the military, and he cooked for a living afterward. He was known to make mad trays of mac 'n' cheese and mad sweet potato pies—the man only knew how to cook in bulk. He added coconut flakes to his sweet potato mixture to give the pie a little crunch, which has become a family tradition.

We like ube, or purple yam, which comes from the Philippines and shows up in desserts like halo-halo (and a shout-out to the Negritos, the Indigenous peoples throughout the Philippines and nearby islands). Sweet potato pie is a staple in many Black American households; we're remixing the spread with purple, which symbolizes abundance and wealth. To your health!

Serves 8

INGREDIENTS

1 pound 2 ounces (500 g) purple sweet potato

⅓ cup plus 2 teaspoons (75 g) cane sugar

½ cup (75 g) date sugar

⅔ cup (40 g) unsweetened coconut flakes

2 tablespoons cornstarch

1 tablespoon ground cardamom

½ to 1 teaspoon (1 to 1.5 g) agar agar powder (a plant-based stabilizer good for mixing)

1½ teaspoons ground nutmeg

1½ teaspoons flaky sea salt

⅔ cup (150 g) coconut milk

3 tablespoons plant-based butter, melted

1 (9-inch/23 cm) piecrust, store-bought or homemade

PREPARATION

Heat the oven to 450°F (230°C).

Roast the sweet potato for 1 hour; you should be able to easily pierce it with a fork when it's cooked. Remove from the oven and allow to cool; reduce the oven temperature to 350°F (175°C). Peel the cooled sweet potato and puree in a food processor.

In a medium bowl, combine the cane sugar, date sugar, coconut flakes, cornstarch, cardamom, agar agar, nutmeg, and salt and stir to combine.

In a separate bowl, mix the coconut milk and the sweet potato puree. Add to the dry mixture and stir to combine, then fold in the melted butter. The consistency should be like a thick cake batter.

Pour the mixture into the piecrust and bake for 50 minutes, rotating the pan after 30 minutes. The crust will be browned when it's ready. Allow the pie to cool before serving. Optional: Garnish with whipped cream. Enjoy.

GUAVA PIÑA

Sweet things don't have to be full of ingredients you can't pronounce. Mix fruit puree and a little sugar, and you've got a treat worthy of any snack bag.

Makes 8 slices

INGREDIENTS

1 lemon, peel and pith removed

2 limes, peel and pith removed

1¾ cups (300 g) coarsely chopped peeled pineapple

⅔ cup (150 g) coarsely chopped peeled Granny Smith apple

1 cup (250 g) guava puree

1 tablespoon plus 2 teaspoons pectin (preferably Pomona's Universal)

1 tablespoon plus ¼ teaspoon cane sugar

5 drops pineapple essential oil (optional)

5 drops guava essential oil (optional)

EQUIPMENT

Juicer

Dehydrator

PREPARATION

Juice all the fruit together. Allow the juice to rest for 30 to 45 minutes. Once rested, the juice will be easy to separate from the foam: Simply tip your pitcher slowly and let the clear juice flow into another container. Pour 11 ounces (325 ml) of the clear juice into a blender pitcher. (Go ahead and drink the leftovers.)

Add the guava puree and blend until smooth. Pass the puree through a fine-mesh strainer into a bowl.

In a small bowl, mix together the pectin and sugar. Sprinkle this mixture into the bowl with the juice, then whisk to combine. Add the essential oils (if using).

After the pectin begins to hydrate, you'll notice the mixture thicken. This part can take about 30 minutes. (You can do this step ahead of time and keep the mixture chilled until ready to dehydrate.) Once the fruit juice has gelled with the pectin, it's ready to dehydrate.

Pour the mixture into a greased sheet pan or nonstick pan and place in a dehydrator. Set the dehydrator to 135°F (60°C) for 6 to 12 hours. When the fruit leather is finished, it will be dry to the touch.

Cut the fruit leather into shapes or roll up and enjoy. It can keep in an airtight container at room temperature for up to 2 weeks.

BARKLEY L. HENDRICKS
TWO!, 1966-67
OIL ON LINEN, 44 in. diameter

AMY SHERALD
INNOCENT YOU, INNOCENT ME,
2016
OIL ON CANVAS,
54 x 43 x 2½ in.

WATERMELON GRANITA

We're going out with that red, black, and green—the colors of the Pan-African flag are symbolic of Black liberation.

This is an easy dish to make with kids, and children are ever-present in the Ghetto Gastro orbit. As sons, dads, and god-papis, we've experienced that some of the best connections with our young people occur when food is being communally prepared. Give them that good game when they're coming up and you won't have to correct them later, ya heard.

Serves 2

INGREDIENTS

4 cups (1 L) watermelon juice (store-bought fresh-pressed or juiced at home)

⅓ cup (80 ml) fresh lime juice

¼ cup (60 ml) agave syrup

Pinch of flaky sea salt

Lime zest, for garnish

PREPARATION

In a bowl or pitcher, stir together the watermelon juice, lime juice, agave, and salt. Strain the mixture through a fine-mesh strainer.

Divide into shallow containers or pour into a rimmed sheet pan and freeze until solid, about 8 hours. Scrape the surface of the ice with a fork to form the granita. This takes a little elbow grease, but you can do it.

Transfer the frozen scraped crystals to a freezer-safe container and cover until ready to serve; it will keep for up to 1 month. Serve the granita in a chilled bowl, garnished with lime zest.

HANK WILLIS THOMAS
HOW TO MARKET KITTY LITTER TO BLACK PEOPLE: EBONY MAGAZINE, 2005/2006
LIGHTJET PRINT, 35 x 28 in.

KIMBERLY DREW

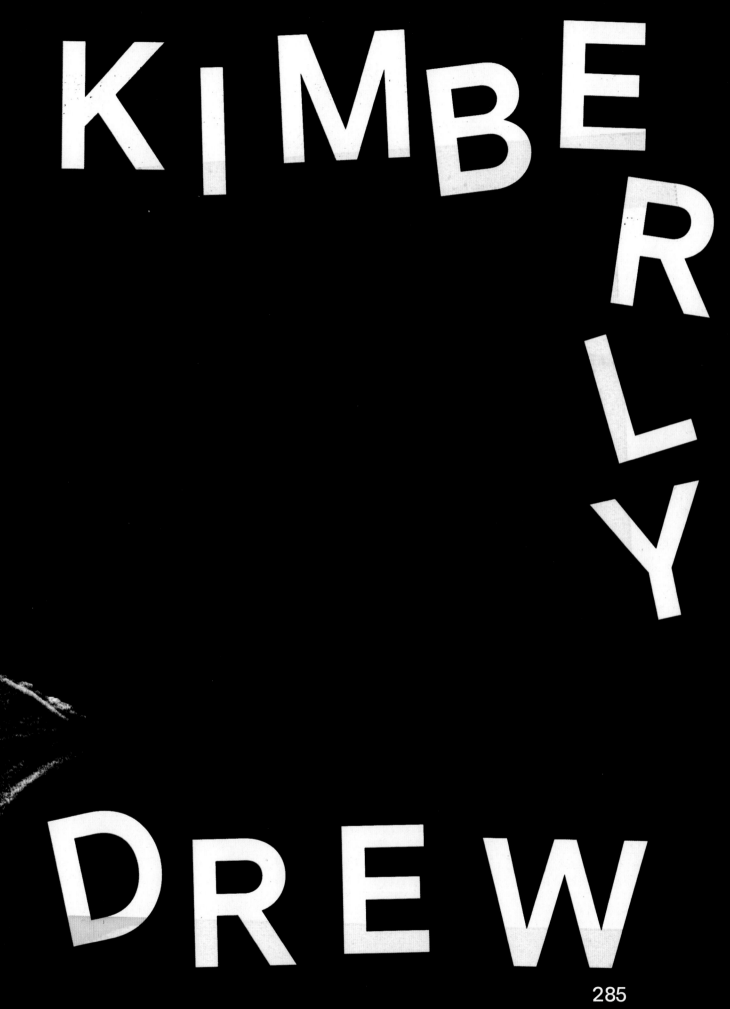

A New York–based writer and curator originally from Orange, New Jersey, Kimberly Drew has lit up the art world, making space for Black creators and the stories their work tells. An early internship at the Studio Museum in Harlem (see the interview with Thelma Golden, page 68) helped Kimberly define her own space in the field. Before shifting focus to writing full-time, she led social media at the Metropolitan Museum of Art after working in various spaces, including the arts magazine *Hyperallergic* and the gallery Lehmann Maupin. Threading activism throughout her work, she is known for challenging institutions and structures that place limitations on what art is, who defines it, and who can profit from it. She is the author of *This Is What I Know About Art* and co-edited *Black Futures*, an anthology of the modern Black experience, with Jenna Wortham.

Ghetto Gastro: When it comes to your creative practice, what does it look like for you to replenish and restore?

Kimberly Drew: As with any other facet of creative practice, I think it's about learning and shifting and maturing. I feel like trying to find a holistic approach to anything is a journey more than a destination. I also think a lot about how whenever we creatives try something new, like, for example, if your work is in multimedia and then you start drawing, but you've had this career where you're looking and seeing, and you have your favorite people who are doing illustration, and then you try to do your own, you're like, *I'm trash!* It's like your aesthetic goals are higher, the further and further you delve into creative practice.

The ways that we learn to care for ourselves are also going to come at a particularly high standard. Because of course, we're also living in this wellness moment that is so co-opted by capitalism and white supremacy. This is so much deeper than getting a manicure-pedicure. It's really, *How am I confronting the parts of myself that really need to be cared for? How am I acknowledging the parts of myself that might not be as strong as I'd like them to be? And what am I going to do about it?*

What does it mean to aim for or achieve benchmarks, and to develop the skills that might help navigate capitalism? Especially when the effort required to do those things can be in direct contradiction to what we need to actually be inside of a holistic model of care. We often don't have access to the structural support that can help fill that gap. How do you think about that in your life?

That's a good question. I think it's really complicated. And definitely something that's custom fit to each person. I can only speak for myself. This is something that I learned from our mutual friend LinYee Yuan, who does *Mold* magazine. LinYee reminded me of the power of community. Sometimes community can be talked about in this vague sense. But I think it's important to have those people in your life whom you can look to that actually see you or are invested in you. Those who can say like, Okay, even if this project fails, our friendship is so much more valuable.

You know, those friends who are like, Did you eat? The people who want to know who you are in both public and private. What I've appreciated so much in my relationship with Jon, and in some ways with Pierre as well, is I really enjoy that these are some of the least performative friendships that I have because I genuinely am invested in the person long before the project. I want to be in a room where people are like, I want to bathe you in so much love that the things that I hope you accomplish are possible. And if they are just as simple as surviving, that's fantastic.

What does it look like throughout the week when you are taking care of yourself?

I have a trainer that I work with twice a week. I love working with her because she's—well, I'm very into astrology, I'll just say that. But we have six of the same placements. And so it's like working with a mirror in many ways, like a very fit mirror. She's the love of my life! And then I also regularly meet with a therapist. Those are things for my brain. And then every day and week, the things that I do to care for myself definitely shift. The biggest act of care is knowing that those things will be in flux. I'm the least invested in trying to do the same thing every day. Giving myself that permission to find rest or find softness is a big part of my practice. Did you ever read those articles in *Forbes* that are like, "Every CEO wakes up at 5:00 a.m."? Relinquishing myself from other people's goals is a daily meditation and practice that I try to take on.

Where do you think that hyper focus on daily regimens comes from? And how did you untangle yourself from it?

It's a mix of things. One is just like, I can't do it! Simply know yourself, know your worth. I am just not that person. I got a lot of that permission from my friend Tourmaline, who is an amazing scholar and artist and thinker. We had a conversation probably five or six years ago, and we were talking about the beauty of messiness. She preaches so beautifully about messiness. Thinking about idols like Marsha P. Johnson as this incredible person who changed the world and was also a very messy person. And how so many systems and structures make us messy, make us crazy, or are crazy making—and how we can find within that our own space and opportunities to thrive.

I like structure to a certain extent, and I am here to applaud people who are, all power to you. But for me, I know that sometimes a meditation might happen at 9:35 p.m. because I was able to leave an event early and needed to find my breath. And I need to find my breath because I was out doing some messy shit. Now I'm going to sit at my altar and try to find some peace, you know? What is more valuable than anything else is that I knew to prioritize that for myself. That took a lot of time to understand, that that is self-worth.

How does food factor in as nourishment for you? Does it?

I feel like you taught me that. I have suffered from eating disorders at multiple points in my life. Going to dinners with Jon when we were first becoming friends, I was like, *Oh my god, food is so beautiful.* It is so nourishing. It's the things on the table, but it's also the conversations that I observed him having with other people in the food space and how much joy it brought them that he would walk in. I was able to separate my own relationship to food and think about it as a system and think about it in connection with other people. It was through our relationship that I saw food as an art form. I appreciate the opportunity to restructure and see the deep joy in it.

Back to the idea of community, that experience of sharing was integral to reframing your relationship to food. Beyond ingredients on a plate or something you have to put in your body at some point.

Yeah, it's not compulsive. It doesn't have to be a compulsory exercise. Any creative structure suffers when it becomes that, like you *have* to go. I grew up in Jersey and we would come into the city, and I think about the difference between when I saw *In the Heights* and when I saw *Les Misérables.* I was so nourished by one, and the other was just a field trip because we had to go see it. They're both incredible products, but one wasn't the right fit for what I was interested in.

What comes up for you with the phrase "Black Power Kitchen"?

It does make sense. In Black art, it's so open. I like it as even with our book, *Black Futures*, we didn't want it to be prescriptive and mean one thing. I like that it's something that can be personal. My handle is @museummammy, and one of the reasons I have maintained this handle, even though it's so awkward when people call me @museummammy, is because I think about the mammy as a powerful domestic figure. What would it mean that there would be space for Black Power or empowerment in a kitchen space?

And then obviously there are commercial kitchen spaces wherein we can find power as well. There are outdoor kitchens where power can mean being next to the beach and being enchanted by that opportunity to be one with nature. I like it as a framework for each person to define for themselves.

It makes me think about how David Adjaye talks about architecture. When David was building the Sugar Hill Development, he said that there's no reason that public housing has to be ugly. Or these assumptions around how spaces that we're in can help us build a sense of worth and worthiness. Of course, that becomes all the more urgent for Black folks and for people who are of lower socioeconomic status. Finding spaces and opportunities to feed others is inherently political. If there can be a space, especially within a Black cultural context, to build a home or create systems that support joy is really valuable because I'm sure we all know of food nonprofits that are bullshit. But thinking about how to have creative interventions to inspire a different relationship to food on a larger scale is valuable.

What does Ghetto Gastro mean to you?

It's an *adventure*. That's it!

PANTRY

GENEVIEVE GAIGNARD
A WOMAN'S PLACE, 2018
MIXED MEDIA COLLAGE ON
PANEL, 36 x 24 in.

AUNT MILLIE'S GREEN SOFRITO

Makes 1 pint (480 ml)

INGREDIENTS

5 tablespoons (90 g) chopped green bell pepper

¾ cup (95 g) chopped yellow onion

3½ tablespoons chopped fresh cilantro

4 teaspoons chopped seeded serrano pepper

4 teaspoons chopped garlic

3½ teaspoons ají dulce

1 tablespoon chopped fresh oregano

1 tomatillo, husked, rinsed well, and chopped

2 teaspoons chopped scallion greens

2 teaspoons lime zest

PREPARATION

In a food processor, combine the bell pepper, onion, cilantro, serrano pepper, garlic, ají dulce, oregano, tomatillo, and scallion greens. Process until the texture is smooth.

Add the lime zest and stir well to incorporate.

Transfer the sofrito to an airtight container and store in the refrigerator for up to 1 week. Alternatively, you can transfer the sofrito to an ice cube tray and freeze, then store the frozen sofrito cubes in an airtight freezer bag for up to 3 months. Use one cube per recipe for your various stews or sauces.

AQUAFABA AIOLI

Makes about 3 cups (700 ml)

INGREDIENTS

¾ cup (180 ml) aquafaba (from one 15-ounce/425 g can of chickpeas; reserve one-third of the drained chickpeas to thicken the aioli, as needed)

1 whole garlic head, roasted and peeled

2 tablespoons champagne vinegar

2 teaspoons Dijon mustard (such as Maille)

2 teaspoons flaky sea salt, plus more if needed

1 Thai chile, seeded and minced to a paste consistency

1 cup (240 ml) grapeseed oil

1 cup (240 ml) extra-virgin olive oil

4 teaspoons fresh lemon juice

Zest of 1 lemon

PREPARATION

In a food processor, combine the aquafaba, roasted garlic, vinegar, mustard, salt, and chile. Puree for 1 minute.

Reduce the blender speed and, with the motor running, slowly add both oils, making sure they're being fully incorporated. If the aioli is too watery, add a few of the reserved chickpeas at a time to firm up the texture.

Add the lemon juice and zest to the blender to finish. Taste for seasoning and adjust the salt to your preference. Store the aioli in an airtight container in the refrigerator for up to 1 week.

SOIL

When we think of abundance in food, the soil is the basis for planting seeds that thrive. This accoutrement of crispy garlic, ginger, and shallots is for finishing dishes. We call it SOIL because of its earthy, golden color and use it liberally as a last layer of flavor and texture.

Makes 1 cup (80 g)

INGREDIENTS

½ cup (120 ml) grapeseed oil
¼ cup (40 g) minced garlic (about 7 cloves)
¼ cup (40 g) minced fresh ginger
½ cup (80 g) minced shallots

PREPARATION

Line a sheet pan with paper towels.

In a saucepan, heat the grapeseed oil over medium heat until it registers 300°F (150°C) on an instant-read thermometer.

Add the garlic to the hot oil and fry until golden brown, 1 to 2 minutes. Use a steel strainer or slotted spoon to remove the garlic from the oil. Let drain on the lined sheet pan and repeat with the ginger and shallots. The ginger should take 1 to 2 minutes; the shallots should take 3 to 4 minutes.

Allow the garlic, ginger, and shallots to cool slightly, then mix them together in a bowl. Once completely cooled, store in an airtight container in a cool place for up to 2 weeks.

CANDIED PEPITAS

Makes 1 cup (200 g)

INGREDIENTS

1 cup (130 g) raw pepitas
¼ cup (55 g) brown sugar
2 tablespoons plant-based butter, melted
1 teaspoon ground cardamom
⅛ teaspoon ground cloves
¼ teaspoon flaky sea salt

PREPARATION

Heat the oven to 300°F (150°C). Line a sheet pan with parchment paper.

In a bowl, combine the pepitas, brown sugar, melted butter, cardamom, cloves, and salt. Mix until the seeds are evenly coated.

Spread the mixture into a thin layer on the lined sheet pan. Bake for 15 to 20 minutes, or until caramelized and crunchy.

Remove from the oven and allow the pepitas to rest and dry on the baking sheet until cooled. Store in an airtight container at room temperature for up to 3 days.

MUSHROOM DASHI

Makes 2 quarts (2 L)

INGREDIENTS

2 quarts (2 L) water
¼ ounce (7g) porcini mushrooms
¼ ounce (7g) dried shiitake mushrooms
3 sheets kombu (about 1 ounce/25 g)

PREPARATION

In a large bowl, combine the water, porcini and shiitake mushrooms, and kombu. Cover and leave at room temperature to infuse overnight.

The next day, pour the contents of the bowl into a saucepan and heat the mixture over medium-low heat until it registers 160°F (70°C) on an instant-read thermometer. Don't allow the liquid to come to a boil. Remove from the heat. Allow the dashi to steep for 1 hour, then strain it through a fine-mesh strainer into an airtight container. Discard the solids. Keep the dashi refrigerated and use it within 3 days.

CHILI OIL

Makes 1 cup (240 ml)

INGREDIENTS

1 cup (240 ml) grapeseed oil
10 dried Thai chiles, stemmed

PREPARATION

In a medium saucepan, heat the oil and chiles over low heat until the oil registers 250°F (120°C) on an instant-read thermometer. Remove from the heat, cover, and set aside to infuse at room temperature overnight.

The next day, transfer the oil and chiles to a blender and blend on high speed for 40 seconds.

Line an airtight container, such as a mason jar, with a coffee filter and *slowly* strain the oil through the filter. Don't rush the flow. You may need to return to the straining incrementally. Don't press the mixture through the filter, just let it drip; it might take 1 to 2 hours to fully strain the oil. Store in an airtight container at room temperature.

LEMONGRASS OIL

Makes ½ cup (120 ml)

INGREDIENTS

½ cup (120 ml) grapeseed oil
¼ cup (60 g) coarsely chopped lemongrass

PREPARATION

In a saucepan, heat the oil and lemongrass over low heat until the oil registers 250°F (120°C) on an instant-read thermometer. Infuse for 5 minutes, then remove from the heat and let the oil sit for 30 minutes. Slowly strain the oil through cheesecloth into a mason jar (or other nonplastic airtight container); discard the solids. Store in an airtight container at room temperature for up to 2 weeks.

GINGER OIL

Makes ½ cup (120 ml)

INGREDIENTS

½ cup (120 ml) grapeseed oil
¼ cup (60 g) coarsely chopped fresh ginger

PREPARATION

In a saucepan, heat the oil and ginger over low heat until it registers 250°F (120°C) on an instant-read thermometer. Infuse for 5 minutes, then remove from the heat and let the oil sit for 1 hour. Slowly strain the oil through cheesecloth into a mason jar (or other nonplastic airtight container); discard the solids. Store in an airtight container at room temperature for up to 2 weeks

PINEAPPLE CONFIT

This dish is great on its own or with treats like Coco Loco (page 36). We serve it with Twerk n Jerk (page 103). If you're doing the same, start this process the same day that the chicken goes into the marinade.

Serves 6 to 10

INGREDIENTS

1 cup (200 g) raw cane sugar
8½ cups (2 L) fresh orange juice
1 pineapple, cored, peeled, and cut into 1-inch-thick (3 cm) slices
8 sprigs lemon thyme
4 cups (1 L) coconut oil

EQUIPMENT

Conical strainer

PREPARATION

In a large saucepan, heat the sugar on medium-low, stirring, until it turns a light amber color, about 3 minutes. Add the orange juice and stir until the sugar has completely dissolved. Increase the heat to medium-high and bring the liquid to a boil. Once it's boiling, reduce the heat by half and cook for 15 minutes.

Place the pineapple and lemon thyme in a casserole dish or Dutch oven. Pour in the orange juice mixture, completely covering the pineapple slices. Place parchment paper over the casserole dish, then cover with a sheet of aluminum foil and refrigerate overnight.

The next day, heat the oven to 300°F (150°C).

Place the covered casserole dish in the oven and bake for 1 hour, until the pineapple is easily pierced with a fork.

Use tongs to remove the pineapple slices from the braising liquid one by one. Work carefully, as the pineapple will be tender. (Don't toss the braising liquid. If preparing this dish for serving with Twerk n Jerk, page 103, save it for the Twerk Sauce, as it will replace the orange and pineapple juices.)

In a large sauté pan, heat the coconut oil over medium heat until it registers 300°F (150°C) on an instant-read thermometer. Carefully place the pineapple slices in the pan and lightly fry until they develop a slight tan hue, about 3 minutes. Transfer the pineapple to a plate and let cool.

Transfer the oil to a separate pan and let cool. When it's cool enough to handle, strain it through a cheesecloth-lined conical strainer.

Combine the cooled pineapple and coconut oil in an airtight container and refrigerate until ready to serve.

Resources

We do our best to shop locally. We have our fave spots and farmers. We urge you to get out into your community and buy from, in particular, the indie retailers that rely on consistent support.

Talk to the folks at your farmers' market. Visit shops owned by people in the African, Asian, Latin, and Arab diasporas. Follow them on social, and sign up for their newsletters. Don't just go once. Go back, and bring a friend.

When you are in the big chains, keep an eye out for signage that lets you know that certain products are from Black-owned businesses or locally made. Walk down different aisles.

Even if you're not in the BX, no matter where in the world you're reading this book, your town is likely made up of a mix of immigrant cultures. If you're not yet familiar with them, get out and explore. Eat their food. See how they do it. Be open.

Beyond that, we know that sometimes online is the way to go. We've got a few retailers here that can help keep your pantry laced. Run it up!

Ancestral Grains

Adda Blooms
addablooms.com

Yolélé
yolele.com

Clairin

Astor Wines & Spirits
astorwines.com

Sea Moss

Lucia Wellness
luciawellness.com

Purple Moss Paradise
purplemossparadise.com

Spices, Seaweed, and Oils

Burlap & Barrel
burlapandbarrel.com

Diaspora Co.
diasporaco.com

Gold Coast Supermarket
goldcoastsupermarket.com

Gustiamo
gustiamo.com

Kalustyan's
kalustyans.com

The Mala Market
themalamarket.com

Sacred Spice
sacredspicebk.com

FURTHER READING

Black Power: The Politics of Liberation by Kwame Ture (formerly known as Stokely Carmichael) and Charles V. Hamilton
(New York: Vintage, 1992)

Building Houses Out of Chicken Legs: Black Women, Food & Power by Psyche A. Williams-Forson
(Chapel Hill: University of North Carolina Press, 2006)

The Color of Law: A Forgotten History of How Our Government Segregated America by Richard Rothstein
(New York: Liveright, 2017)

High on the Hog: A Culinary Journey from Africa to America by Jessica B. Harris
(New York: Bloomsbury, 2011)

Soul Food: The Surprising Story of an American Cuisine, One Plate at a Time by Adrian Miller
(Chapel Hill: University of North Carolina Press, 2013)

The Sword and the Shield: The Revolutionary Lives of Malcolm X and Martin Luther King Jr. by Peniel E. Joseph
(New York: Basic Books, 2020)

Women, Race & Class by Angela Davis
(New York: Random House, 1981)

Acknowledgments

Without our community, this book doesn't exist. A special thank-you to our families and team members over the years who've helped shape Ghetto Gastro. Throughout this journey, you have been loyal to the soil and there for us since day one.

To our writer, Osayi Endolyn, thank you for crafting and distilling our message into this offering for the people. Your patience and grace during this project have been exceptional.

We're grateful to Carter Media Group, especially Courtney Carter and Lauren Elias. You are the engine that keeps this machine moving.

To New Studio, Nayquan Shuler, Myesha Evon Gardner, Joshua Woods, Harold Kenyon, Jakevian Matthews, Sonia Rentsch, and Vegas Giovanni, Stikxz, and Sabella, thank you for helping us bring our creative vision to life.

Thank you to our recipe testers Zoe Maya Jones and the team led by Elle Simone Scott for your diligence and feedback. Special thanks to Janae Folami, Shaina Juliana, and Diana Lee for always being our backbones and for bringing your creativity and thoughtfulness to our kitchens over the years.

Gratitude to the featured contributors, our beloved friends, griots, artists, coconspirators, and mentors who each generously shared their creations, wisdom, and time in these pages.

And a huge thank-you to the team at Artisan Books, particularly our editor Judy Pray, for your commitment in helping us make the best book we could make, as well as Lia Ronnen, Nina Simoneaux, Suet Chong, Bella Lemos, Zach Greenwald, Nancy Murray, and Allison McGeehon.

To Dr. Jessica B. Harris, when we turned the pages of *High on the Hog*, it all started to make sense. Thank you for illuminating our stories, for spreading your wings, and for allowing us to take refuge in the shade of them.

To the Bronx: We did it!!!

Thank you to my mother, my brother Chad, and my nana, Gaga. This is dedicated to my father, Lester Walker, who is gone but will never be forgotten. I'm grateful for my son, Tre, for saving me and giving me a reason to be a positive role model.

Thank you to the teachers who doubted me and gave me the fire and desire I needed to be great. To Chef Richard Grausman at NYC's Careers Through Culinary Arts Program (C-CAP), and to Chef Anthony Ricco, thank you for believing in me and being encouraging when I needed it. To Chef Floyd Cardoz, may you rest in peace, thank you for being an inspiring teacher on my journey.

—LESTER WALKER

A special thank-you to my parents, Roxanne and Andrew, for persevering as a supportive unit all these years. To my aunties Dawna, Sandy, Valarie, Marcie, Tina, Beverly, and Karen, your lessons and love have gotten me this far. To my uncles Gary, Brian, and Dicka, you've taught me how to put the muscle into my hustle. All the Serraos, Mendeses, and cousins by the dozens out there from Hartford, you are my heartbeat!

To my siblings Alana, Ian, and Rondell, who were my first and most honest recipe and taste testers. To my teachers in high school who tried to suspend me for hustling deli sandwiches to my classmates in their lockers during class, look at me now.

To all my Barbadian family who have taught me everything about being a Bajan Yankee and how to properly season my food. To Ms. Jackie and Pat Miller, the years I spent in the kitchens getting fed by the both of you have inspired my cooking beyond belief. Ishma, Teff, Jaicko, Shane McClean, and Spragga my bredrin, you all have believed in me since I was exploring my opportunities as part chef, part DJ. Manners and respect, 246 to the world!

Lastly to Devon, I love you, more than words can describe. You are my biggest fan, devil's advocate, lover, best friend, and, most important, the cosmic mother of our spicy Sagittarius Saige. The two of you are my keys to happiness, and I can't wait to continue to explore the world as a family.

—PIERRE SERRAO

Big love to the women who raised me: my mother Denise, grandmoms Ursula aka Ursluv, my aunt Akai who got me ready for outside, my aunt Sheila who gave me the game, and my great-grandma Helen for teaching me that variety is the spice of life.

To my great-grandpops, Bishop John Arthur Jones, whose legacy inspires me to pursue entrepreneurial and community building in the Bronx, thank you for giving me the blueprint. Uncle Jeff for the flavor. My brothers O and P who influenced the relentless hustle from a distance. RIP Howard, thanks for the unlimited mac 'n' cheese and sweet potato pie.

CC, you've been my right hand since '07. Jose Mejia, those squares that kicked us out of All Hallows High, they can look at us now. Thank you Nicole Sr. for the cookware, furniture, and for linking us with Yaz for our first dinner gig. To Jas for working the decks. To Nick and JT for letting us hold that Marta kitchen down. Brooks and WD for the freezer space. Joe and Marissa for making Cannes happen. Samira and Michele Lamy for the Paris takeover. To Lauren Carothers for unwavering support with the RL gigs that enabled us to learn and experiment. The Conrad clan, you know the vibes. And to Banna my Nega, stay sturdy and worthy baby.

Kyle, Kev, Kawami, Shawn and Paul. Black, DJ, Young, Ty Jenkins, and my lil bros Tashon and Dale. Joshua Woods, we'll be globetrotting until we leave the planet. Coodie & Chike, let's keep winning. Andrea, thank you for Savannah. To Mecca, Reggie, Nes, Facts, Born, Jesse, Chico, B.O., you already know. RIP M DOT, RIP CHEO. Axel, Rita, Louis. New Studio on the set protect your neck.

—JON GRAY

Index

Pages in *italics* indicate photographs.

Ghetto Gastro

is the Bronx-born culinary collective from Jon Gray, Pierre Serrao, and Lester Walker. The group has notably defined its own lane, merging food, fashion, music, art, and design. Claiming both the beauty and grit from the streets with the aspiration and aesthetics of the finer things, Ghetto Gastro's interdisciplinary approach celebrates the Bronx as a driver of global culture. The crew masterfully blends influences from the African diaspora, Global South ingredients, and the pulse of hip hop to create offerings that address race, identity, and economic empowerment.

Since launching in 2012, Ghetto Gastro has gone from hosting underground parties to spearheading large-scale brand campaigns and events with leading fashion designers, artists, and entrepreneurs. Their collaborators and partners include figures like Virgil Abloh, Nike, Cartier, the Serpentine, the Museum of Modern Art, and many more.

During the onset of the pandemic in 2020, Ghetto Gastro prioritized Bronx grassroots initiatives and mutual aid. In recognition for feeding their community, the group was nominated for the Basque Culinary World Prize. In 2021, Ghetto Gastro launched its namesake consumer goods brand of pantry items inspired by ancestral ingredients. The collective released a custom line of kitchen appliances, CRUXGG, across Target stores nationwide, and recently launched their cookware line with Williams Sonoma. *Black Power Kitchen* is their first cookbook.

OTIS KWAME KYE QUAICOE
JON GRAY, 2021
OIL ON CANVAS, 95 x 72 in.

AMOAKO BOAFO
PIERRE SERRAO, 2019
OIL ON CANVAS, 200 X 160 cm

ALVIN ARMSTRONG
SAY LES, 2021
ACRYLIC ON CANVAS, 24 x 36 in.

Jon Gray is cofounder of Ghetto Gastro. He aims to shift social narratives by celebrating the culinary, blending a background in fashion to create immersive experiences, product design, and unique storytelling.

From Co-op City, Gray's mother and grandmother taught him about the arts and challenged him to innovate as a way of life. When a rebellious adolescence almost put him behind bars, Gray used the experience to imagine a greater vision for himself. Inventorying his passions and pastimes, he made Bronx-driven gastro-diplomacy his career and mission.

In 2019, Gray delivered the TED Talk "The Next Big Thing Is Coming from the Bronx, Again." Gray is a Civic Practice Partnership Artist in Residence at the Metropolitan Museum of Art. In 2021, he served as guest curator at the Cooper Hewitt, Smithsonian Design Museum, where "Jon Gray of Ghetto Gastro Selects" featured an Afrofuturist theme.

Pierre Serrao is chef and cofounder of Ghetto Gastro. Serrao uses food to create immersive culinary experiences incorporating storytelling and product design to advance health sovereignty.

Raised between Barbados and Connecticut, Serrao worked in restaurants throughout high school, then graduated from culinary school and the Italian Culinary Institute for Foreigners in Piemonte. He worked at award-winning restaurants in New York, Barbados, and Italy, styling an approach to cooking influenced by ancestral practices and innovation.

The desire to create a culturally sound and iterative expression of food led Serrao to join forces with Jon Gray and Lester Walker, rounding out Ghetto Gastro. Fueled by international travel, enthusiasm for learning, and sheer curiosity, Serrao explores ways to bridge the global pantry with creative entrepreneurship.

Lester Walker is chef and co-founder of Ghetto Gastro. Walker brings unrelenting imagination, competition-ready technique, and skill at layering flavors to Ghetto Gastro's iconic events, offerings, and storytelling.

A native of the Bronx's Co-op City, Walker discovered cooking at a pivotal moment in his teen years. New York City's Careers Through Culinary Arts Program inspired him to pursue a career in food. Spurred by the speed, focus, and creativity of cooking, Walker worked up the fine-dining line in award-winning kitchens in New York, Washington, D.C., and Miami.

Walker's cooking merges the roots of NYC-based Black American foodways with the cuisines he studied professionally: French, Italian, Indian, and Southeast Asian. In 2012, he won *Chopped* on the Food Network. That same year, seeking ways to explore historic and modern Black culture through food, he partnered with Jon Gray, fellow Co-op City native, to launch Ghetto Gastro. With Ghetto Gastro, Walker aims to create art by intentionally pairing food with ideas that represent and celebrate where he comes from.

Osayi Endolyn is a James Beard Award–winning writer whose work explores food and identity. She's been published in the *New York Times*, the *Washington Post*, the *Los Angeles Times*, the *Wall Street Journal*, and *Time*, among others. Endolyn is coauthor, with Marcus Samuelsson, of the national bestseller *The Rise: Black Cooks and the Soul of American Food*.

She's appeared on Netflix's *Chef's Table* and *Ugly Delicious*, and Hulu's *The Next Thing You Eat*. Her writing is featured in the Museum of Food and Drink's *African/American: Making the Nation's Table*, as part of the historic exhibit's Legacy Quilt. Endolyn is the recipient of the UC Berkeley–11th Hour Food & Farming Journalism Fellowship and was named to *Southern Living*'s list of 30 Women Moving Southern Food Forward. Endolyn is on the board of trustees for the Edna Lewis Foundation and Radical Xchange and worked with PepsiCo's inaugural Dig In initiative in support of Black-owned restaurants.

Along with forthcoming book collaborations, Endolyn is writing a narrative that explores American restaurant and dining culture. A California native and former resident of the South, she lives in New York.

Credits

Listed by page number

14: from the authors' personal archive
14: © Andy Hur, courtesy of FirstWeFeast .com
17: from the authors' personal archive
18 (foreground): © Ibrahem Hasan
22: © Henry Taylor, courtesy the artist and Hauser & Wirth; photo: Jeff McLane
23: © Chase Hall, image courtesy of Chase Hall Studio
31 (foreground): © Jordan Casteel, courtesy of the artist and Casey Kaplan, New York
34 (top right): © Lynette Yiadom-Boakye, courtesy of the artist and Jack Shainman Gallery, New York
35: © Tyler Mitchell, courtesy of the artist and Jack Shainman Gallery, New York
38: © Barkley L. Hendricks, courtesy of the Estate of Barkley L. Hendricks and Jack Shainman Gallery, New York
39 (bottom right): © Bryan Fernandez
55 (bottom): © Larissa De Jesús Negrón, courtesy of the artist
61: © Hugo McCloud. Photo: Jason Wyche, New York. Courtesy: Sean Kelly, New York
66 (top left foreground): © Henri Paul Broyard
72–73 (center, repeated): © Kim Dacres; photo: Gene Ogami
72–73 (lower left and upper right, repeated): © Rashid Johnson
74: © Ming Smith, courtesy of the artist and Nicola Vassell Gallery
79 (bottom right foreground): © John Rivas and LNkoth Studios
83 (right): © LNkoth Studios
87: © Sophia-Yemisi Adeyemo-Ross
91 (top): © Alvaro Barrington, courtesy Sadie Coles HQ, London; photo: Eva Herzog
94 (top left, foreground): The Metropolitan Museum of Art, New York. 2020.7. www.metmuseum.org
94 (bottom right, foreground): © Hugh Hayden, courtesy ICA Miami; photo: Zachary Balber
100–101: © Paul Anthony Smith, courtesy of the artist and Jack Shainman Gallery, New York
115 (bottom right, foreground): © Miguel Luciano
119: The Metropolitan Museum of Art, New York. 31.6.17. www.metmuseum.org
122: © Lynette Yiadom-Boakye, courtesy of the artist and Jack Shainman Gallery, New York
123: © Sophia-Yemisi Adeyemo-Ross
125: © Ibrahem Hasan
130: © Cheyenne Julien, courtesy of the artist and Chapter NY, New York; photo: Charles Benton
139 (bottom right, foreground): © Raelis Vasquez
151 (top right): © Cheyenne Julien, courtesy of the artist and Chapter NY, New York; photo: Charles Benton
162: © Kerry James Marshall, courtesy of the artist and Jack Shainman Gallery, New York
166 (top): © Renell Medrano
166 (bottom): © Hank Willis Thomas, courtesy of the artist and Jack Shainman Gallery, New York
171: © Larissa De Jesús Negrón, courtesy of the artist
172–174: © Oasa DuVerney, courtesy of the artist
179: © Alvin Armstrong, courtesy of the artist and Anna Zorina Gallery, New York City; photo: Stan Narten
182: © Emmanuel Massillon, courtesy of Emmanuel Massillon and Swivel Gallery
183: © Emmanuel Massillon, courtesy of Emmanuel Massillon and Swivel Gallery
189 (top left): © Renell Medrano
198–199: © Hank Willis Thomas, courtesy of the artist and Jack Shainman Gallery, New York
206: © Aya Brown
207: © Ibrahem Hasan
211: © Arthur Jafa, courtesy of the artist and Gladstone Gallery
215 (top): © Larissa De Jesús Negrón, courtesy of the artist
215 (bottom): Ibrahem Hasan
222: © Martine Syms, courtesy of the artist and Bridget Donahue, NYC
223: © Toyin Ojih Odutola, courtesy of the artist and Jack Shainman Gallery, New York
241: © Awol Erizku, commissioned by Public Art Fund for "Awol Erizku: New Visions for Iris"
249: © Wangechi Mutu, courtesy of the artist and Gladstone Gallery, New York and Brussels, The Metropolitan Museum of Art; photo by Joseph Coscia, Jr.
250 (top left): © Reginald O'Neal
250 (bottom left): © Garrett Bradley
251 (top right): © Derek Fordjour; photo: Daniel Greer
251 (bottom right): © Derrick Adams, courtesy of the artist
261: © Toyin Ojih Odutola, courtesy of the artist and Jack Shainman Gallery, New York
264–265: © Kerry James Marshall, courtesy of the artist and Jack Shainman Gallery, New York
271: © Bony Ramirez, courtesy of the artist and REGULARNORMAL
273: © Cheyenne Julien, courtesy of the Artist and Chapter NY, New York; photo: Charles Benton
278: © Barkley L. Hendricks, courtesy of the Estate of Barkley L. Hendricks and Jack Shainman Gallery, New York
279: © Amy Sherald, courtesy the artist and Hauser & Wirth; photo: Thomas Barratt
283: © Hank Willis Thomas, courtesy of the artist and Jack Shainman Gallery, New York
289: © Genevieve Gaignard, courtesy of the artist and Vielmetter Los Angeles
303 (top): © Otis Kwame Kye Quaicoe; photo by Mario Gallucci
303 (middle): © Amoako Boafo, courtesy the artist; photo: Jorit Aust
303 (bottom): © Alvin Armstrong, courtesy of the artist and Anna Zorina Gallery, New York City; photo: Stan Narten
Endpapers: Inspired by *African American Flag*, 1990 by David Hammons